D0620086

Homeland Security

Homeland Security
Policy and Politics

Nancy E. Marion
UNIVERSITY OF AKRON

Kelley A. Cronin
NOTRE DAME COLLEGE

Willard M. Oliver
SAM HOUSTON STATE UNIVERSITY

CAROLINA ACADEMIC PRESS
Durham, North Carolina

Copyright © 2015
Carolina Academic Press
All Rights Reserved.

Library of Congress Cataloging-in-Publication Data

Marion, Nancy E.
  Homeland security : policy and politics / Nancy E. Marion, Kelley Cronin,
and Willard M. Oliver.
    pages cm
  Includes bibliographical references and index.
  ISBN 978-1-61163-482-2 (alk. paper)
  1. Terrorism--United States--Prevention. 2. United States. Department of
Homeland Security. 3. National security--United States. 4. Internal security-
-United States. 5. Emergency management--United States. I. Cronin, Kelley.
II. Oliver, Willard M. III. Title.

  HV6432.M367 2015
  363.325'1560973--dc23

                        2014049832

Carolina Academic Press
700 Kent Street
Durham, NC 27701
Telephone (919) 489-7486
Fax (919) 493-5668
www.cap-press.com

Printed in Canada

This book is dedicated to our children:

NM: Jacob and Anthony
KC: Serena and Leo
WMO: Paul, James, Mark, & Sarah

May you all have healthy and happy futures.

Table of Contents

Introduction

On September 11, 2001, terrorists attacked the US in New York City and Washington, D.C., killing almost 3,000 innocent people. While homeland security was a minor concern prior to that event, the issue immediately leaped to the forefront of the minds of most Americans in the days following the attack. Politicians quickly began debating different policy actions in the following weeks, allocating millions of dollars to build up infrastructure geared toward identifying potential terrorist activity and preventing a future attack. As the new policies were created and implemented, the controversy surrounding the new policies grew. What should the policies be? Should the government be able to read citizen's e-mails and track the books they check out of the library or the websites they visit? Should illegal immigrants be permitted to come into the country and under what circumstances? Should border security be increased at the expense of tourism? How much power should the government have in the name of protecting the homeland?

This book contains more information about these and other controversies related to homeland security. In Chapter 1, the reorganization of the Federal Emergency Management Agency (FEMA), an agency established to assist citizens after disasters such as the 9/11 attacks, is considered. The agency was reorganized after the terrorist attacks, leading some to argue that the new agency became ineffective and unable to respond as it should. What should the future hold for this group? Another question raised by many politicians concerns the costs of our new homeland security policies. It is clear that the new policies are expensive and the US must pay more for the new programs designed to ensure Americans' safety. But do these increased costs mean we are safer? Are they truly preventing a future attack? This controversial debate is the topic of Chapter 2.

Chapters 3, 4, and 5 are related to law enforcement's role in homeland security after 9/11. In the days after the attack, many state and local law enforcement agencies created fusion centers as a way to gather and analyze intelligence on homeland security. The question soon became, are fusion centers a proper role for local police? This question remains unanswered but described in Chapter 3. While local police were developing new policies, federal law enforcement agencies were reorganized and expanded. Many continue to wonder if this expansion has succeeded in protecting Americans and if it is worth the increased budgets. The question of whether a larger federal law enforcement is effective is debated in Chapter 4. Another technique adopted by police in the post-9/11 period is Intelligence-Led Policing. Under this approach, law enforcement collects information about a crime and uses that as a basis for action. However, does this lead police to violate the civil rights of innocent people? This controversy is the basis of Chapter 5.

Chapter 6 poses the question, is the threat of terrorism on the rise? Have the agents within the Department of Homeland Security succeeded in keeping Americans safe from terrorists? What should they do in the future? Chapter 7 concentrates on the role of citizen volunteers in providing aid and assistance to those injured in the event of a disaster, either natural or man-made. To what extent should citizens be involved in responding to emergencies, or should we rely on volunteers at all during such a critical time?

The question posed in Chapter 8 is one that has received a substantial amount of attention since 9/11. What should be the US policy toward holding those individuals detained in the War on Terrorism? At this point, we hold detainees in Guantanamo Bay, Cuba. Some have alleged that the inmates are held unfairly, without formal charges or being given basic human rights. Should the US continue to maintain this facility? And if not, what do we do with the detainees?

More controversy surrounds the law passed by Congress in the weeks immediately following the terrorist attacks called the USA Patriot Act. This statute gave law enforcement increased power of surveillance over citizens. Should the police be able to do things like track communications and search a person's personal records without their knowledge? This and other provisions are debated in Chapter 9.

One of the most controversial policies in the US at this time is immigration at the American-Mexican border, especially related to thousands of unaccompanied children entering the US. What should the US do with all of these people who seek to come into the country illegally?

Each chapter of this book examines a different controversy by providing the reader with a history of the issue along with evidence supporting all perspectives. While these disputes will undoubtedly continue for many years, debate will help to clarify what our policies should be regarding the security of the homeland.

Homeland Security

Chapter 1

Should FEMA Be Reorganized?

Introduction

FEMA, or the Federal Emergency Management Agency, is the nation's lead agency that oversees the federal response to disasters, both natural and man-made.[1] FEMA has multiple responsibilities. Most importantly, the agency coordinates activities by all organizations that provide assistance and aid to those people and places affected by a disaster in order to save lives and property. The agency also funds and oversees reconstruction to homes, buildings, and other infrastructure that are damaged in a disaster. More recently, agency personnel have been assigned the task of designing hazard mitigation programs that are designed to reduce potential damage in future disasters.

Since its inception, FEMA has often been criticized for its lack of quick response after a disaster. Complaints also revolve around the agency's ineffectiveness, wastefulness, and a lack of communication. Many have called for the reorganization of FEMA or even its complete elimination. This chapter provides a history of FEMA and explains some of the controversy surrounding the agency.

History of FEMA

FEMA is a relatively new federal agency. It was established by President Jimmy Carter in 1979 when he reorganized all federal agencies that played a role in disaster relief into one. Through Executive Order 12127 ("Federal Emergency Management Agency"), Carter brought together five different agencies to become a new independent agency called FEMA.[2] These agencies included the Pentagon's Defense Civil Preparedness Agency and the Department of Housing and Urban Development's Federal Disaster Assistance Administration, among others. Carter explained the reorganization by saying, "For the first time, key emergency management and assistance functions would be unified and made directly accountable to the president and Congress."[3] The new agency was given the task of overseeing the emergency management functions that were carried out by federal, state, and local governments.

In the early years, the response to FEMA was generally positive. One of the first federal disasters that required FEMA's assistance was the cleanup of the underground toxic waste dumps in an area called the "Love Canal" in Niagara Falls, New York, in the late 1970s. In August of 1978, President Carter declared the area to be a national disaster. He authorized the use of federal relief aid and asked FEMA to assist with the cleanup. This was the first time federal money was used to help victims of a man-made disaster.[4] One year later, in 1979, FEMA also assisted in helping those who lived around Three Mile Island, a nuclear power station near Harrisburg, Pennsylvania, after a meltdown and release of nuclear waste into the atmosphere. For the most part, the agency's assistance after both disasters was viewed as helpful.[5]

When President Reagan took office in the early 1980s, he attempted to bring new life to the agency by again reorganizing the unit, this time giving it new responsibilities. He assigned the agency a broader mandate so that FEMA became responsible for handling evacuation and warning programs in the case of a nuclear attack as well as prevention programs and responses to floods, fires, tornados, and other natural disasters.

However, FEMA's reputation deteriorated in September 1989 when Hurricane Hugo hit Charleston, South Carolina, causing great devastation to the area. Residents of the state criticized FEMA for its slow response in providing assistance to those who needed food, housing, and other emergency supplies. Just a few months later, in November 1989, the Loma Prieta earthquake hit San Francisco, California, during the baseball World Series. Sixty-three people were killed and thousands of buildings and homes were damaged. As the federal response agency, FEMA was expected to step in to help the victims. It was not long before critics complained that FEMA personnel failed to provide adequate housing assistance for many of the earthquake victims, especially those who were from lower incomes. Once again, FEMA appeared to be unprepared to respond to those needing assistance in the days after the emergency.

FEMA's ability to respond was tested again when another disaster hit the US in 1992. This time, Hurricane Andrew struck the southern portion of the country. Once again, victims complained that FEMA's response was slow and disorganized.[6] In answering the critics, President George H. W. Bush was forced to ask Transportation Secretary Andrew Card to oversee the response efforts.

Because of the lack of adequate response to these disasters, FEMA's credibility with the public was grim. The agency was viewed as unable to respond quickly and effectively in helping victims of disaster.[7]

Upon becoming president in 1993, Bill Clinton addressed FEMA's poor reputation and inability to serve victims of disasters in an effective way. He again reorganized the agency in hopes that FEMA could become an operational organization. This time, Clinton raised FEMA to a Cabinet-level agency and hired a new director for the agency, James Lee Witt, along with other personnel who had experience in emergency management. Clinton also increased the agency's budget and streamlined the types of response methods. As a centerpiece of the reorganization, Witt used an "all-hazards, all phases" approach indicating that FEMA would be prepared to respond to all types of hazards, and in all phases of a crisis (before, during and after).[8] He established crisis management teams that delivered assistance to those who were injured. In the end, Witt was able to transform the agency into one that was much more capable and more effective at responding to a wide variety of possible disasters.

The changes Clinton made were quickly apparent. FEMA stepped up to the task and in 1993 reacted effectively to help victims during the floods in the Midwestern US. This time, the agency responded with emergency teams and coordinating officers that came to the disaster areas immediately, some of whom arrived at the scene in less than twelve hours. FEMA officials in the field made suggestions about how they could provide help to victims rather than waiting for victims to request help. They also consulted with local officials throughout the disaster relief, asking for guidance and suggestions for assistance. They had constant contact with state and regional emergency managers throughout the crisis.[9]

The following year, FEMA officials responded effectively to provide help to the victims of a 6.7 magnitude earthquake that hit Los Angeles, California. FEMA successfully oversaw relief and reconstruction efforts after the disaster hit the city. Once again, the federal government (and FEMA) showed that it could act effectively and efficiently to help the victims and rebuild structures after disasters.

It appeared as if Clinton's changes had saved FEMA. Its reputation as a competent agency continued to grow, especially as they responded to provide assistance to the victims of the Oklahoma City bombings on April 19, 1995. This time, the crisis was the result of an attack on the US by a domestic terrorist. Because of their quick response to this event, FEMA's role in responding to possible terrorist attacks was added to its agenda. However, it was soon recognized that FEMA lacked sufficient resources to address terrorism concerns such as weapons of mass destruction when added to their original task of responding to disasters.[10]

When President George W. Bush was elected to the office, he again sought to reorganize the agency. Early in 2001, prior to the terrorist attacks against the US on September 11, Bush changed the focus of FEMA so that the agency's emphasis would be more on civil defense and counterterrorism efforts. When the terrorist attack occurred, it was obvious that FEMA needed to adapt their role to concentrate on their response to possible future terrorist acts. Bush sought additional changes in the agency to make it more narrowly focused on security, terrorism preparedness, and mitigation. Bush believed that FEMA should be prepared to respond quickly to provide assistance following a terrorist attack, a nuclear, chemical, or biological attack, as well as a natural disaster.

Thus, as part of the Homeland Security Act of 2002, Bush moved FEMA out of the President's Cabinet and into the newly established Department of Homeland Security (DHS). This was a significant change for FEMA, and one that reduced its autonomy. As part of DHS, agency officials were unable to work as closely with the president or other federal agencies as in the past. Bush also reduced the agency's budget and subjected it to more spending accountability and oversight. Any requests for resources or support now had to be approved by DHS.[11] Essentially, Bush stripped FEMA of much of its authority, money, and essential staff and also made a political appointment to the director's position rather than a leader with experience in disaster response.

The reorganization concerned many experts who were uneasy about the agency's new role and whether it would be capable of an effective response to a disaster. Emergency managers from many states warned President Bush that the reorganization could weaken FEMA's ability to respond to disasters given the new constraints placed on it. They argued that the time FEMA would be forced to spend on preparing a response to a terrorist attack would mean that it would be less prepared to respond to disasters effectively.

The first test of the reorganized agency was in 2005 when Hurricane Katrina hit Louisiana and the Southern US. Two days before the hurricane hit land (on August 27), President Bush declared a state of emergency for Louisiana, making it eligible for federal assistance. Then, when Katrina made landfall and caused such horrendous damage, Bush issued a federal "declaration of emergency" that put the country's disaster plan into place to provide assistance to those who needed it.

When it was over, Hurricane Katrina had left a path of destruction about 250-miles long along the Gulf Coast. Even though the levees that held back water from New Orleans were supposed to withstand Category III conditions

(Katrina's classification when it made landfall), the strong winds, enormous amounts of water, and storm surges as high as twenty-eight feet caused approximately fifty levees to breach or break within the city of New Orleans, leaving the area submerged in water up to twenty feet deep. At the height of the storm, about 80 percent of Orleans Parish, 99 percent of St. Bernard Parish, and 40 percent of Jefferson Parish were under water. Even two weeks after the hurricane, about 50 percent of New Orleans remained flooded, and the water did not recede for over forty days. About 100,000 families were left homeless and approximately 90 percent of the city buildings were destroyed.

Many area residents did not evacuate before the hurricane hit because local officials waited too long to issue an evacuation order. Mayor Ray Nagin ordered a mandatory evacuation on August 28, just hours before the hurricane came ashore. About 1.4 million people listened to him and left the area, but about 150,000 did not. Many who stayed were the city's poorest residents who lacked the resources to leave. They had no car or other means of transportation. Many who did not evacuate had to be rescued by federal, state, and local government efforts or by non-governmental organizations.[12] Those who chose to remain in their homes were advised to take shelter in the Superdome, and about 20,000 people took that advice. There, they were faced with insufficient food and water supplies as well as inadequate medical assistance. There were only 40,000 meals and five trucks of water on the scene, despite plans by FEMA to provide 360,000 ready-to-eat meals and fifteen truckloads of water.

Even though there was an obvious need for federal assistance in the aftermath of Hurricane Katrina, FEMA's response was again slow and confused. There was clear mismanagement and a lack of preparation. Many workers had no prior training and had to be instructed on the spot. Victims did not receive the assistance they needed. Many residents faced a lack of safe water, food, and shelter. Many people died because of thirst and other conditions. There was also widespread looting throughout the city as people sought ways to survive. It was clear that there was little preparation by FEMA or others.[13]

Residents and local officials complained that FEMA asked victims to register online or via phone before they could receive help, noting that this was unrealistic to those who had no power or electricity, nor were they likely to have access to a phone or computer. Moreover, the federal aid hotline that was described by President Bush in a speech to the nation was not able to handle the massive number of calls that came in. To add to the frustration, only eight of the forty federal help centers promised to Louisiana residents were ever opened.[14]

To make matters worse, it seemed that no one seemed to know who was in charge. Debate ensued about the roles that federal, state, and local government officials should play in providing help to those who desperately needed it. There seemed to be no interagency cooperation, and when help finally arrived, it was not coordinated well.[15] There was also a massive failure of communication within and between all levels of government.[16] The existing communications efforts were inadequate and faulty for the disaster. By the time the crisis ended, more than 1,000 people died. Many complained that a faster response by FEMA would have prevented so many citizen deaths.

Some other people put the blame on the director of FEMA at this time, Michael Brown. He was sharply criticized for FEMA's slow response to aid victims. He later admitted underestimating the impact of Hurricane Katrina on Louisiana. At one point, he appeared to blame the victims for their injuries and deaths because they failed to evacuate. He also blamed other government officials for the lack of response. He told others in Washington that the state's governor, Kathleen Babineaux Blanco, and her staff were incapable of organizing a coherent state effort. He said, "I truly believed the White House was not at fault here."[17]

Brown's comments were not received well, and he resigned as the director of FEMA on September 9. The position was filled temporarily by R. David Paulison, a former fire chief from Miami-Dade County, Florida. Paulison had previous experience in emergency management situations. Eventually, Coast Guard Vice Admiral Thad W. Allen became the official leader of the agency.

Some critics argued that the ineffective response to Hurricane Katrina by Brown and FEMA was the result of Bush's reorganization of the agency and placement into DHS. As predicted, this move took away FEMA's ability to respond. They argued that FEMA was too focused on protecting against a possible terrorist attack and thus were not prepared to launch a response to a natural disaster along the lines of Hurricane Katrina. The agency also had a smaller budget, which prevented a full response. Moreover, because of the changes, many FEMA personnel had quit and the agency had lost many of its most experienced leaders. These new personnel did not know the state and local officials and procedures. Reports that came out after the hurricane clearly note that the agency had been unprepared to deal with a catastrophe the size of Katrina and was not able to respond.[18]

In their defense, FEMA pointed to the procedures in place for responding to a disaster. At that time, it was FEMA's policy to defer to emergency teams in the states and local governments to respond to disasters. If a city did not have the resources to respond as needed, then the county or the state would step in to provide assistance. If the state lacked the ability to assist, then the federal government would respond. This would only happen if the state governor requested federal help, and if the FEMA director from that region agreed that help was needed. In order to receive resources from FEMA, the governor of the state was to submit a letter to the president of the US in which a formal request was made to invoke the Robert T. Stafford Disaster Relief and Emergency Assistance Act. This act guarantees that all victims of a disaster would receive help from FEMA. The governor was also required to provide an estimate of what resources were needed to respond to the situation.[19]

In addition, although a new system for responding to national emergencies, called the National Incident Management System, or NIMS, had been created by this time, many first responders had not been trained in the system. They were not aware of the response procedures outlined in NIMS that were designed to increase the efficiency of first responders. Because they lacked the training, their response was, therefore, lacking.

Nonetheless, the slow response from the federal government continued even after the immediate needs were addressed. Two weeks after Katrina, Bush promised to rebuild the Gulf Coast region. But months later, no major federal reconstruction projects had commenced. Two months after Katrina, at least 20,000 public school students in the state were still not attending school. Hundreds of thousands of people were still displaced. About 200,000 evacuees were living in local hotels. The government had provided only 7,308 temporary trailers and 10,940 housing units for victims who had lost their homes. Six months after the storm, FEMA had provided only 3,000 of the 21,000 trailers requested by residents to use as temporary shelter while they rebuilt their own homes. FEMA also decided to cut off temporary housing assistance to those victims who were living in apartments and hotels. As a result, many Katrina victims had no safe place to live.[20] Many Medicaid recipients were unable to pick up needed medications and receive other medical assistance in their new locations.

Investigations into the lack of assistance after Hurricane Katrina were carried out by the 109th Congress, the White House, the Inspector General, and the Government Accountability Office (GAO). In general, the findings of the reports indicated that the damage and deaths after the hurricane were largely the result of questionable leadership decisions, organizational failures, a lack of preparation, and a failed communication system. A common theme was the major shortcomings that existed within FEMA that led to the lack of response, alongside the loss of personnel and a small budget. FEMA was also criticized for not making investments in the infrastructure necessary to prevent the damage. The reports indicated that DHS did not focus on an "all-hazards" approach to disaster relieve, focusing too much on terrorism, which limited the ability to respond to a domestic emergency. As noted in one report, "While terrorism may occur again, we know hurricanes and other types of disasters will."[21] This indicated the need for FEMA to be prepared to respond to all types of disasters, not just terrorism.[22] The reports urged that Congress reconsider existing policies and practices regarding FEMA.[23]

The Senate Homeland Security and Governmental Affairs Committee investigated the slow response to Katrina, making a list of 86 recommendations for improving the agency. One of the top recommendations included a proposal to create a National Preparedness and Response Authority that would replace FEMA.[24]

FEMA was even critical of itself after the failed response. A report was issued in April 2006 by the agency in which it admitted that the criticism lodged against them was largely deserved. The Inspector General of the Department of Homeland Security agreed that the criticism was warranted. Their reports indicated that it took about three days after the hurricane hit land for officials in FEMA to truly understand the magnitude of the destruction caused by the storm. Moreover, they admitted that the events of Katrina showed them that their response plan was deficient. Specifically they noted that FEMA and officials from Louisiana could not communicate, that they did not provide adequate housing for victims, did not carry out a sufficient search-and-rescue operation to find survivors, and did not provide, nor track, needed supplies. The report included thirty-eight recommendations for improvement.[25]

To make matters worse, in December 2006, it was announced that FEMA mistakenly gave out an estimated $1 billion in fraudulent or unjustified monetary awards after Hurricane Katrina. They admitted that at as much as eight percent of the money that had been distributed was in error. FEMA explained that they were under pressure to help residents after the hurricane, and they were not as careful as they should have been in providing money so that victims could purchase food, clothing, housing, and medicine. This resulted in large amounts of fraud. Although FEMA officials sought repayment of the funds, the agency recouped less than one percent of the money.[26]

In response to the findings of the investigations, members of the 109th Congress (2005–2006) proposed different laws regarding policies for the nation's federal emergency management, seeking to reorganize FEMA once again. They wanted to clarify the agency's mission, functions, and leadership. In May 2006, the House Transportation and Infrastructure Committee and the Government Reform Committee approved a bill (HR 5316) to reorganize FEMA and move it out of DHS, making it once again an independent or Cabinet-level agency. The House Homeland Security Committee approved another bill that would overhaul FEMA but leave it as part of DHS.[27] In July 2006, the Senate endorsed the idea of keeping the FEMA as an agency within DHS, but overhauling the agency.

By the end of 2006, Congress had passed a proposal to revamp the agency. The overhaul of FEMA was part of the fiscal 2007 Homeland Security Appropriations bill for fiscal year 2007.[28] The changes were part of Title VI, which was officially named the "Post-Katrina Emergency Management Reform Act of 2006," or more commonly referred to as the Post-Katrina Act. The new law contains many changes that will have long-term consequences for FEMA.

The Post-Katrina Act reorganized FEMA, expanded its authority, and imposed new conditions and requirements on how the agency carried out its responsibilities.[29] Under the new law, FEMA would remain part of DHS but the agency would have an elevated status and more autonomy. The agency's administrator was asked to undertake a variety of activities to prepare both prior to a disaster occurs and afterwards. The agency was given the responsibility to lead all efforts that are intended to protect lives and limit property damage that may result from all hazards. These responsibilities include, among other things, establishing emergency alert systems, providing for a continuity of operations, and building a national emergency management system. There would be ten regional offices created, each one with distinct responsibilities. There were new leadership positions created, including a Disability Coordinator and a Small State and Rural Advocate. Other positions established include an Assistant Secretary for Cybersecurity and Communications, US Fire Administrator, Chief Medical Officer, and a Director of the Recovery Office. Other positions were abolished, including the Under Secretary for Federal Emergency Management, who was replaced with the position of FEMA Administrator. Under the new law, the FEMA administrator would provide recommendations regarding emergency management activities directly to Congress (after informing the DHS Secretary).

A National Advisory Council (NAC) was established by the Post-Katrina Act. As defined in the legislation, the NAC was to be comprised of up to thirty-five members who would be appointed by, and served at the pleasure of, the FEMA administrator. As much as possible, the members were to be geographically diverse and represent multiple officials, including emergency managers and response providers from state, local, and tribal governments, as well as representatives from the private sector and nongovernmental organizations. The administrator would have the authority to appoint one member to serve as the chair and one member to serve as the vice chair.

The role of the council was to ensure effective and ongoing response by the federal government to emergencies. This included all aspects of preparedness, protection, response, recovery, and mitigation for natural disasters, acts of terrorism, and other manmade disasters. The NAC members were to be an integral component in the development and revision of the National Preparedness Goal, the National Preparedness System, the National Incident Management System, and other related plans and strategies.[30] The council membership also had the responsibility to advise the FEMA administrator on all aspects of emergency management.

The Post-Katrina law addressed some of the administrative problems that became readily apparent after Hurricane Katrina. The FEMA administrator was given the task of developing a logistics system that would track the location of goods and services as they are transported from FEMA to the disaster site. The administrator was also tasked with establishing a pre-positioned equipment program in at least eleven places as a way to be prepared for disaster assistance operations. Additionally, the administrator was asked to update and improve the agency's information technology systems. The new law had some other provisions to assist after a disaster. They are listed in Table 1.1.

Table 1.1: Provisions of the Post-Katrina Act

- The development of a system to locate missing family members after a disaster. The new system was called the National Emergency Family Registry and Locator System and the Child Locator Center.
- The creation of recovery offices in five states to allow for provisions of needed assistance in a timely and effective manner after a future disaster.
- The creation of a "Housing Strategy" that would provide a list of housing resources that would be available for disaster victims for all incomes and specifically for those populations with special needs.
- The establishment of training programs to ensure that first responders are effective, grants are supervised, the National Response Plan was administered and implemented.
- The creation of a new National Integration Center within FEMA to manage both the National Incident Management System (NIMS) and the National Response Plan (NRP). In addition, NIC is responsible for coordinating volunteer activity and first responders.
- The creation of ten regional offices within FEMA, each to be headed by a Regional Administrator. Each Administrator is to work alongside non-federal partners to develop resources related to the national catastrophic response system. They are also tasked with establishing emergency communications systems, overseeing regional strike teams that coordinate initial response efforts, developing regional plans that support the National Response Plan, developing mutual aid agreements in the region, identifying special response modes for those with special needs, and maintaining a Regional Response Coordination Center. Every Regional Administrator must also create a Regional Advisory Council to provide advice on emergency management issues and identify gaps in response plans.

The reorganization of FEMA under the Post-Katrina Act became effective in 2007. In 2012, the new FEMA was tested before and after Hurricane Sandy (also known as "Superstorm Sandy") hit the Northeast US in October 2012. While all states along the east coast were affected, the hurricane hit New Jersey and New York the hardest, causing $65 billion in damages.[31] Between 117–159 people died.* Before the storm hit, President Obama signed an emergency declaration for those states identified as being impacted by the storm, which would allow officials there to request federal aid as needed.

For the most part, there was a general agreement that the federal response to victims in those communities affected by Hurricane Sandy was far improved as compared to the response after Hurricane Katrina. It was obvious that officials from DHS and FEMA established stronger partnerships with state and local governments and were more prepared prior to the disaster. The mayor of New Jersey, Chris Christie, despite being of the opposite political party to the president, praised the administration for their quick response and assistance. Even survivors of the storm recognized how helpful FEMA was before the storm and immediately after. They reported that FEMA provided bottled water, food, and places to stay.[32]

In the days after Hurricane Sandy, Obama created the Hurricane Sandy Rebuilding Task Force and asked the members to devise a strategy for rebuilding the areas that were damaged by the storm. The task force issued a report in August 2013, in which it made 69 recommendations for new policies. They recommended that neighborhoods located along the coast should assume that floods will happen again, and will probably be more frequent. They also recommended that a more advanced electrical grid be developed so power outages are less likely to occur, as well as methods that will maintain cellular service. Moreover, communities should take protective measures now and make plans to help prevent damage during future storms.[33]

Even though it was a marked improvement, the federal response to Sandy was not perfect. There were fuel shortages and power outages that remained longer after Sandy than Katrina. Rudy Giuliani, the former Mayor of New York, spoke against the government's response and President Obama, comparing the New York neighborhoods affected by Sandy to those in New Orleans after Katrina. Nonetheless, it was obvious to most people that the

---

* The exact number of people who died as the result of Hurricane Sandy is unknown. While data from the Centers for Disease Control and Prevention, which used data from the American Red Cross, estimates that 117 died, the National Oceanographic and Atmospheric Administration indicates that 159 people died directly or indirectly by the storm.

government's response to Sandy clearly demonstrated marked advancements from Katrina.[34]

FEMA Today

Today, FEMA is much more effective than in past years in preparing for, and responding to, disasters. There have been many changes that have made it a more effective agency and better able to respond to emergencies. Craig Fugate, the agency's administrator, is a veteran emergency manager. Before working at FEMA, he was the head of Florida's emergency office where he was given high marks for his response to several hurricanes that hit the state, including Hurricane Katrina. In FEMA, Fugate has hired other personnel who have backgrounds related to state and local emergency management positions.

Under Fugate, FEMA has become more focused on getting personnel to the site as early as possible and providing needed assistance quickly. They are also working with communities to prepare for events so that when they do occur, communities will be better able to deal with the crises.[35]

According to FEMA, today's agency "coordinates the federal government's role in preparing for, preventing, mitigating the effects of, responding to, and recovering from all domestic disasters, whether natural or man-made, including acts of terror." The agency has many offices that specialize in different areas related to responding to future events. They include an Office of Policy and Program Analysis, Office of Disability Integration and Coordination, Office of National Capital Region Coordination, Office of External Affairs, Regional Operations, Protection and National Preparedness, Office of Response and Recovery, Office of Senior Law Enforcement Advisor, and the Office of Equal Rights.

FEMA's mission "is to support our citizens and first responders to ensure that as a nation we work together to build, sustain, and improve our capacity to prepare for, protect against, respond to, recover from, and mitigate hazards."[36] To do this, personnel within the agency help to "identify actions that should be taken before, during, and after an event that are unique to each hazard."[37]

FEMA is now actively involved in two vital areas: planning, preparing, and mitigating the effects of a disaster, and response and recovery (Disaster Survivor Assistance).

Plan, Prepare, and Mitigate

FEMA works directly with individuals in local communities to help them prepare for possible disasters, both natural and man-made, and then mitigate or lessen the possible effects of those events. For example, FEMA officials work with homeowners, contractors, architects, and even engineers to build safer homes and buildings that can withstand natural events through the FEMA Building Science Branch. Through the National Flood Insurance Program, FEMA provides homeowners, renters, and business owners with ways to protect themselves financially from losses due to catastrophic floods.[38]

While FEMA helps communities prepare for events, they also work to help prepare for a potential national disaster. The Mitigation Directorate is the office within FEMA that has the responsibility to oversee planning and preparations for a possible national disaster. They help to identify potential risks found in a community, and make plans to reduce potential injuries, deaths, or loss of property that could result.

Part of the planning, preparing, and mitigating stage is National Preparedness. According to FEMA, everyone can play a role to help ensure that the nation is protected from an attack. FEMA helps all communities be prepared for a disaster, and be ready to implement their programs effectively. To do this, FEMA relies on the National Preparedness Goal, written in September 2011, which defines what it means for the whole community to be prepared for all types of disasters and emergencies. The goal is: "A secure and resilient nation with the capabilities required across the whole community to prevent, protect against, mitigate, respond to, and recover from the threats and hazards that pose the greatest risk."[39]

Disaster Response

The second role of FEMA is to respond quickly to assist all victims of natural disasters or acts of terrorism throughout the US. FEMA provides victims with immediate needs like food, water, and housing. They assist victims locate family and friends who may be missing. In many situations, FEMA operates disaster recovery centers in those areas that have been affected by an event. The centers are operated by trained workers and FEMA officials who provide information, legal advice, and financial assistance to those who need help.[40] FEMA's emergency response services are described in Table 1.2.

Table 1.2: FEMA's Response Services

National Disaster Medical System (NDMS): comprised of medical professionals who provide medical assistance to victims of a disaster.

Urban Search and Rescue (USAR): involves locating, rescuing, and stabilizing any victims trapped in confined spaces.

Disaster Mortuary Operations Response Team (DMORT): comprised of individuals who have specialized training in recovery, identification, and processing of deaths at a disaster scene, and provide mortuary and forensic services after a crisis.

Disaster Medical Assistance Team (DMAT): composed of doctors and paramedics who provide assistance to burn victims, children, or victims who have been crushed.

National Medical Response Teams (NMRT): addresses the medical needs of victims in the aftermath of accidents involving chemical, biological, or nuclear weapons or materials.

Mobile Emergency Response Support (MERS): provides multi-media communications, information processing, logistics, and operational support to agencies during emergencies to support recovery efforts.[41]

Veterinary Medical Assistance Teams (VMAT): made up of veterinarians, pathologists, animal health technicians, microbiologists, and others who assist animal disaster victims and provide care to search dogs.

International Medical Surgical Response Teams (IMSuRTs): trained to quickly establish a surgical facility anywhere in the world to assist victims.

Others: National Nursing Response Teams (NNRT) and the National Pharmacy Response Teams (NPRT).[42]

Source: FEMA, August 17, 2012. "Mobile Emergency Response Support" https://www.fema.gov/mobile-emergency-response-support; FEMA, July 16, 2012. "National Disaster Medical System." http://www.fema.gov/news-release/2004/04/21/national-disaster-medical-system; FEMA, Oct 28, 2012, "Urban Search and Rescue" http://www.fema.gov/urban-search-rescue.

Should FEMA Be Reorganized?

As the US has faced different disasters and emergencies throughout its history, it has become clear that there is a need for an organization that can provide the things that individuals need to survive during a disaster or to rebuild in the time after a disaster. Short-term assistance is often needed to ensure that victims have the medical assistance, food, water, and housing they require. Long-term assistance is also needed to allow a community to rebuild its infrastructure (roads, schools, and parks) that are necessary for a functioning and safe society. Assistance is also important to protect people from health, environmental, and disaster risks. Help can mean that people and communities are able to restore some level of normalcy and decency to their lives. In the end, it is essential that the US has a competent agency that can provide both short-term and long-term services. There is a need for an agency that is prepared to assist citizens, communities, and the nation plan and prepare for events so when they happen, everyone is prepared for, and can respond to, a wide variety of disasters as needed.

FEMA was created to meet this need and to ensure that those affected by disasters were provided with assistance needed to survive, remain safe, and rebuild their lives. The agency has gone through many changes since it was first created in 1978 by President Carter. As it has gone through these changes, its effectiveness has varied. Given the problems that FEMA has faced, the question often arises: what should the structure of FEMA look like? Should it be reorganized? If so, there are two obvious choices. It could remain as part of DHS, as currently structured. Or it could once again be given more autonomy and returned to a Cabinet-level agency. Another option would be to abolish the agency altogether and the task of responding to a disaster returned to the individual states.

A clear argument exists for leaving FEMA as a part of DHS. As a stand-alone agency, FEMA is overloaded by the responsibility of being asked to perform both disaster preparation and response. Either one of these tasks separately is monumental, but to give one agency both responsibilities may be overwhelming. DHS has many more resources and is better equipped to respond to a disaster in any part of the country in a coordinated and organized way. DHS personnel are trained and prepared to respond at a moment's notice to a variety of situations. Further, the federal government can provide a more consistent response to disasters. Some states, especially smaller states, may not have the resources to respond quickly to a disaster or emergency situation. The federal government has more money, personnel, equipment, and technology to respond much more quickly than states. They have more means of communication, more available personnel and the equipment and supplies needed to assist those in need.

However, the argument has been made that FEMA has shown itself to be an effective agency in both preparing for, and responding to, disasters of all kinds as an independent agency. It was obvious that when it was provided with adequate resources (budget) and support, along with effective leadership and personnel, the agency was clearly capable of responding quickly and effectively to both acts of terrorism (9/11 and Oklahoma City) and natural disasters (Hurricane Sandy). When given an appropriate budget, personnel, autonomy, and organization, the organization was able to provide the services it was called on to provide, and in a timely fashion.

At the same time, the arguments for abolishing the agency and reassigning disaster response tasks to the states are compelling. The first is simply that neither FEMA nor DHS is effective in providing immediate relief to those who have suffered after a disaster. There have been many instances where FEMA's response has been slow and uncoordinated, whether as an independent agency or as part of DHS. There has also been a lack of communication on many levels: within the federal government, between the federal government and the states, between the government and victims, and with service agencies. People have suffered, or even died, because of a lack of action by FEMA. In many cases, state officials may be able to respond more quickly to disasters that occur within their boundaries. They are closer to the location and can respond in a more timely fashion. Moreover, states are more aware of their own needs and capabilities. From that perspective, disaster training and response should be provided by states, not by FEMA either as an independent agency or as part of DHS.

Conclusion

At this point, the future of FEMA is unknown. Whether it stays within DHS or is reorganized once again to be an independent agency, or even dissolved altogether and the responsibilities given to the individual states, remains to be seen. While it is clear that there is a need for the nation to have a response plan in the case of a disaster or attack, the best way to do that is yet to be determined.

Endnotes

1. Federal Emergency Management Agency Website, "FEMA: 35 Years of Commitment" Retrieved from http://www.fema.gov/fema-35-years-commitment.
2. Carter, Jimmy. "Executive Order 12127—Federal Emergency Management Agency." (March 31, 1979). Online by Gerhard Peters and John T. Woolley, *The American Presidency Project.* http://www.presidency.ucsb.edu/ws/?pid=32127.
3. Taylor, Andrew. (September 12, 1992). "Andrew is Brutal Blow for Agency." *CQ Weekly:* 2703. Retrieved from http://library.cqpress.com/cqweekly/WR102408159.
4. Carter, Jimmy. "Environmental Priorities and Programs Message to the Congress." (August 2, 1979). Online by Gerhard Peters and John T. Woolley, *The American Presidency Project.* Retrieved from http://www.presidency.ucsb.edu/ws/?pid=32684.
5. Walker, Samuel J. (2005). *Three Mile Island: A Nuclear Crisis in Historical Perspective.* Berkeley: University of California Press.
6. Prah, P. M. (November 18, 2005). "Disaster Preparedness." *CQ Researcher* 15: 981–1004. Retrieved from Http://library.cqpress.com/cqresesarcher/document.php?id=cqresrre2005 111800&type=hitli.

7. Taylor, Andrew. (September 12, 1992). "Andrew is Brutal Blow for Agency." *CQ Weekly*: 2703. Retrieved from http://library.cqpress.com/cqweekly/WR102408159; Roberts, Patrick S. (June/July 2006). "FEMA After Katrina" *Policy Review* pp. 15–33.

8. Roberts, Patrick S. (June/July 2006). "FEMA after Katrina" *Policy Review* pp. 15–33.

9. Veron, Ilyse J. (July 17, 1993). "High Marks for FEMA—for Now." *CQWeekly*: 1862. Retrieved from http://library.cqpress.com/cqweekly/WR103401932.

10. Prah, P. M. (November 18, 2005). "Disaster Preparedness" *CQ Researcher* 15: 981–1004. Retrieved from Http://library.cqpress.com/cqresesarcher/document.php?id=cqresrre2005111800&type=hitli.

11. Adams, Rebecca. (September 12, 2005). "FEMA Failure a Perfect Storm of Bureaucracy" *CQ Weekly* 2378–2379. http://library.cqpress.com/cqweekly/weeklyreport109-000001853459; Roberts, Patrick S. (June/July 2006). "FEMA after Katrina" *Policy Review* pp. 15–33.

12. Pierre, John K. and Gail S. Stephenson. (2008). "After Katrina: A Critical Look at FEMA's Failure to Provide Housing for Victims of Natural Disasters." *Louisiana Law Review* vol 68: 443–495.

13. "The Federal Response to Hurricane Katrina: Lessons Learned" (February 2006); Washington, D.C.: Government Printing Office. Retrieved from http://georgewbush-whitehouse.archives.gov/reports/katrina-lessons-learned/.

14. Lipton, Eric. (9/17/2005). "FEMA, Slow to the Rescue, Now Stumbles in Aid Effort." Retrieved from http://www.nytimes.com.

15. Roberts, Patrick S. (June/July 2006). "FEMA after Katrina" *Policy Review* pp. 15–33.

16. "The Federal Response to Hurricane Katrina: Lessons Learned" (February 2006). Washington, D.C.: Government Printing Office.

17. Kirkpatrick, David D. and Scott Shane. (September 15, 2005). "Ex-FEMA Chief Tells of Frustration and Chaos." Retrieved from *New York Times* http://www.nytimes.com/2005/09/15/national/nationalspecial/15brown.html.

18. Prah, P. M. (November 18, 2005). "Disaster Preparedness" *CQ Researcher* 15: 981–1004. Retrieved from Http://library.cqpress.com/cqresesarcher/document.php?id=cqresrre2005111800&type=hitli; Hsu, Spencer S. and Susan B. Glasser. (September 6, 2005). "FEMA Director Singled Out by Response Critics." *Washington Post.* Retrieved from http://www.washingtonpost.com/wp-dyn/content/article/2005/09/05/AR2005090501590.html; Crittenden, Michael R. (September 10, 2007). "Emergency Plan Deemed a Disaster-in-Waiting" *CQWeekly*: 2551. Retrieved from http://library.cqpress.com/cqweekly/weeklyreport110-000002580266.

19. Shoup, Anna. (September9, 2005). "FEMA Faces Intense Scrutiny" PBS Newshour; Retrieved from http://www.pbs.org/newshour/updates/government_programs-july-dec05-fema.

20. Drier, Peter. (2006). "Katrina: A Political Disaster." National Housing Institute, Shelterforce Online. Issue 145; Retrieved from http://www.nhi.org/online/issues/145/political disaster.html; see also Drier, Peter. March 2006. "Katrina and Power in America." *Urban Affairs Review.*

21. Fischer, Henry W., Kathryn Gregoire, John Scala, Lynn Letukas, Joseph Mellon, Scott Romine and Danielle Turner. (2006). "The Emergency Management Response to Hurricane Katrina" Millersville, PA: Center for Disaster Research and Education. Retrieved from http://www.colorado.edu/hazards/research/qr/qr189/qr189.html.

22. Fischer, Henry W., Kathryn Gregoire, John Scala, Lynn Letukas, Joseph Mellon, Scott Romine and Danielle Turner. (2006). "The Emergency Management Response to Hurricane Katrina" Millersville, PA: Center for Disaster Research and Education. Retrieved from

http://www.colorado.edu/hazards/research/qr/qr189/qr189.html.

23. Library of Congress, Congressional Research Service. (March 6, 2007). "Federal Emergency Management Policy Changes after Hurricane Katrina: A summary of Statutory Provisions." Retrieved from http://www.fas.org/sgp/crs/homesec/RL33729.pdf.

24. Starks, Tim. May 1, 2006. "Senators Say Scrap FEMA and Start Over." *CQ Weekly* 1186. Retrieved from http://library.cqpress.com/cqweekly/weeklyreport109-000002168014.

25. Ahlers, Mike M. (April 14, 2006). "Report: Criticism of FEMA's Katrina response Deserved" Retrieved from CNN.com.

26. Lipton, Eric (December 6, 2006). "Report Finds New Problems in FEMA Aid Distribution." *New York Times*; Retrieved from http://www.nytimes.com/2006/12/06/us/06fraud.html; Zeller, Shawn. (February 18, 2013). "Finding Fraud in FEMA Funds." *CQWeekly*: 320. Retrieved from http://library.cqpress.com/cqweekly/weeklyreport113-000004222618; Kunzelman, Michael and Ryan J. Foley. (6/1/11). "FEMA to Demand that Hurricane Katrina Victims Return Aid Money." *Huff Post Politics*. Retrieved from http://www.huffingtonpost.com/2011/06/01/fema-to-demand-that-hurricans-869584.html.

27. Yoest, Patrick. (July 17, 2006). "Senate Keeps FEMA in its Place" *CQWeekly*: 1971. Retrieved from http://library.cqpress.com/cqweekly/weeklyreport109-000002334169; Starks, Tim. (May 22, 2006). "House Panels Take Differing Approaches to 'Fixing' FEMA." *CQWeekly*: 1412. Retrieved from http://library.cqpress.com/cqweekly/weeklyreport109-000002230429.

28. Yoest, Patrick. (December 18, 2006). "2006 Legislative Summary: FEMA Restructuring." *CQWeekly*: 3355. Retrieved from http://library.cqpress.com/cqweekly/weeklyreport109 000002418336.

29. Library of Congress, Congressional Research Service. (March 6, 2007). "Federal Emergency Management Policy Changes after Hurricane Katrina: A summary of Statutory Provisions." Retrieved from http://www.fas.org/sgp/crs/homesec/RL33729.pdf.

30. FEMA. "National Advisory Council" Retrieved from http://www.fema.gov/nationa-advisory-council.

31. National Oceanic and Atmospheric Administration (2013). "Billion-Dollar Weather/Climate Disasters". *National Climatic Data Center*.

32. Naylor, Brian. (November 3, 2012). "Lessons From Katrina Boost FEMA's Sandy Response." NPR. Retrieved from http://www.npr.org/2012/11/03/164224394/lessons-from-katrina-boost-femas-sandy-response.

33. Caruso, David B. and Meghan Barr. (August 19, 2013). "Hurricane Sandy Rebuilding Task Force: Coasts Should Prepare for Rising Seas" *Huffington Post* Retrieved from http://www.huffingtonpost.com/2013/08/19/hurricane-sandy-rebuilding-task-force_n_3778310.html; Jackson, David. (August 19, 2013). "Hurricane Sandy Task Force Urges Better Construction" *USA Today* Retrieved from http://www.usatoday.com/story/news/politics/2013/08/19/obama-hurricane-sandy-rebuilding-task-force/2670407/.

34. Starks, Tim. (December 31, 2012). "Katrina's Lessons Seen in Response to Sandy." *CQWeekly*: 2551. http://library.cqpress.com/cqweekly/weeklyreport112-000004197197.

35. Naylor, Brian. (August 27, 2010). "Has FEMA Recovered from Hurricane Katrina? NPR Morning Edition; Retrieved from http://www.npr.org/templates/story/story.php?storyId=129466751.

36. FEMA, "About the Agency." Retrieved from http://www.fema.gov/about-agency.

37. FEMA. "Plan, Prepare and Mitigate" Retrieved from http://www.fema.gov/plan-prepare-mitigate.

38. FEMA. "Protecting Homes" Retrieved from http://www.fema.gov/protecting-homes.

39. FEMA. "National Preparedness Goal" Retrieved from http://www.fema.gov/national-preparedness-goal.

40. Blair, Kimberly (May 9, 2014). "FEMA Disaster Recovery Centers Opening This Weekend" *Pensacola News Journal*. Retrieved from http://www.pnj.com/story/news/2014/05/09/femas-disaster-recovery-center-opens-saturday/8911747/.

41. Federal Emergency Management Administration. (August 17, 2012). "Mobile Emergency Response Support." Retrieved from https://www.fema.gov/mobile-emergency-response-support.

42. Federal Emergency Management Administration (July 16, 2012). "National Disaster Medical System." Retrieved from http://www.fema.gov/news-release/2004/04/21/national-disaster-medical-system; Federal Emergency Management Administration, (October 28, 2012). "Urban Search and Rescue" Retrieved from http://www.fema.gov/urban-search-rescue.

Chapter 2

The Costs of Homeland Security: Are We Safer?

Introduction

On April 15, 2013, at 2:49 pm, an improvised explosive device (IED) detonated near the finish line of the Boston Marathon. The attack claimed the lives of three observers and injured nearly three hundred more; many lost limbs or suffered horrific wounds. Within minutes, Boylston Street became the scene of a war zone. First responders and the public at large reacted quickly in what has become known colloquially as "Boston Strong."[1] The Boston Marathon bombings closed down businesses and the subsequent manhunt for the two suspects shut down the entire city as the governor requested citizens to "shelter in place." The number of law enforcement agencies called into action included the Boston and Watertown Police Departments, FBI, ATF, Massachusetts State Police, Massachusetts Bay Transportation Authority Police, and the National Guard. There was an NHL hockey game scheduled at TD Garden that evening. It was cancelled along with an NBA basketball game scheduled for the next night. The FAA instituted flight restrictions in the area and the Amtrak service was suspended. On April 18, the FBI released photographs and surveillance videos showing the two suspects. They were later identified as brothers Tamerlan and Dzhokhar Tsarnaev, but not before they killed a police officer and hijacked a civilian. A firefight with police in Watertown resulted in the death of one of the brothers, Tamerlan. Dzhokhar escaped in a stolen SUV. He was later captured hiding in the bottom of a boat in the backyard of a Watertown, Massachusetts, home on Friday evening, April 19. By the end of the 18-hour manhunt numerous first responders, law enforcement agencies, and medical personnel had lent their expertise to the event.

So how much did the ordeal cost the state of Massachusetts? It was estimated that it cost up to $333 million to shut down Boston for a day to catch the marathon bombing suspects.[2] The response to the bombings was well executed—a result of years of planning and coordination. It spanned geographic boundaries, levels of government (local, state, and federal), professional disciplines, and the public and private sectors.[3]

The work leading up to the Boston Marathon, as well as the quick action following the event, highlights the significant progress that the US, as a nation, have made since the 9/11 attacks.[4] These efforts, however, are costly. Many of the capabilities demonstrated in Boston and in the immediate aftermath of the bombings were built or enhanced through grant monies secured from the Homeland Security Grant Programs (HSGP), including the Urban Areas Security Initiative (UASI) Grant Program and the State Homeland Security Program (SHSP). Since 2002 the Commonwealth of Massachusetts received more than $943 million in FEMA preparedness grant funds. Since 2003, Boston received more than $369 million through eight grant programs, including $179 million through the Urban Areas Security Initiative (UASI) grants.[5]

While both Massachusetts and Boston invested state, local, and federal grant funds in systems that were critical during the response, the fact remains that these measures are costly. Since September 11, 2001, the US has spent a reported $635.9 billion on homeland security. Furthermore, in recent years, federal funding for state homeland security efforts to respond to emergencies has decreased. The largest DHS formula grant program for states went from a high of $2 billion in 2003 to just $294 million in 2012. In 2013, the sequestration produced additional cuts to the Homeland Security Grant program, some of the effects were immediate, but most will be felt long term and are difficult to quantify.[6]

A look into homeland security funding since 9/11 raises almost as many questions as it answers. How is the money apportioned? Are we spending enough—and how would we know? Do the costs of homeland security keep us safer? This chapter will attempt to answer these questions. First it will address the history of DHS funding and the Homeland Security Grant Programs (HSGP). It will then discuss trends and controversies surrounding funding. The chapter will conclude with a discussion of whether or not the high costs of homeland security actually keep us safer as a nation.

DHS Funding

In the aftermath of September 11, 2001, our country has worked to strengthen and promote homeland security efforts and, specifically, how to deal with a crisis like the Boston Marathon Bombings. Many of these efforts have been geared towards mitigation of a terrorist attack. Preparation, training, effective leadership, and a coordinated response plan are the hallmarks of homeland security. But how much does it cost to keep America safe? What does it cost to prepare for and then respond to a crisis such as the Boston bombings? In this next section we will examine the DHS budget, its history, and how monies are distributed through the Homeland Security Grant Programs (HSGP).

DHS Appropriations FY2004–FY2014

The Homeland Security Appropriations Act of 2004 was an act of Congress that gave the authority to the president to fund the operations of the Department of Homeland Security (DHS) for each year. The act was first passed in June 2003 and authorized $29.4 billion dollars for homeland security. Each year, Congress passes the DHS appropriations bill which includes funding for all components and functions of the department. Table 2.1 presents DHS discretionary appropriations, as enacted for FY2004 through FY2014. Overall, annual appropriations for DHS rose from the establishment of the department, peaking in FY2010. However, the structural changes affected by the Budget Control Act allowed disaster funding to be included in regular appropriations bills without being scored against the bill's allocation. This altered the downward trend as funding that might have been provided in a supplemental appropriations bill was now provided in the annual process.[7] Minus the impact of disaster relief funding, the level of annual appropriations for the department has declined each year since FY2010. Supplemental funding, which frequently addressed congressional priorities such as disaster assistance and border security, varies widely from year-to-year and as a result distorts year-to-year comparisons of total appropriations.[8]

The total budget authority for DHS includes funding for sixteen organization components. The most heavily funded organization is FEMA followed by Customs and Border Protection (CBP), the US Coast Guard (USCG), Transportation Security Agency (TSA) and Immigration and Customs Enforcement (ICE). Organizations with smaller DHS funding include the US Secret Service (USSS) and the Science and Technology Directorate (S&T). Table 2.2 presents this information for the years FY2013–FY2015.

The DHS budget focuses resources on key capabilities in each of the Department's five mission areas. These are: preventing terrorism and enhancing security, securing and managing our borders, enforcing and administering our immigration laws, safeguarding and securing cyberspace, and preparing for and responding to disasters.[9] Additionally, the DHS budget reflects funding proposals for a portion of the Federal Emergency Management Agency's (FEMA) and National Protection and Programs Directorate's (NPPD) activities through the President's Opportunity, Growth and Security Initiative.[10] The following

Table 2.1. DHS Appropriations FY2004–FY2014
(Billions of dollars of budget authority)

	Nominal Appropriations				Constant Dollar Appropriations		
	Regular	Supplemental	Total	GDP Price Index	Regular	Supplemental	Total
FY2004	$29,411	$7.418	$36.829	0.969	$30.368	$7.659	$38.027
FY2005	29.557	67.328	96.885	1.000	29.557	67.328	96.885
FY2006	30.995	8.195	38.190	1.034	29.976	7.926	37.901
FY2007	34.047	4.560	38.607	1.065	31.981	4.283	36.264
FY2008	37.809	0.897	38.706	1.089	34.709	0.823	35.533
FY2009	40.070	3.143	43.213	1.103	36.318	2.849	39.167
FY2010	42.817	5.571	48.388	1.115	38.418	4.999	43.417
FY2011	42.477	0	42.477	1.138	37.329	0.000	37.329
FY2012	40.062	6.400	46.462	1.159	34.572	5.523	40.095
FY2013	46.247	12.072	58.319	1.183	39.093	10.205	49.298
FY2013 post-sequester	44.971	n/a	n/a	1.183	38.014	n/a	n/a
FY2014	45.123						

Source: Painter, W.L. Department of Homeland Security Appropriations: FY2014 Overview and Summary. (CRS Report R43193), p.6.

examples represent some of the funding requests in these five mission areas for FY2105:

Preventing Terrorism and Enhancing Security

- $3.8 billion for the Transportation Security Administration (TSA) screening operations to continue improving aviation security effectiveness by aligning passenger screening resources based on risk.
- $112 million for Secure Flight, under which DHS conducts passenger watch list—now vetting more than 14 million passengers weekly.

Table 2.2. DHS Total Budget Authority by Organization FY 2013–FY 2015

	FY 2013	FY 2014	FY 2015 (Pres. Budget)
Departmental Operations	$708,695	$728,269	$748,024
Analysis and Operations (A&O)	301,853	300,490	302,268
Office of the Inspector General (OIG)	137,910	139,437	145,457
US Customs & Border Protection (CBP)	11,736,990	12,445,616	12,764,835
US Immigration & Customs Enforcement (ICE)	5,627,660	5,614,361	5,359,065
Transportation Security Administration (TSA)	7,193,757	7,364,510	7,305,098
US Coast Guard (USCG)	9,972,425	10,214,999	9,796,995
US Secret Service (USSS)	1,808,313	1,840,272	1,895,905
National Protection and Programs Directorate (NPPD)	2,638,634	2,813,213	2,857,666
Office of Health Affairs (OHA)	126,324	126,763	125,767
Federal Emergency Management Agency (FEMA)	11,865,196	11,553,899	12,496,517
FEMA: Grant Programs	2,373,540	2,530,000	2,225,469
US Citizenship & Immigration Services (USCIS)	3,378,348	3,219,142	3,259,885
Federal Law Enforcement Training Center (FLETC)	243,111	258,730	259,595
Science & Technology Directorate (S&T)	794,227	1,220,212	1,071,818
Domestic Nuclear Detection Office (DNDO)	302,981	285,255	304,423
Total Budget Authority	59,209.964	60,655.168	60,918.787

Source: US Dept. of Homeland Security "Budget-in-Brief Fiscal Year 2015" Retrieved from www.dhs.gov.

- $187.6 million for Enhanced Explosives Screening to ensure screening of 100 percent of all checked and carry-on baggage for explosives.
- $106.9 million for Air Cargo Screening to ensure that 100 percent of all cargo transported on passenger aircraft that depart from or arrive at US airports is screened.
- More than $1 billion for FEMA's preparedness grants.
- $86 million for Infrastructure Security Compliance funding to secure America's high-risk chemical facilities.[11]

Securing and Managing Our Borders

- Salaries, benefits, and operating costs for 21,370 Border Patrol agents and 25,775 CBP officers.
- $362 million to maintain necessary infrastructure technology along the nation's borders to ensure that law enforcement personnel are supported with effective surveillance.
- $27 million in operations and maintenance for six new Coast Guard Fast Response Cutters (FRCs), which provide critical maritime border security along the Southeast and Gulf Coast.
- US Coast Guard port security screening to secure key transportation nodes through security/background checks.
- 35 Border Enforcement Security Task Force units that partner with DHS law enforcement with Federal, state, local, tribal, and foreign law enforcement agencies to combat illicit activities along the borders and major seaports.[12]

Enforcing and Administering Our Immigration Laws

- Authority to use $3.1 billion in fee collections to process the millions of immigration benefit applications expected to be received in FY2015.
- $184.9 million to support the transformation of the US immigration process from a paper-based filing system to an efficient, customer-focused, electronic filing system.
- $124.8 million to continue expansion and enhancement of the E-Verify program.
- $2.6 billion to support Immigration and Customs Enforcement (ICE) activities to identify, apprehend, and remove illegal aliens from the US. Specifics include:
- Funds to supervise over 60,000 illegal aliens.
- $1.8 billion to provide safe, secure, and humane detention of removable aliens who are held in government custody because they present a risk of flight, a risk to public safety, or are subject to mandatory detention.
- $322.4 million to identify and remove criminal aliens.[13]

Safeguarding and Securing Cyberspace

- $1.25 billion for cybersecurity activities to include:
  - $377.7 million for Network Security Deployment.
  - $143.5 million for the Continuous Diagnostics and Mitigation program.
  - $173.5 million to support cyber and cyber-enabled investigations carried out by ICE related to programmatic areas such as cyber-economic crime and identity theft.
  - $8.5 million to establish a voluntary program and an enhanced cybersecurity services capability to support Executive Order 13636, Improving Critical Infrastructure Cybersecurity.

Preparing for and Responding to Disasters

- $10.2 billion to support disaster resiliency through the grants programs that are administered by FEMA and the Disaster Relief Fund (DRF). This includes:
  - $2.2 billion in total grants funding to state and local governments to prevent, protect against, and respond to and recover from incidents of terrorism and other catastrophic events.
  - $7 billion in DRF funding to provide immediate and long-lasting assistance to individuals and communities stricken by emergencies and major disasters.
- National Flood Insurance Program (NFIP)—$4.5 billion of mandatory budget authority, of which $150 million will be used for flood mitigation grants to increase our nation's resiliency to floods.
- Continued funding for the recovery and reconstruction efforts for the effects of Hurricane Sandy.[14]

A Brief History of Homeland Security Funding

The federal government began providing counter-terrorism assistance to the states and localities following the bombings of the World Trade Center in 1993 and the Alfred P. Murrah federal building in 1995.[15] In 1996, Congress enacted The Defense Against Weapons of Mass Destruction Act (also known as the Nunn-Lugar-Domenici Act) which left open the question of who would be the lead agency in terrorism. Several agencies—including the FEMA, Department of Justice (DOJ), Department of Health and Human Resources (DHHS), Department of Defense (DoD), and the National Guard—were involved in the terrorism issue and all were jockeying for the leadership position.[16] The largest distinction between these agencies was related to the levels of funding they received. Since DoD and DOJ controlled the majority of what was allocated, DoD became the lead agency for the establishment of the Nunn-Lugar Domenici Program (NLD).[17] This new program provided financial assistance to over 150 major US cities. The focus was on helping first responders prepare for, prevent, and respond to terrorist attacks involving weapons of mass destruction.[18] In 2000, the NLD-DPP was transferred to the DOJ's Office of Domestic Preparedness (ODP). Here, assistance programs that enhanced state and local emergency response capabilities, including terrorist attack responses, were administered.

At the time of the 9/11 terrorist attacks, funding for emergency preparedness was primarily through ODP. In addition to working with state and local first responders, ODP was responsible for directing terrorism preparedness grant programs at the federal level for all emergency response providers and for measuring programmatic performance and improvements in domestic preparedness.[19] For example, in 2002, ODP offered training to law enforcement in such areas as weapons of mass destruction (WMD) awareness, response to hazardous materials events or incidents involving WMD, and incident management.[20]

The enactment of the Homeland Security Act of 2002 transferred the ODP to the newly created Department of Homeland Security (DHS). Initially, ODP and its terrorism preparedness programs were administered by the Border and Transportation Security Directorate and all-hazards preparedness programs were in the Federal Emergency Management Agency (FEMA). ODP and all assistance programs were transferred to the Office of the Secretary in 2004 due to state and local criticism of DHS not having a "one-stop shop" for grant programs assistance.[21] The Post-Katrina Emergency Management Reform Act of 2006 (P.L. 109-295) further consolidated grant administration authority under FEMA led by the Grants Program Directorate (GDP). GDP is now the primary DHS and FEMA entity responsible for managing the majority of DHS assistance to states and localities.[22] Each year, the GPD announces the availability of program funding opportunities in the Funding Opportunity Announcements (FAO). This bulletin provides details on the various preparedness grant programs being made available for that fiscal year. The FOA released on March 18, 2014 represented $1,616,346,000 in FY 2014 federal assistance for six grant programs:

- Homeland Security Grant Program (HSGP)
- Tribal Homeland Security Grant Program (THSGP)
- Nonprofit Homeland Security Grant Program (NSGP)
- Intercity Passenger Rail—Amtrak (IPR) Program

- Port Security Grant Program (PSGP)
- Transit Security Grant Program (TSGP)[23]

The following discussion explains the Homeland Security Grant Program (HSGP) and how this grant program is allocated to the states.

Homeland Security Grant Program (HSGP)

In FY 2003, DHS administered eight assistance programs and expanded the total to fifteen programs in FY 2010. This expansion and scope of homeland security assistance programs are the result of congressional and executive branch actions.[24] Over the years, the number of programs administered by DHS has fluctuated. Moreover, the formula for how much funding is provided to the states has changed from a fair-share non-discretionary allocation to a risk based discretionary funding. In this section we will examine homeland security grant funding and the controversies surrounding these allocations to the states.

The FY 2014 HSGP supports core capabilities across the five mission areas of Prevention, Protection, Mitigation, Response, and Recovery based on allowable costs. HSGP is comprised of three interconnected grant programs:

- State Homeland Security Program (SHSP)
- Urban Areas Security Initiative (UASI)
- Operation Stonegarden (OPSG)[25]

State Homeland Security Program (SHSP)

The purpose of the SHSP is to support the implementation of risk driven, capabilities-based State Homeland Security Strategies to address capability targets set in urban area, state, and regional Threat and Hazard Identification and Risk Assessments (THIRAs).[26] The capability targets are established during the THIRA process and assessed in the State Preparedness Report (SPR) and inform planning, organization, equipment, training, and exercise needs to prevent, protect against, mitigate, respond to, and recover from acts of terrorism and other catastrophic events.[27] The State Administrative Agency (SAA) is the only entity eligible to apply to FEMA for SHSP funds. In FY 2014, the total amount of funding available was $401,346,000. Eligible applicants include all 50 states, the District of Columbia, Puerto Rico, American Samoa, Guam, the Northern Mariana Islands, and the US Virgin Islands. Table 2.3 illustrates the breakdown of these allocations for FY 2014.

Table 2.3. FY 2014 SHSP Allocations

State/Territory	FY 2014 Allocation	State/Territory	FY 2014 Allocation
Alabama	$3,733,000	Montana	$3,733,000
Alaska	$3,733,000	Nebraska	$3,733,000
American Samoa	$854,000	Nevada	$3,733,000
Arizona	$4,568,000	New Hampshire	$3,733,000
Arkansas	$3,733,000	New Jersey	$8,354,000
California	$60,035,000	New Mexico	$3,733,000
Colorado	$3,979,000	New York	$76,742,000
Connecticut	$3,978,000	North Carolina	$5,489,000
Delaware	$3,733,000	North Dakota	$3,733,000
District of Columbia	$4,119,000	Northern Mariana	$854,000
Florida	$11,010,000	Ohio	$7,698,000
Georgia	$6,807,000	Oklahoma	$3,733,000
Guam	$854,000	Oregon	$3,837,000
Hawaii	$3,733,000	Pennsylvania	$10,026,000
Idaho	$3,733,000	Puerto Rico	$3,733,000
Illinois	$16,357,000	Rhode Island	$3,733,000
Indiana	$3,978,000	South Carolina	$3,733,000
Iowa	$3,733,000	South Dakota	$3,733,000
Kansas	$3,733,000	Tennessee	$3,978,000
Kentucky	$3,978,000	Texas	$21,448,000
Louisiana	$3,978,000	US Virgin Islands	$854,000
Maine	$3,733,000	Utah	$3,733,000
Maryland	$6,125,000	Vermont	$3,733,000
Massachusetts	$5,622,000	Virginia	$7,414,000
Michigan	$6,658,000	Washington	$6,493,000
Minnesota	$3,978,000	West Virginia	$3,733,000
Mississippi	$3,733,000	Wisconsin	$3,978,000
Missouri	$3,978,000	Wyoming	$3,733,000
Total			$401,346,000

Sources US Dept. of Homeland Security FEMA Grant Program Directorate Information Bulletin No. 394, March 18, 2014.

Urban Areas Security Initiative (UASI)

The UASI program provides funding to metropolitan areas, counties, and mutual aid partners. Designated urban areas may use UASI funds to purchase specialized homeland security equipment, plan and execute exercises, and to pay for first responder overtime costs and training.[28] All funding allocations are based on risk analysis and anticipated effectiveness of funding. Eligible applicants must come from high-threat, high-density urban areas. To determine this, the DHS conducts vulnerability and threat assessments that evaluate the location of critical infrastructure and the population density of all major population areas. Based on these assessments, selected metropolitan areas are then grouped into two categories, Tier I and Tier II. The seven highest risk urban areas are designated as Tier I and receive a larger portion of funding; the remaining areas are designated as Tier II and receive less funding. In FY 2014, the total funding available was $587,000,000.[29]

Operation Stonegarden (OPSG)

The intent of the Operation Stonegarden Program (OPSG) is to enhance cooperation and coordination among various law enforcement agencies in a joint mission to secure the US' borders along routes of ingress from international borders to include travel corridors in states bordering Mexico and Canada, as well as states and territories with international water borders. Local entities can apply for funding through their State Administrative Agency (SAA). The total funding available in FY 2014 was $55,000,000 (see Table 2.4).[30]

Until 2012, the Citizen Corps Program (CCP) and Metropolitan Medical Response System (MMRS) were funded under the SHSP. While this is no longer the case, states may request funding for mass casualty incident preparedness and citizen preparedness programs but they must meet the allowability requirements of the SHSP and UASI programs.[31]

Funding Trends and Controversies

Tracking funding trends over the years has been especially challenging. This is partially a result of the fragmented nature of the grant administration process and because of inconsistent data on expenditures and reimbursements.[32]

To improve the grant administration process, DHS and some state governments initiated several new procedures in 2005. For example, some states developed centralized purchasing systems that allowed local governments to

Table 2.4. Key Homeland Security Grant Programs

Grant Program	Purpose	Funding
State Homeland Security Program (SHSP)	Supports the implementation of the State Homeland Security Strategy to address the identified planning, equipment, training, and exercise needs for acts of terrorism. SHSP also supports the implementation of NIMS.	Funds are allocated based on a minimum guarantee of 0.75% to each state of total appropriations (all eligible states). The remaining funds are allocated based on an individual state's population. In FY 2014, the SHSP provided $401,346,000 in support of building and sustaining core capabilities.
Urban Areas Security Initiative (UASI)	Supports the unique planning, equipment, training and exercise needs of high threat, high density urban areas, and assist them in building an enhanced and sustainable capacity to prevent, protect against, respond to, and recover from acts of terrorism. UASI grant program was established in 2003. UASI funds are also used to establish and operate fusion centers.	Funding is allocated to 50 major urban areas and 25 mass transit systems nationwide that DHS determined in 2004 were at high risk of terrorist attacks. DHS uses risk and vulnerability assessments, as well as data on population density and placement of critical infrastructure to determine the level of funding for each state. In FY 2014, the UASI program provided $587,000,000 in support.
Operation Stonegarden (OPSG)	Provides funding to enhance cooperation and coordination among local, state, and federal law enforcement agencies to secure the nation's land borders.	Funds are allocated competitively to designated localities within the US border states based on risk analysis and the anticipated feasibility and effectiveness of proposed investments by the applicants. In FY 2014, OPSG provided $55,000,000 in support.

Sources: Davis, L.M., Polland, M., Ward, K., Wilson, J.M., Varda, D.M., Hansell, L., Steinberg, P. (2010) Long Term Effects of Law Enforcement's Post-911 Focus on Counterterrorism and Homeland Security. Report prepared for the National Institute of Justice, p. 23–24.

FY 2014 Homeland Security Grant Program (HSGP) retrieved from www.FEMA.gov.

bypass local procurement requirements by having state governments purchase services and equipment on their behalf. In addition, DHS arranged for states and localities to be able to purchase products directly from DoD vendors, thus expediting the procurement process.[33] In a final adjustment, DHS allowed states and localities the opportunity to obtain grant funds prior to making expenditures rather than having to wait for reimbursement.

Distribution of the Homeland Security Grant Program (HSGP) has not been without criticism. Similar to the funding for education and highways, the HSGP distributes 60 percent of their funds based upon population and the other 40 percent is spread evenly across recipients regardless of population.[34] Prior to 2006, many homeland security grants were distributed by formula. Under this initial disbursement process, each state received a base level of funding—0.75 percent of the total distribution for a given grant program. The remaining funds were distributed proportionately based on a state's population. This process was used to allocate funds for three of the grant programs: the State Homeland Security Grant Program (SHSP), the Law Enforcement Terrorism Prevention Program (LETPP), and the Citizens Corp Program (CCP). A fourth program—the Urban Areas Security Initiative (UASI), distributes funds based on risk.[35]

Relying on a population-based template and not risk analysis proved to be an inefficient distribution of funds. To address these issues, the Department of Homeland Security Appropriations Act of 2006 changed the procedures. While still awarding each state a base of 0.75 percent of the total distribution for a respective program, the remaining SHSP and LETPP funds are now allocated based on risk. While the 2006 legislation allowed the DHS to have more discretion over the distribution of funds, the discrepancies in allocations continue to persist. In some cases, funding has been sent to places with little to no terrorist risk while some of America's high-risk jurisdictions received less funding than they should have. For example, under the 2012 allocations, the lowest Urban Areas Security Initiative (UASI) allocation of $1.25 million went to both Indianapolis and San Antonio; Denver received $2.5 million, Las Vegas got $1.8 million; Charlotte pulled in $1.5 million; and Portland earned $2.2 million. Yet Wyoming, which has fewer people than all of those cities, received $2.8 million. In fact, over one-third of the 31 high-risk UASI cities received less funding than Wyoming.[36] A key change in FY 2013 eliminated some of these eligible cities in response to congressional mandate. Hence the number of urban areas receiving funding under the UASI program was decreased from 31 to 25, thereby maximizing the funding to America's riskiest cities.[37] While in essence this makes sense, the reality is that the baseline distribution of funds is still unbalanced in favor of small population states. States with high populations and population densities receive relatively little funding per capita compared to states with low populations and population densities.

Much of the criticism surrounding the HSGP revolves around the improper use of funds. Reports of misused grant monies and outlandish purchases have included the following: surveillance cameras in a small Alaskan fishing village; a $98,000 underwater robot for the landlocked city of Columbus, Ohio; an armored vehicle for a tiny New Hampshire town that uses it to patrol the annual pumpkin festival; and the purchase of thirteen Sno-Cone machines in Montcalm County, Michigan, to prevent heat-related illnesses during emergencies.[38]

Despite reports of "wasteful" spending, it is alleged that political considerations are driving funding. Some claim that politicians, fighting for monies on behalf of their constituents, have superseded the objective of preventing terrorist attacks and that DHS grants are being distributed as "pork-barrel projects."[39]

Take for instance, South Dakota—a landlocked state with only 800,000 people. Since 2003, roughly $100 million dollars in homeland security grants were given to various South Dakota agencies. However, whether the money was used to make the state safe from terrorism is an open question. A list of expenditures reveals that money was spent on fire trucks and ambulances for small towns, for surveillance cameras for schools and police stations, on communications gear for local and county police, on anti-cyber-attack security, on electronic fingerprinting technology, and to increase bomb squad capabilities.[40] The state of South Dakota has very little threat of terrorism and the most recent South Dakota strategic plan implicitly acknowledges that lack of threat. According to the state strategic plan, the only potential threats facing South Dakota come from white supremacist groups, environmentalists opposed to uranium mining, and the Keystone XL pipeline.[41]

Since 2007, the Department of Homeland Security Office of the Inspector General has audited states and urban areas to determine whether they have implemented their HSGP grants efficiently and effectively, achieved program goals, and spent funds according to grant requirements.[42] An audit conducted by the DHS Office of Inspector General found that South Dakota's strategic plans from 2010 to 2012 did not establish measurable goals and objectives to address significant threats and vulnerabilities, or a context (baseline) for measuring capability improvements. The state prepared two strategic plans for the audit period of FY 2010 through FY 2012: a plan prepared in 2009 covered the period 2010 and 2011 and a plan prepared in 2011 covered 2012–14. Neither plan contained goals, objectives, or a baseline that could be easily measured.[43] But South Dakota is not alone. A recent study by the DHS Inspector General revealed that many states' homeland security strategies did not include specific goals and objectives and were outdated. According to

DHS guidelines, states that received HSGP grants are to create and use strategies aimed at improving preparedness and response to natural and manmade disasters. The goals and objectives in these strategies should be specific, measurable, achievable, results-oriented, and time-limited. The problem was that many states had established goals which were too general for them to use effectively in measuring their performance and progress towards improving preparedness and response capabilities.[44] A 2012 audit found that strategies for Arkansas, Florida, Georgia, Kansas, Louisiana, Minnesota, Montana, New Mexico, US Virgin Islands, and Washington did not include some or all of the elements for a successful strategy. Minnesota and New Mexico also had outdated strategies.

So, what does this mean for calculating the costs of homeland security? Because of inadequate monitoring of grant spending, many states are unable to determine the extent to which the federal homeland security grants enhanced the state's ability to prepare for and respond to disasters and acts of terrorism. It is clear that despite specified requirements, very few states actually have a system in place to measure preparedness. Furthermore, this lack of accounting of the effectiveness of the millions already spent could very well result in the uncertainty of future funding.

Regionalism

An important trend in homeland security funding is regionalization.[45] This is a consistent trend in both grant funding and federal and state guidance to encourage the adoption of a regional approach to homeland security and preparedness. Rather than simply funding individual departments, entire regions are considered in the funding formulas. This translates into less flexibility in terms of how the funding is used. The Urban Areas Security Initiative (UASI) is the best illustration of this trend which focuses on metropolitan areas. The program provides opportunities for large urban areas to apply for UASI grants with adjacent counties and municipalities. The goal is to encourage regionalization and improve coordination among agencies in large urban areas.[46] In addition to assisting participating jurisdictions in developing integrated regional systems for prevention, protection, response, and recovery, the UASI requires that states dedicate at least 25 percent of UASI appropriated funds to law enforcement terrorism prevention activities.[47] Some of the advantages of regionalization are improvements in inter-jurisdictional coordination and planning, mutual agreement on roles and responsibilities, and regional consolidation of administrative functions and procurement activities.[48]

Regionalization also presents challenges. Conflicting missions, concerns regarding jurisdiction and control over resources, and incompatible processes or systems are but some of the potential problems. UASI regions may also be inconsistent with existing mutual aid and emergency management structures at the state and local levels. This would require reconciling the various systems into one unified system—which would be costly. Furthermore, such arrangements have the potential to create competition among mutual aid law enforcement partners for grant dollars and may drive a wedge between the departments that had received UASI grant funds versus those mutual aid partners that had not.[49]

Costs: Defining Homeland Security

Perhaps the difficulty in determining the overall costs of homeland security lie in this problem: there is no agreed-upon definition for just what homeland security is. In the early days it was defined strictly from a terrorism perspective. This strong focus on terrorism resulted in a disaster: Hurricane Katrina and its aftermath. Congress immediately tackled the apparent emergency management shortfalls resulting in the Post-Katrina Emergency Management Reform Act (PKEMRA) which served to reconfigure the leadership hierarchy of DHS and to return many functions into FEMA (see Chapter 1). Hence, the homeland security approach was broadened to include an all-hazards perspective. In doing so, the ability to track spending became a major challenge. There is obviously political advantage in labeling an initiative as crucial homeland security.

It has been argued that homeland security, at its core, is about coordination because of the disparate stakeholders and risks.[50] Many have also asserted that homeland security is about the coordination of the strategic process policymakers use in determining the risks, the stakeholders and their missions, and the prioritization of those missions.[51]

The 2010 *Quadrennial Homeland Security Review Report* (QHSR) revised the definition of homeland security to incorporate a more global and comprehensive approach.[52] The Executive Summary of the QHSR elaborates on the definition of homeland security as "the intersection of evolving threats and hazards with traditional governmental and civic responsibilities for civil defense, emergency response, law enforcement, customs, border control, and immigration."[53]

Without a general consensus on the literal and philosophical definition of homeland security, some believe that there will continue to be the potential for disjointed and disparate approaches to securing the nation.[54]

The Costs of Homeland Security—Are We Safer?

In seeking to evaluate the effectiveness of the massive increases in homeland security expenditures since the terrorist attacks of September 11, 2001, the common question has become, "Are we safer?" While homeland security dollars were unable to prevent the Boston Marathon Bombings, it theoretically could have been worse. Many of the capabilities demonstrated in Boston and in the immediate aftermath of the bombings were built or enhanced— and have been sustained—through the preparedness suite of Homeland Security Grant Programs (HSGP).[55] Without these monies, the response may not have been as effective. In his testimony before the Senate Committee on Homeland Security and Governmental Affairs, Massachusetts Undersecretary for Homeland Security Kurt N. Schwartz remarked, "The response to the events surrounding the Boston Marathon once again demonstrated the value of our investments of money, time and resources in local, state, and federal security since 2001. Within seconds of the bomb blasts at the finish line of the Boston Marathon, an array of personnel, resources, and capabilities—many funded with federal homeland security grant dollars—were brought to bear to triage and care for the wounded, communicate with the public, provide situational awareness for decision makers, ensure the safety and security of the public and critical infrastructure, set up a joint command center, and ultimately identify and apprehend the suspected terrorists."[56]

Other expenses proved to be key factors that contributed to the effectiveness of the response operations. For example, interoperability was a success story. Over the years, millions of dollars have been invested under local, regional, and state interoperability plans, and Boston's investments in mutual aid channels, tactical channel plans, radio towers, new radios, and specialized training allowed first responders, as well as command level personnel, to effectively communicate by radio between agencies, between disciplines, and between jurisdictions.[57] In the first few hours after the bomb blasts, the availability of interoperable radio systems was critical to first responders because cell phone and land-line telephone systems in the greater Boston area were overloaded.

Boston also benefited from their investments in regional exercise programs, such as the Urban Shield exercises conducted by the Boston Urban Area Security Initiative (UASI) and other programs using federal funding. These trainings set a framework for multiple jurisdictions to work seamlessly with one another in a highly effective manner. According to the testimony of Boston Police Commissioner Edward F. Davis, III before the Senate Committee on Homeland Security, "Urban Shield training with Boston's law enforcement and medical professionals was one of the most important steps we took to prepare for this day. The significance of this can be not better illustrated than by looking at the facts: the scene was cleared of all spectators and nearly 300 injured within 22 minutes; the 19 critically injured victims admitted to hospitals all survived, due to exceptional medical care and backed up by the response and use of tourniquets."[58] Additionally, UASI funding also provided highly trained analysts in the Boston Regional Intelligence Center (BRIC) who were critical to daily decision-making and intelligence gathering. Funding also provided important technology such as armored vehicle, robots, harbor patrol vehicles, and other safety equipment. According to Chief Davis, "This equipment allowed us to take Dzhokhar Tsarnaev into custody alive."[59]

Conversely, many would argue that the increased costs on homeland security have not made us safer as a nation. Extreme examples, such as paying for first responders to attend a HALO Counterterrorism Summit at a California island spa resort featuring a simulated zombie apocalypse, have made headlines.[60] The underwater robot purchased in Columbus, Ohio, using $98,000 in UASI grant monies and the remote control helicopter purchased by the City of Seattle for traffic surveillance are other examples. It has been reported that this country has spent a jaw-dropping $791 billion on homeland security since 9/11.[61] Furthermore, with all of this spending, some have argued that there are still many gaps in security. For example, reports have found a myriad of vulnerabilities in our port security, which include gaps in screening for nuclear and radiological materials. Issues still exist with our screening of individuals crossing into the country and as we have found, simply throwing money at programs to absorb illegal immigrants does not solve the problem. The recent crisis of unaccompanied children crossing into the US has created a costly political and humanitarian crisis.[62]

Still others have argued that asking the question "Are we safer?" is not the correct question to pose. Rather we should be asking, "Are the gains in security worth the funds expended?"[63] In a 2011 study conducted on balancing the costs and benefits of homeland security, John Mueller and Mark G. Stewart concluded that the US government always overestimates the risk of terrorism.[64] It is estimated that federal expenditures on domestic homeland security have increased by some $360 billion over those in place in 2001.[65] By 2009, these increases totaled roughly $75 billion per year.[66] In their analysis, they assumed that the risk reduction caused by the security measures in place before 9/11 and by the extra vigilance of the public after the event reduced risk by 50 percent. Moreover, the increase in US expenditures on homeland security since 2001 reduced the remaining risk by 45 percent.[67] Putting this all together, Mueller and Stewart concluded that in order to justify the $75 billion enhanced expenditures on homeland security, they would have to deter, prevent, foil, or protect against 1,667 Times-Square-style attacks every year.[68] That equates to more than four major attacks every day.

Conclusion

Since the attacks of 9/11, America has spent an enormous amount of money on homeland security. Estimates on the total costs venture into the trillions. This chapter has addressed the issues surrounding homeland security spending and the controversial high costs of keeping us safe. The successful response to the Boston Marathon Bombings illustrates that homeland security dollars have been put to good use. However, it is clearly time to examine the massive homeland security expenditures in a careful and systematic way. Perhaps agreeing upon the definition of homeland security would be the best start — thus enabling policymakers to determine exactly where costs are most needed. Funding a department that encompasses an all-hazards approach leaves too much room for waste, fraud, and abuse. The challenge is for government to fully adopt risk management approaches to determine where homeland security dollars should be spent. At some point, we may have to ask the question, "When is the homeland secure enough?"

Endnotes

1. Cole, Christine M., Arnold M. Howitt and Philip B. Heymann. (2014). Harvard Kennedy School, Program on Crisis Leadership Report. *Why Was Boston Strong? Lessons from the Boston Marathon Bombing.*

2. Green, J. & Winter, C. (2013). It Costs $333 Million to Shut Down Boston for a Day. *Bloomsberg Businessweek.* Retrieved online at http://www.businessweek.com/articles/2013-04-19/it-costs-333-million-to-shut-down-boston-for-a-day.

3. Cole, Christine M., Arnold M. Howitt and Philip B. Heymann. (2014). Harvard Kennedy School, Program on Crisis Leadership Report. *Why Was Boston Strong? Lessons from the Boston Marathon Bombing.*

4. U.S. Congress. (2013). *Lessons Learned From The Boston Marathon Bombings: Preparing For and Responding To The Attack: Hearing before the U.S. Senate Committee on Homeland Security And Government Affairs,* 113th Congress, 1st Sess..

5. U.S. Congress. (2013). *Lessons Learned From The Boston Marathon Bombings: Preparing For and Responding To The Attack: Hearing before the U.S. Senate Committee on Homeland Security And Government Affairs,* 113th Congress, 1st Sess..

6. Kimery A. (2014). Sequestration Takes Toll on DHS, With Lasting Effects, GAO Audit Says. *Homeland Security Today.* Retrieved from www.hstoday.us.

7. Painter, W. L. (2014). *Department of Homeland Security Appropriations: FY2014 Overview and Summary.* (CRS Report No. R43193). Washington DC: Library of Congress, Congressional Research Service. Retrieved from http://fas.org/sgp/crs/homesec/R43193.pdf.

8. Painter, W. L. (2014). *Department of Homeland Security Appropriations: FY2014 Overview and Summary.* (CRS Report No. R43193). Washington DC: Library of Congress, Congressional Research Service. Retrieved from http://fas.org/sgp/crs/homesec/R43193.pdf.

9. U.S. Department of Homeland Security, "Budget in Brief Fiscal Year 2015" Retrieved from http://www.dhs.gov/publication/fy-2015-budget-brief.

10. U.S. Department of Homeland Security, "Budget in Brief Fiscal Year 2015" Retrieved from http://www.dhs.gov/publication/fy-2015-budget-brief.

11. U.S. Department of Homeland Security, "Budget in Brief Fiscal Year 2015", p. 11 Retrieved from http://www.dhs.gov/publication/fy-2015-budget-brief.

12. U.S. Department of Homeland Security, "Budget in Brief Fiscal Year 2015", p. 12–13 Retrieved from http://www.dhs.gov/publication/fy-2015-budget-brief.

13. U.S. Department of Homeland Security, "Budget in Brief Fiscal Year 2015", p. 13–14 Retrieved from http://www.dhs.gov/publication/fy-2015-budget-brief.

14. U.S. Department of Homeland Security, "Budget in Brief Fiscal Year 2015", p. 15–16 Retrieved from http://www.dhs.gov/publication/fy-2015-budget-brief.

15. Reese, S. (2009) *Department of Homeland Security Assistance to States and Localities: A Summary and Issues for the 11th Congress.* (CRS Report No. R40246). Washington D.C.: Library of Congress, Congressional Research Service. Retrieved from http://www.fas.org/sgp/crs/homesec/R40246.pdf.

16. Bullock, J.A., Haddow, G.D., Coppola, D.P. (2013) *Introduction to Homeland Security* 4th edition.

17. Davis, L.M., Polland, M., Ward, K., Wilson, J.M., Varda, D.M., Hansell, L., Steinberg, P. (2010*) Long Term Effects of Law Enforcement's Post-911 Focus on Counterterrorism and Homeland Security.* Report prepared for the National Institute of Justice. Rand Safety and Justice.

18. P.L. 104-201, Title XIV, Subtitle A, Sec. 1412, 110 Stat. 2718.

19. Davis, L.M., Polland, M., Ward, K., Wilson, J.M., Varda, D.M., Hansell, L., Steinberg, P. (2010) *Long Term Effects of Law Enforcement's Post-911 Focus on Counterterrorism and Homeland Security.* Report prepared for the National Institute of Justice. Rand Safety and Justice.

20. Davis, L.M., Polland, M., Ward, K., Wilson, J.M., Varda, D.M., Hansell, L., Steinberg, P. (2010) *Long Term Effects of Law Enforcement's Post-911 Focus on Counterterrorism and Homeland Security.* Report prepared for the National Institute of Justice. Rand Safety and Justice.

21. Reese, S. (2009). *Department of Homeland Security Assistance to States and Localities: A Summary and Issues for the 11th Congress.* (CRS Report No. R40246). Washington D.C.: Library of Congress, Congressional Research Service. Retrieved from http://www.fas.org/sgp/crs/homesec/R40246.pdf.

22. Reese, S. (2009) *Department of Homeland Security Assistance to States and Localities: A Summary and Issues for the 11th Congress.* (CRS Report No. R40246). Washington D.C.: Library of Congress, Congressional Research Service. Retrieved from http://www.fas.org/sgp/crs/homesec/R40246.pdf.

23. U.S. Department Homeland Security FEMA Grant Programs Directorate Information Bulletin No. 394. March 18, 2014.

24. Reese, S. (2009). *Department of Homeland Security Assistance to States and Localities: A Summary and Issues for the 11th Congress.* (CRS Report No. R40246). Washington D.C.: Library of Congress, Congressional Research Service. Retrieved from http://www.fas.org/sgp/crs/homesec/R40246.pdf.

25. FY 2014 Homeland Security Grant Program (HSGP) retrieved from www.FEMA.gov.

26. FY 2014 Homeland Security Grant Program (HSGP) retrieved from www.FEMA.gov.

27. FY 2014 Homeland Security Grant Program (HSGP) retrieved from www.FEMA.gov.

28. Reese, S. (2009) *Department of Homeland Security Assistance to States and Localities: A Summary and Issues for the 11th Congress*. (CRS Report No. R40246). Washington D.C.: Library of Congress, Congressional Research Service. Retrieved from http://www.fas.org/sgp/crs/homesec/R40246.pdf.

29. FY 2014 Homeland Security Grant Program (HSGP) retrieved from www.FEMA.gov.

30. FY 2014 Homeland Security Grant Program (HSGP) retrieved from www.FEMA.gov.

31. FY 2013 Homeland Security Grant Program (HSGP) retrieved from www.FEMA.gov.

32. Davis, L.M., Polland, M., Ward, K., Wilson, J.M., Varda, D.M., Hansell, L., Steinberg, P. (2010) *Long Term Effects of Law Enforcement's Post-911 Focus on Counterterrorism and Homeland Security*. Report prepared for the National Institute of Justice.

33. Davis, L.M., Polland, M., Ward, K., Wilson, J.M., Varda, D.M., Hansell, L., Steinberg, P. (2010) *Long Term Effects of Law Enforcement's Post-911 Focus on Counterterrorism and Homeland Security*. Report prepared for the National Institute of Justice.

34. Homeland Security Presidential Directive—HSPD/8.

35. Prante, T. & Bohara A. (2008). What Determines Homeland Security Spending? An Econometric Analysis of the Homeland Security Grant Program. *The Policy Studies Journal, Vol. 36, No. 2*, p. 245.

36. Mayer M. (2012) Homeland Security Grants: Greater Focus Needed with Finite Federal Funding. *The Heritage Foundation* Issue Brief No. 3681.

37. Mayer M. (2012) Homeland Security Grants: Greater Focus Needed with Finite Federal Funding. *The Heritage Foundation* Issue Brief No. 3681.

38. Solomon, J. (2013). "Senator Slams Homeland Program for Wasteful, Frivolous Spending." *The Washington Times*. Retrieved from www.washingtontimes.com.

39. Prante, T. & Bohara A. (2008). What Determines Homeland Security Spending? An Econometric Analysis of the Homeland Security Grant Program. *The Policy Studies Journal, Vol. 36, No. 2*, p. 245.

40. O'Sullivan J. (2014). State gets millions in homeland security grants, but where does it go? *The Rapid City Journal* Retrieved from www.rapidcityjournal.com.

41. O'Sullivan J. (2014) State gets millions in homeland security grants, but where does it go? *The Rapid City Journal* Retrieved from www.rapidcityjournal.com.

42. Statement of Anne L. Richards, Assistant Inspector General for Audits DHS before the Subcommittee on Emergency Preparedness, Response and Communications, Committee on Homeland Security U.S. House of Representatives *concerning* Homeland Security Grants: Measuring Our Investments (March 19, 2013).

43. U.S. Department, Office of Homeland Security Inspector General *South Dakota's Management of Homeland Security Grant Program Awards for Fiscal Years 2010–2012* (May, 2014).

44. Statement of Anne L. Richards, Assistant Inspector General for Audits DHS before the Subcommittee on Emergency Preparedness, Response and Communications, Committee on Homeland Security U.S. House of Representatives concerning Homeland Security Grants: Measuring Our Investments (March 19, 2013).

45. Davis, L.M., Polland, M., Ward, K., Wilson, J.M., Varda, D.M., Hansell, L., Steinberg, P. (2010) *Long Term Effects of Law Enforcement's Post-911 Focus on Counterterrorism and Homeland Security*. Report prepared for the National Institute of Justice.

46. Davis, L.M., Polland, M., Ward, K., Wilson, J.M., Varda, D.M., Hansell, L., Steinberg, P. (2010) *Long Term Effects of Law Enforcement's Post-911 Focus on Counterterrorism*

and Homeland Security. Report prepared for the National Institute of Justice. Rand Safety and Justice.

47. Davis, L.M., Polland, M., Ward, K., Wilson, J.M., Varda, D.M., Hansell, L., Steinberg, P. (2010) *Long Term Effects of Law Enforcement's Post-911 Focus on Counterterrorism and Homeland Security*. Report prepared for the National Institute of Justice. Rand Safety and Justice.

48. Davis, L.M., Polland, M., Ward, K., Wilson, J.M., Varda, D.M., Hansell, L., Steinberg, P. (2010) *Long Term Effects of Law Enforcement's Post-911 Focus on Counterterrorism and Homeland Security*. Report prepared for the National Institute of Justice. Rand Safety and Justice.

49. Davis, L.M., Polland, M., Ward, K., Wilson, J.M., Varda, D.M., Hansell, L., Steinberg, P. (2010) *Long Term Effects of Law Enforcement's Post-911 Focus on Counterterrorism and Homeland Security*. Report prepared for the National Institute of Justice. Rand Safety and Justice.

50. Kettl, D.F. (2007) *System Under Stress: Homeland Security and American Politics*, 2nd ed, Washington DC, CQ Press, p. 82.

51. Painter, W.L. (2013) *Issues in Homeland Security Policy for the 113th Congress*. (CRS Report No. R42985). Washington DC: Library of Congress. Retrieved from http://fas.org/sgp/crs/homesec/R42985.pdf.

52. Bullock, J.A., Haddow, G.D., Coppola, D.P. (2013) *Introduction to Homeland Security* 4th edition.

53. Quadrennial Homeland Security Review Report: A Strategic Framework for Secure Homeland, DHS, February 2010.

54. Painter, W.L. (2013) *Issues in Homeland Security Policy for the 113th Congress*. (CRS Report No. R42985). Washington DC: Library of Congress. Retrieved from http://fas.org/sgp/crs/homesec/R42985.pdf.

55. *Lessons Learned From The Boston Marathon Bombings: Preparing For and Responding To The Attack: Hearing before the U.S. Senate Committee on Homeland Security And Government Affairs*, 113th Congress, 1st Sess., (2013), p. 4.

56. *Lessons Learned From The Boston Marathon Bombings: Preparing For and Responding To The Attack: Hearing before the U.S. Senate Committee on Homeland Security And Government Affairs*, 113th Congress, 1st Sess., (2013), p. 1.

57. *Lessons Learned From The Boston Marathon Bombings: Preparing For and Responding To The Attack: Hearing before the U.S. Senate Committee on Homeland Security And Government Affairs*, 113th Congress, 1st Sess., (2013).

58. *Lessons Learned From The Boston Marathon Bombings: Preparing For and Responding To The Attack: Hearing before the U.S. Senate Committee on Homeland Security And Government Affairs*, 113th Congress, 1st Sess., (2013), p. 9.

59. *Lessons Learned From The Boston Marathon Bombings: Preparing For and Responding To The Attack: Hearing before the U.S. Senate Committee on Homeland Security And Government Affairs*, 113th Congress, 1st Sess., (2013), p. 10.

60. Coburn, T. (2013) "Safety at Any Price: Assessing the impact of homeland security spending in U.S. cities" Report by Senator Tom Coburn, Member Homeland Security and Governmental Affairs Committee.

61. Kramer, M. & Hellman C. (2013, February 28) "Homeland Security: The Trillion Dollar Concept That No One Can Define." Retrieved online at www.thenation.com.

62. Rappleye, H. (2014, July 9). "Undocumented and Unaccompanied: Facts, Figures on Children at the Border." *NBC News.*

63. Mueller J. & Stewart M.G. (2011) "Does the United States Spend Too Much on Homeland Security?"

64. Mueller J. & Stewart M.G. (2011) "Balancing the Risks, Benefits, and Costs of Homeland Security" *Homeland Security Affairs,* vol vii.

65. Mueller J. & Stewart M.G. (2011) "Balancing the Risks, Benefits, and Costs of Homeland Security" *Homeland Security Affairs,* vol vii.

66. Mueller J. & Stewart M.G. (2011) "Balancing the Risks, Benefits, and Costs of Homeland Security" *Homeland Security Affairs,* vol vii.

67. Mueller J. & Stewart M.G. (2011) "Balancing the Risks, Benefits, and Costs of Homeland Security" *Homeland Security Affairs,* vol vii.

68. Mueller, J. & Stewart M.G. (2011) "1,667 Times Square-Style Attacks Every Year."

Chapter 3

Are Fusion Centers a Proper Role for Local Police?

Introduction

There are many stories about the failure of law enforcement before 9/11 that are often contrasted with the success of law enforcement in a post-9/11 world. The most often told story of that failure before 9/11 is the case of Maryland State Trooper Joseph Catalano, who pulled over a red Mitsubishi for speeding 90 in a 65-mile-per-hour zone on Interstate 95. He checked the license and registration, issued the ticket and let the driver go. Two days later, the speeding driver, Ziad Jarrah, boarded United Airlines Flight 93.[1]

In the post-9/11 environment, there are many stories of law enforcement's success, such as the case of another state trooper, this time from the state of Colorado. This state trooper pulled over a green Toyota driving recklessly, and after checking the driver's license and registration discovered that the vehicle was used in the attempted bombing of a bookstore. The fusion center has been credited with the arrest of David Lawless for a series of attempted bombings. Lawless was later convicted and sentenced to 20 years in prison.[2]

The failure of law enforcement before 9/11, and their success after 9/11 with the establishment of fusion centers, tells a simple story that fusion centers are useful and they work. The reality, however, may be something entirely different.

The case of the Maryland State Trooper letting one of the 9/11 hijackers go two days before that tragic attack makes it appear as if the trooper failed in the performance of his job. That is just not the case. The failure was entirely on the part of the intelligence community for not sharing their concerns with law enforcement about the possibility that Ziad Jarrah was a potential terrorist. In fact, according to the 9/11 Commission Report, there were ten opportunities for law enforcement to have thwarted the hijackers on 9/11. Yet, not one of the failures had anything to do with a breakdown of traditional law enforcement practices. Every one of the failures was attributed to a mistake on the part of intelligence officials refusing to share information that they had collected, blocked by bureaucratic rules, policies, and procedures overseeing the dissemination of classified material.[3]

In the case of David Lawless, while fusion centers have taken credit for the capture of this attempted bomber, once again we find this was just not the case. Lawless had attempted to set off a bomb at a Borders Bookstore. After setting off the burglar alarm, police officers arrived on scene and discovered the doorway shattered and two explosive devices. On the busted glass they found blood. The police soon received calls for two more similar incidents. At one location they obtained a video of a Toyota Tacoma that appeared to be involved. Then later that day, the police responded to a one-car crash from a DUI and the suspect, David Lawless, attempted to stab the officers with a pair of scissors. Taken into custody and his Toyota Tacoma impounded, the police realized he might be a suspect in the bombings. The blood from the glass matched that of Lawless and he was arrested. The case was solved from good old-fashioned police work, and while the fusion center may have helped pass along information, the crime would have been solved without the center's assistance.

While there seems to be some controversy over the success and failure of law enforcement, the controversies surrounding the fusion centers go much deeper than this. In order to explore the controversies of fusion centers, this chapter will first define fusion centers and discuss their function as it relates to Homeland Security. It will then address the many implementation issues they have faced since 9/11. The chapter will then focus on the greatest issues surrounding the fusion centers and that is the violation of civil rights and personal privacy. It will then end with a brief discussion of the efficacy of fusion centers.

Fusion Centers

The concept for fusion centers came in the wake of the 9/11 terrorist attacks on America.[4] Although it has been noted that most state police organizations had run intelligence or analytic units prior to 9/11, most of these tended to be small units focused primarily on crime analysis.[5] As the US recovered from the attacks, there was a strong initial reaction to enhance the national security apparatus against future terroristic threats. Initially the Federal Bureau of Investigation focused on expanding its use of Joint Terrorism Task Forces (JTTFs) to share intelligence between federal, state and local law enforcement agencies.[6] The problem, however, was the fact JTTFs were always run by federal agents and information always traveled up, but rarely did it ever travel down. The local and state law enforcement fed the federal government information and intelligence, but the federal government rarely ever provided state and local governments with the same. In fact, in some cases, it was illegal for state and local police to share information, as local police did not have the necessary security clearances to receive classified information, in essence, the very same information that the state and local law enforcement agencies provided federal law enforcement could not in turn be given back to the state and local law enforcement officers by federal agents because it was now classified. Hence, there was a strong desire on the part of state and local law enforcement to begin collecting their own information, conducting their own analysis, and creating their own intelligence.

As a few centers that were similar in nature to fusion centers existed prior to 9/11, these became the template for state and local agencies to create state, local, and regional fusion centers. They developed independently of one another at first because there were so few of them. However, once the 9/11 Commission made the recommendation that the federal government support the fusion centers and Congress began to allocate funds through the Department of Homeland Security, the fusion centers quickly grew and they began communicating with each other.[7] They were also further supported by the National Governor's Association, which, in 2007, made the creation of a fusion center a central part of the key steps in providing homeland security, noting that these centers would become "the focal point for information and intelligence sharing among local, state, and federal agencies from a variety of disciplines."[8]

The idea behind the new network of fusion centers was that it would lead to a number of beneficial outcomes.[9] The first was that the federal government would be able to have a more local context to the information provided by local law enforcement and it could integrate that information into the homeland security apparatus. The second was that they would be an entity that could satisfy the needs of the state and local jurisdictions, one that could work more closely with the private sector.[10] Third, they would provide a more holistic approach to gathering information and intelligence because it would satisfy all levels of needs: federal, state, local, tribal, and territorial.

As a result of the federal government's involvement, various standards and guidelines were created for all of the "independent" fusion centers to follow. These guidelines also began to define what a fusion center was, thus creating the default definition used by nearly everyone today: "Fusion Centers are a collaborative effort of two or more agencies that provide resources, expertise, and information to the center with the goal of maximizing their ability to detect, prevent, investigate, and respond to criminal and terrorist activity."[11] Further clarifying the mission of the fusion centers, then Department of Homeland Security Janet Napolitano, testifying before the US House of Representatives Committee on Homeland Security, explained:

> These centers analyze information and identify trends to share timely intelligence with federal, state, and local law enforcement including DHS, which then further shares this information with other members of the Intelligence Community. In turn, DHS provides relevant and appropriate threat information from the Intelligence Community back to the fusion centers. Today, there are 72 state and locally run fusion centers in operation across the nation, up from a handful in 2006. Our goal is to make every one of these fusion centers a center of analytic excellence that provides useful, actionable information about threats to law enforcement and first responders.[12]

Napolitano is also on record as stating that, "Fusion Centers will be the centerpiece of state, local, federal intelligence-sharing for the future,"[13] and later, in 2009, "Fusion centers are and will be a critical part of our nation's homeland security capabilities. I intend to make them a top priority for this Department of support them, build them, improve them, and work with them."[14] US Attorney General Eric Holder stated in 2010 that, "We are at war. This is the reality in which we live. And our fusion centers are on the frontlines of America's best, and more effective, efforts to fight back."[15] And in 2011, the Department of Homeland Security issued a report on the anniversary of 9/11 detailing the implementation status of the 9/11 Commission's recommendations and it noted: "Fusion centers are uniquely situated to empower front-line law enforcement, public safety, fire service, emergency response, public health, critical infrastructure protection, and private sector security personnel to understand local implications of national intelligence, thus enabling local officials to better protect their communities."[16]

Since those statements were made, the number of fusion centers have continued to rise. In 2007, there were forty-three fusion centers with fifteen more in development.[17] By 2011, it was noted that "every state has a fusion center, as well as twenty-two urban areas"[18] for a total of at least 77 fusion centers.[19] According to 2012 data, "Fusion centers are staffed by anywhere from three to 250 individuals—averaging, in 2008, twenty-seven full-time personnel—the majority of whom are state law enforcement officers and analysts."[20] And the most recent report cites that "with the January 2013 designation of a fusion center in Guam, there are now 78: 52 State and territorial and 26 Major Urban Area Fusion Centers."[21] Yet, despite all of these official counts of fusion centers, a US Senate investigation into fusion centers found that several of the fusion centers that DHS reported to exist did not. These included the alleged fusion centers in both Wyoming and Philadelphia.[22]

When fusion centers do exist, the majority of the personnel that work in the centers are law enforcement. When the personnel are not from the state law enforcement agency, the overwhelming majority have come from the largest city police departments in that state/region due to the fact they have more resources and may already have their own intelligence unit from which to draw personnel to send them to the fusion center.[23] Most of these personnel claim to be playing a preventive role, as many have described themselves as maintaining situational awareness and playing a support role to the emergency operation centers during active investigations and events.[24] While most of the fusion centers also claim to be more proactive, a departure from traditional law enforcement practices, research into the fusion centers have shown that most are actually reactive in practice.[25]

Because of the grass-roots nature of the fusion centers being created by local and state law enforcement, each fusion center was allegedly created to serve local and regional needs. This meant that each fusion center was to be different. As W. Ross Ashley III, the executive director of the National Fusion Center Association described it with a wry sense of humor, "If you've seen one fusion center, you've seen one fusion center."[26] He explained that every fusion center in the US should look different and he argued that every fusion center was, in fact, different. Yet, when Congress passed the 9/11 Commission Act, it required the Secretary of Homeland Security to create the local and state Regional Fusion Center Initiative.[27] It also mandated the DHS establish guidelines for fusion centers including standards for providing operational standards and privacy training.[28] This resulted in the US Department of Justice contracting with the Global Justice information Sharing Initiative to create the *Fusion Center Guidelines,* an operational standards template for the fusion centers, which was later supplemented with a follow up document in 2008.[29] In addition, the actual fusion process technical assistance programs and services also has a template that is currently in the 7th edition of revisions providing specific guidelines for the fusion centers. A federally driven investigation into how the network of fusion centers were working was released in 2012.[30] It has been noted that "the emphasis during the period 2006–2010 as reflected in these initiatives was on developing a more 'standardized model' fusion center."[31] In a sense, the fusion centers which were supposed to be very different from one another and controlled locally are being controlled nationally and are supposed to all look the same. In fact, a 2013 report by the US House of Representatives Committee on Homeland Security noted that "The strength of the

National Network lies in individual fusion center's unique expertise," but then cites "the lack of a comprehensive State and locally-driven National Strategy for Fusion Centers" as being a problem.[32] Their individuality is great, but they all need to be the same in what is being communicated. This notion of local origins versus federal control has added to the questions surrounding who is actually in charge of the fusion centers.

Although the fusion centers are supposed to be a state and local creation, and the personnel derived from state and local governments, the federal government sends its representatives to work in the fusion centers. As of July 2010, the Department of Homeland Security had assigned fifty-eight intelligence officers to work in the various fusion centers.[33] In addition, the US Department of Justice's Federal Bureau of Investigation also assigned seventy-four special agents and analysts to work full time in 38 of the fusion centers.[34] This is actually down from previous years, for in 2007 there were over 200 agents working with the 36 fusion centers at the time. Regardless, it is clear that the federal government has been concerned about maintaining a presence in the fusion centers across the country. In fact, it has also been noted that 30 percent of the fusion centers are actually located in federal agency offices which clearly diminishes their independence from federal government intervention.[35]

In 2009, directors of the many fusion centers across the US came together to create the National Fusion Center Association (NFCA), a nonprofit organization. According to its mission statement, as found on its website, the NFCA exists:

> To represent the interests of state and major urban area fusion centers, as well as associated interests of states, tribal nations, and units of local government, in order to promote the development and sustainment of fusion centers to enhance public safety; encourage effective, efficient, ethical, lawful, and professional intelligence and information sharing; and prevent and reduce the harmful effects of crime and terrorism on victims, individuals, and communities.[36]

Clearly, the purpose of the NFCA is to serve as a lobbying group most likely aimed at continuing to secure federal funds in order to remain in existence, called "sustainment" in the mission statement.

The reported success of the fusion centers, as described in the introduction, raises questions about the actual success of the fusion centers. When the director of the NFCA was asked to highlight the achievements of the fusion centers, rather than focus on particular events, he stated explained it this way: "When was the last time you've seen an autonomous network stand up with federal support in a very successful way without a formal program? Here, you have a grass roots program where seventy-two fusion centers work together focusing on similar issues, sharing information horizontally and vertically in both directions. It's a heck of a success story."[37] Yet merely standing up seventy-two organizations does not make for a success story, especially when the Department of Homeland Security dangled the money to incentivize local and state police to initiate the creation of the fusion centers. And sharing information horizontally and vertically does not make for a success story for even the passing of gossip is the sharing of information. What makes for a success story is the sharing of actionable intelligence. This chapter now turns to the many issues the fusion centers have faced that challenge this so-called success story.

Implementation Issues

Terrorism vs. Crime

When the fusion centers were created, the emphasis was to prevent terrorism through developing an inter-connected intelligence system that derived from local law enforcement upward.[38] It has been described as trying to bring the fictitious television show 24 to life by emulating the exciting adventures and even the physical look of the Counter Terrorist Unit (CTU), replete with dozens of flat screen TVs, multiple computer monitors, and snazzy Sport Utility Vehicles.[39] Many of these fusion centers found that they had built the mechanisms to fight the war on terror, but then seldom played much of a role in that war. Just as the militarization of the police in America has seen the Special Weapons and Tactics teams (SWAT) find a wider array of applications, so too have fusion centers.[40] Operating under the idea that if you have a tool you should use it, fusion centers have expanded into the area of what they call an "all-hazards" mission which allows them to focus on not only terroristic threats, but threats by natural disasters and crime.[41] Other fusion centers have adopted what they call an "all-crimes" approach, which means that any crime or terrorist threat falls under their mission, just not natural disasters in this case.[42] A 2013 study found that out of fusion center personnel surveyed, only 5 percent reported their fusion center being focused on "terrorism only," and 29 percent were focused on "all-crimes," while the majority (52 percent) were focused on "all-crimes, all-threats, all-hazards."[43] As one police chief explained the move to the all-crimes concept, "No chief ever lost their job for a terrorist strike, but they lose their jobs every day for a spike in the crime rate."[44] While the concept behind the fusion centers was to create a center dedicated to fighting the war on terror at the local level, the reality appears to be more akin to the fusion centers being another mechanism for fighting the local war on crime.[45]

In a survey of fusion center personnel, one respondent noted, "Most of our intelligence functions still deal with every-day criminal activity."[46] Another noted that "Relevant counterterrorism information products are not shared proactively. General products like 'watch out for people stealing propane tanks' are shared, but not 'a group of Somali refugees are attempting to purchase small arms.' "[47] So, while the fusion centers are touted as fighting terrorism, they are really about crime, which is why many have adopted the "all-crimes" focus, rather than "terrorism only." The explanation for the focus on traditional law enforcement is, as one fusion center employee explained, "Law enforcement partners built the fusion center and dominate its executive board. Further, the Statewide Integrated Intelligence Plan focuses on law enforcement activities."[48]

Another reason for this expansion in focus, according to some of the leadership at the fusion centers, was so they could apply for more grants, and to overcome the reluctance on the part of some local law enforcement. As one director explained, "[I]t was impossible to create 'buy in' amongst local law enforcement agencies and other public sectors if a fusion center was solely focused on counterterrorism, as the center's partners often didn't feel threatened by terrorism, nor did they think that their community would produce would-be terrorists."[49]

What this has effectively done is allowed the law enforcement personnel manning the fusion centers to continue operating in their role as law enforcement officers by conducting criminal investigations and using the collection and dissemination of information and intelligence for the purposes of investigating routine crime. This is what is known as "mission creep"[50] or "mission drift."[51] Rather than staying focused on a specific mission, the agency broadens its mission so that it remains relevant and it helps to secure the existence (often called sustainability) of the organization.

There has also been a proposal by the Department of Homeland Security to create at least one more fusion center, this one a federal fusion center. The mission of the federal version would not be limited to terrorism or all-crimes, but as the DHS's own proposal states, it would collect and analyze data related to "All-threats and all-hazards, law enforcement activities, intelligence activities, man-made disasters and acts of terrorism, natural disasters and other information collected or received from federal, state, local, tribal and territorial agencies and organizations; foreign governments and international organizations; domestic security and emergency management officials; and private sector entities or individuals."[52] In other words, it could collect information and analyze this data from nearly any sources possible, making it the most powerful entity to protect our freedom, while the most dangerous threat to our civil liberties.

Funding

According to a Government Accountability Office (GAO) investigation, "Fusion centers have cited DHS grant funding as critical to achieving the baseline capabilities—the standards the government and fusion centers have defined as necessary for centers to be considered capable of performing basic functions in the national information sharing network."[53] In fact, the majority of money that the fusion centers have received for their funding comes from the Department of Homeland Security's Homeland Security Grant Program (HSGP), and it has been noted that 20 to 30 percent of all fusion center funding comes from this program.[54] For instance, in fiscal year 2010, the HSGP consisted of five different grants directing toward state and local jurisdictions. Two out of the five grants could be used for fusion center funding and, as a result, 61 percent of all of the fusion centers' funding came from the Department of Homeland Security. When looking at the budgetary allocations of the Department of Homeland Security across time, the amount has fluctuated, but remains in the area of $65 million per year (See Table 3.1). Despite this being a state and local initiative, nearly two-thirds of the funding came from the federal government. Regardless of the appearance of hard numbers, however, there is a word of caution. In 2011, a US Senate investigation uncovered that DHS was unable to "produce a complete

Table 3.1. Department of Homeland Security Funding for Fusion Centers

Fiscal Year	Funding Reported by Fusion Centers
2004	$100,320,799
2005	$57,246,542
2006	$62,664,343
2007	$78,723,783
2008	$61,864,080
2009	$65,402,360

Source: U.S. General Accountability Office. (2010). Information sharing: Federal agencies are helping fusion centers build and sustain capabilities and protect privacy, but could better measure results. Washington, D.C.: U.S. GAO, p. 14.

and accurate tally of the expense of its support for fusion centers," so the amount and percentage of funding may indeed be even higher.[55]

John Rollins, in his research into fusion centers for the US Congress, found that fusion centers were highly dependent upon federal funding in order to remain in existence. One of the fusion center officials he interviewed stated, "if federal funding went away, his fusion center would continue to operate, albeit with less staff and possibly with a more limited scope."[56] Rollins argued, based on his research, that there is a possibility that if federal funding ceased, so too would the fusion centers. Others have echoed this sentiment, including the Kennedy School for Government's report which noted that "DHS does not guarantee consistent funding streams to fusion centers, calling into question each center's long-term viability."[57]

Classified Material

One issue that surfaced as fusion centers began to stand up was related to classified material. In order to handle classified material, fusion center personnel must have security clearances issued by the federal government.[58] The process for obtaining clearances was often slow, and many personnel working in fusion centers today still do not have security clearances. Thus, in meetings of a classified nature, they are prevented from attending. One fusion center employee highlighted this fact in 2012 when he explained, "I am designated as Homeland Security Coordinator for our Fusion Center, but am excluded from briefings given to top level officials including the Governor."[59] He was excluded because, despite being the homeland security coordinator, he did not have the proper security clearance.

Another issue related to security clearances is the transfer of information and its return as intelligence. For instance, if raw data is collected and sent to the FBI or DHS, no security clearance is required. When that raw information is analyzed, it becomes intelligence, and then to receive it, a person needs a security clearance. So, if a fusion center employee sends the FBI information, that same employee may not be able to receive the intelligence report because they lack the security clearance, even though it may roughly be the same information they sent up the chain.

The fact that most fusion center employees are law enforcement personnel causes problems for sharing intelligence even with the agency for which they work because other personnel in that department may not have the proper security clearance.[60] Even if the police chief had a security clearance, he or she could not necessarily share it with members of their own department because they lack the necessary security clearances. As Washington, D.C., Police Chief

Cathy Lanier lamented, "It does a local police chief little good to receive information—including classified information—about a threat if she cannot use it to help prevent an attack."[61]

Civil Liberty Issues

One of the greatest concerns regarding the establishment of fusion centers has been the loss of civil liberties by an intrusive collection of data and the level of surveillance over innocent civilians who have committed no crime nor are under any reasonable suspicion.[62] The issue of balancing on one hand the need to protect American citizens against terroristic threats and actions, versus protecting their civil liberties and freedoms, is not an easy one, but one that is important to the American way of life. The fact that the fusion centers are about the combination of multiple streams of data means that they have the capabilities, or potential capabilities, of having the means to track many people. And while every fusion center makes the claim to have a strong civil liberties component, as the Constitution Project noted, "In such an interconnected system, fusion centers—even those with the best civil liberties practices—can inadvertently perpetuate or exacerbate the problematic activities of other fusion centers or law enforcement agencies."[63] Many civil liberties groups have explained that because the fusion centers are so new and developing so fast, they may be developing without the necessary oversight to insure they are not violating the law. As Shane Harris of the American Civil Liberties Union made clear, "We're setting up essentially a domestic intelligence agency, and we're doing so without having a full debate about the risks to privacy and civil liberties."[64]

One investigation into the violation and threat to civil liberties regarding fusion centers came from the American Civil Liberties Union (ACLU).[65] The authors of that report raised five major issues with regard to the fusion centers. The first had to do with the ambiguous lines of authority. While they recognized the rhetoric that no two fusion centers are alike and so it is difficult to generalize, they raised concerns that the very nature of there being no clear lines of authority raised issues with accountability. In other words, if there is no specific agency responsible (say the Department of Homeland Security on the federal level or the state police on the state level), there is less chance to hold any entity accountable. In fact, one analyst likened the rapid development and expansion of the fusion centers to the "wild west" since the directors were free to "use a variety of technologies before 'politics' catches up and limits options."[66]

While many believe that the ACLU is a biased organization and is often opposed to any government program, in 2012, the US Senate's Committee on Homeland Security and Government Affairs requested that the Permanent Subcommittee on Investigations conduct an assessment of the fusion centers. Their findings were not all that different from the ACLU's. The Senate report highlighted that "The Subcommittee Investigation found that DHS-assigned detailees to the fusion centers forwarded 'intelligence' of uneven quality—oftentimes shoddy, rarely timely, sometimes endangering citizens' civil liberties and Privacy Act protections, occasionally taken from already-published public sources, and more often than not unrelated to terrorism."[67]

What the ACLU fears the most is that each fusion center will have the capability of "policy shopping" or law shopping. In other words, if the fusion center consists of local, state, and federal representatives, when it comes to something like privacy violations, they will look to the agency's set of laws that will allow them the most latitude to search or gather information. For instance, to record a phone conversation in most states, both parties must consent (or there must be a warrant). However, in the state of Texas the law requires the consent of only one person. Therefore, a Texas fusion center with local police that have local ordinances mandating one party consent and federal agents who are bound by federal law for two party consent, may opt to say that they will follow the representative from the Texas State Department of Public Safety and apply Texas laws because they give the fusion center more latitude in their investigation.

Another way that fusion centers can get around privacy concerns is by not actually hosting the data at their location, but rather accessing the data located in some other location.[68] Federal law has very strict privacy requirements when personal data is stored at a federal location. Specifically, Title 28 Part 23 of the Code of Federal Regulation states what information law enforcement can place and store on a database.[69] Thus, fusion centers can have local law enforcement agencies, or even private companies, maintain the database and then the analysts can access the data without actually maintaining them, hence, circumventing the law.[70] As one Texas fusion analyst explained, "of particular interest … was the way the Center accesses and uses data from local agencies; it does not host the data, but rather refreshes them regularly. That means analysts are not subject to the Freedom of Information Act (FOIA) or being dragged into court."[71] Yet, it still allows fusion center analysts to search through personal data and make the necessary connections in order to convert information into intelligence that may be used against not just terrorists, but innocent citizens as well. Then, by not storing that information, there is no way that the fusion center can be scrutinized for violating anyone's civil rights because there is no evidence stored on the fusion center databases.[72] According to the Fourth

Amendment, Title 28, and many Supreme Court decisions, law enforcement can only launch an investigation if they have a reasonable suspicion. If they then suspect a violation of the law, they must go before a judge or magistrate to request a search warrant. There is the potential that both of these legal concepts, these constitutional rights, can simply be bypassed by the fusion centers.

The second concern raised is the use of private sector participation. Fusion centers have held up the incorporation of private sector entities in the information sharing process as being a shining example of cooperation. Yet, just as the concern of using an entity because the laws do not cover them as strictly, the use of private sector businesses opens this opportunity up to a much greater extent. As has been revealed by Edward Snowden, various businesses such as Google, Microsoft, Yahoo, Facebook, Youtube, Skype, AOL, and Apple have all entered into agreements with the federal government (via the National Security Agency) through a program called PRISM that allowed the federal government to have access to the private databases of these companies.[73] If the private companies willingly give access to their customer's information, than there is no requirement for these agencies to secure a search warrant and, hence, there is no means for holding the federal government accountable in violating privacy rights. The argument stands that when a person obtains services from these companies, such as surfing the Internet via Google or using Facebook, they have waived their privacy rights.

The report lists a number of additional reasons why having the private sector become involved in the fusion centers could be potentially disastrous, and they include the fact that the companies involved may be given an unfair business advantage, citizen's private information that the private company holds could be turned over to the government without their consent, businesses then become involved in spying on Americans creating a surveillance state, and as described before, the private companies maintaining the databases may cover up illegal activity on the part of law enforcement. Just the fact that one fusion center may buy access to credit reports, while another buys access to car-rental databases, the fact that these fusion centers then share this information with other fusion centers opens up a greater potential for the data of the average citizen, who has committed no crime, to be scrutinized for every aspect of the digital life which can be fused together to provide an enormous level of detailed information about any given person.[74] Still further, companies could obtain business information based on what law enforcement is requesting, private companies may then use this information to target individuals, and private company employees may be enlisted to provide information to the fusion centers on potential activities in their place of business or in their neighborhoods, thus having citizens snitch on one another.

The third concern raised by the ACLU investigators was the fact that military personnel were being used to staff some of the fusion centers.[75] Since 1878, when the US Congress passed the Posse Comitatus Act, it has been against the law for US military personnel to be used in a law enforcement capacity on US soil. This was a result of many abuses in the Reconstruction era when military soldiers were used to police communities in the South. Yet, there is clear evidence that in at least one fusion center, the Maryland Coordination and Analysis Center (MCAC), a regional fusion center, US Army personnel have been used as analysts. In addition, National Guard troops, although not federal military until activated, have been used in some fusion centers. In fact, the fusion center in North Dakota is located in a National Guard Armory.[76] Perhaps most egregious is the case in Washington state, where a member of the US Army managed to infiltrate an anti-war protest group in Olympia, Washington, in 2007, and then provided intelligence for the Washington State Fusion Center which shared that information across the network.[77]

The fourth concern of the ACLU has to do with the fact that as data is fused together, it opens up the opportunity for data mining. The head of the Delaware fusion center explained: "The fusion process is to take law enforcement information and other information—it could be from the Department of Agriculture, the Department of Transportation, the private sector—and fuse it together to look for anomalies and push information out to our stakeholders in Delaware who have both a right and a need to know."[78] To understand this, think about your own circumstances, such as your checking account and the checks you write. They are one piece of information about you. By itself, it is rather innocuous. Your credit cards and spending patterns are probably the same. Where you drive to and from in any given day is probably the same (think license plate readers and cameras recording your movements), as is your cell phone usage, and your Internet surfing history. But think about what happens if every point of these data are pulled together, and the data system can now connect all the dots in your life, where you go, who you talk to, what you say, what you buy, what you look at, and what you do at most any given moment. Anyone that has access to that level of data now knows more about you than you probably do yourself. Now imagine how that can be used against you. We have already seen it used against certain conservative groups and members of the Tea Party who have been singled out by the federal government for investigations and Internal Revenue Service (IRS) audits. All of this starts to raise concerns for how the fusion of data at the fusion centers may be giving too much power, information, and intelligence into the hands of the government, without the proper safeguards to our civil liberties that we used to enjoy in the US through our Bill of Rights. When that same director was asked about the limitations of the data collection, rather than thinking in terms of how far law enforcement should be allowed to go, he responded based upon the limitation of resources. "I don't want to say it's unlimited, but the ceiling is very high ... When we have the money, we'll start going to those other agencies and say, 'Are you willing to share that database and what would it cost.' "[79]

The fifth and last concern that the ACLU report raised was the fact that fusion centers have claimed that their work is secret and often classified, but there are very limited mechanisms in place for the purposes of public oversight of their work.[80] The fusion centers have been very secretive about the nature of their work and have only reluctantly divulged information when forced to do so through Freedom of Information Act (FOIA) requests.[81]

While concerns for violations of civil liberties are real, it is the actual violations of civil liberties that drive home the point that these violations are real. There are a number of documented violations already by fusion centers, despite the fact their development and activities have been kept relatively quiet.[82] In a February 2009 bulletin, a Texas fusion center warned of Muslim lobbying groups posing a terroristic threat, yet this was a clear violation of religious freedom. Another report from a Missouri fusion center noted that any group possessing the "Don't Tread on Me" flag, the symbol of the Tea Party, may be a domestic terroristic threat, as well as those advocating against abortion who are members of pro-life groups.[83] Blanket statements by fusion centers that these groups who are peacefully assembling may pose a terror threat is a violation of their constitutional rights to assemble with like-minded groups. Labeling one side of an issue as being signs of belonging to a domestic terrorist group amounts to government picking sides in a political debate.

Another fusion center report in 2009, coming from one located in Virginia, presented their analysis that student groups from historically black colleges may actually serve as potential breeding grounds for future terrorists.[84] One other, and perhaps the most egregious violations of civil rights, was discovered by way of a FOIA request from a Maryland fusion center. This Center had the Maryland State Police conduct an undercover investigation of 53 peace activists and anti-death penalty opponents over a period of 14 months because they were dubbed to have been potential domestic terrorists because of the views they held.[85] All of this was also supported by the US Senate investigation into the fusion centers which found 40 reports over a one year period that had to be either recalled or nixed because they were violations of individual's civil liberties and violated privacy protections.[86]

A Congressional Research Service report raised a number of issues revolving around the fusion centers and encouraged the US Congress to consider a number of options to address these shortcomings. One option was to draft a national fusion center strategy, which would place all of the fusion centers on a more professional level and require to all centers to meet the same requirements. However, this would amount to federal control over the centers. A second option was to address the funding of the fusion centers, which again, if funded by the federal government, the state and local nature of the fusion centers all but vanishes. Another option was training, not only in intelligence gathering and analysis, but in regard to privacy concerns as well. Once again, this raises the same concern. Federally mandated training means federal government control over the program. And yet another option is how best to organize the growing network of fusion centers, which again raises issues of federalism, or who is ultimately in control.

Are Fusion Centers a Proper Role for Police?

Finally, the last thing, perhaps the most important aspect of understanding fusion centers, is to ask whether or not they have been successful. In light of all of the problems with implementing fusion centers and with the issue of violating civil liberties, it is important to know the efficacy of this local and state initiated and federally funded initiative. Do fusion centers thwart the terroristic attacks they claim to be about?

Fusion centers have been credited with being an influential component of American's Homeland Security apparatus in fighting the war on terror.[87] Many have cited the fusion centers with helping to disrupt the planned terrorist attack on New York City's subway system and assisting in the investigation of bomb threats against US airlines.[88] Yet, these are fusion center personnel crediting fusion centers with being influential in the war on terror. They are not exactly the best evidence of their success for they are certainly biased toward what they do.

Even if we relied upon these anecdotes, as in the opening to this chapter, we have to be cautious. When fusion center personnel were asked to identify the greatest success story of the use of a fusion center, they articulated the arrest of a Muslim man who was videotaping the Chesapeake Bay Bridge.[89] Yet, in a *Washington Post* report, they noted that the person in question was a US citizen and he was quickly released and was never charged with any crime.[90] Not exactly a best example scenario to justify the vast expenditures of the fusion centers.

All of the anecdotes about the success of fusion centers aside,[91] there is simply no empirical evidence to date that they have truly been instrumental in thwarting a terrorist attack in the US.[92] The US Senate investigation explained that during their period of investigation, 610 reports were drafted by the 77 fusion centers of which many had to be cancelled for violating civil liberties. Of those remaining, only 94 were said to be related to suspected terrorism and it found "the utility of many of the 94 terrorism-related reports was questionable."[93]

Still further they noted that they "could identify no reporting which uncovered a terrorist threat."[94] Taylor and Russell perhaps have summed it up best, "although fusion centers ... are flourishing, evidence suggests they are perhaps another illustration of a criminal justice response which is good in theory but bad in practice."[95]

Conclusion

The rapid creation of fusion centers, largely unchecked and unsupervised, has created a system without much thought into how to balance the issue that law enforcement has always faced: protecting people, while protecting their freedoms. This chapter has addressed the issues facing America in regard to fusion centers. The controversial issue that needs to be addressed, the one that needs to be openly debated, is whether or not fusion centers are a good idea? Will they truly help to protect us from future terrorist attacks, all-hazards, and all-crimes, or will they simply take away more of our civil liberties and more of our freedoms?

Endnotes

1. Cilluffo, F.J., Clark, J.R., Downing, M.P., & Squires, K.D. (2012). *Counterterrorism intelligence: Fusion center perspectives*. Washington, D.C.: Homeland Security Policy Institute; Rosenbach, E. & Peritz, A.J. (2009). *Confrontation or collaboration? Congress and the intelligence Community: State and Local Fusion Centers*. Boston, MA: Harvard Kennedy School of Government.

2. Cilluffo, F.J., Clark, J.R., Downing, M.P., & Squires, K.D. (2012). *Counterterrorism intelligence: Fusion center perspectives*. Washington, D.C.: Homeland Security Policy Institute.

3. 9/11 Commission. (2004). *The 9/11 commission report*. New York, NY: W.W. Norton & Company.

4. Rollins, J. (2008). *Fusion centers: Issues and options for congress*. Washington, D.C.: Congressional Research Service.

5. Rollins, J. (2008). *Fusion centers: Issues and options for congress*. Washington, D.C.: Congressional Research Service.

6. German, M. & Stanley, J. (2007). *What's wrong with fusion centers?* Washington, D.C.: American Civil Liberties Union; U.S. Senate Permanent Committee on Investigations. (2012). *Federal support for and involvement in state and local fusion centers*. Washington, D.C.: U.S. Senate.

7. 9/11 Commission. (2004). *The 9/11 commission report*. New York, NY: W.W. Norton & Company; Newkirk, A.B. (2010). The rise of the fusion-intelligence complex: A critique of political surveillance after 9/11. *Surveillance & Society, 8*, 43–60.

8. National Governor's Association Center for Best Practices. (2007). *A governor's guide to homeland security*. Washington, D.C.: National Governors Association Center for Best

Practices, p. 8; Rollins, J. (2008). *Fusion centers: Issues and options for congress*. Washington, D.C.: Congressional Research Service, p. 19.

9. Johnson, B. (2009). Fusion centers: Engaging law enforcement in the nation's homeland security enterprise. *Sheriff*, March/April, 37–39; U.S. House of Representatives Committee on Homeland Security. (2013). *Majority staff report on the national network of fusion centers*. Washington, D.C.: U.S. House of Representatives, pp. Iv–v.

10. Carter, D.L. & Carter, J.G. (2009). The intelligence fusion process for state, local, and tribal law enforcement. *Criminal Justice and Behavior, 36,* 1323–1339.

11. Bureau of Justice Assistance. (2006). *Fusion center guidelines: Developing and sharing information and intelligence in a new era*. Washington, D.C.: U.S. Department of Justice. See also German, M. & Stanley, J. (2007). *What's wrong with fusion centers?* Washington, D.C.: American Civil Liberties Union; Johnson, B.R. (2007). A look at fusion centers: Working together to protect America. *FBI Law Enforcement Bulletin,* December, 28–32, p. 29.

12. Napolitano, J. (2011). *Testimony of Secretary Janet Napolitano.* Retrieved online at https://www.dhs.gov/news/2011/02/09/secretary-napolitanos-testimony-understanding-homeland-threat-landscape.

13. Napolitano, J. (2009). Remarks to the national fusion center conference. Retrieved online at https://www.dhs.gov/news/2009/03/13/napolitanos-remarks-national-fusion-center-conference.

14. U.S. Senate Permanent Committee on Investigations. (2012). *Federal support for and involvement in state and local fusion centers*. Washington, D.C.: U.S. Senate, p. 15.

15. As quoted in Monahan, T. (2010). The future of security? Surveillance operations at homeland security fusion centers. *Social Justice, 37,* 84–98, p. 85.

16. U.S. Department of Homeland Security. (2011). *Implementing 9/11 commission recommendations: Progress Report*. Washington, D.C.: U.S. Department of Homeland Security.

17. German, M. & Stanley, J. (2007). *What's wrong with fusion centers?* Washington, D.C.: American Civil Liberties Union.

18. Kanable, R. (2011). Fusion centers grow up. *Law Enforcement Technology,* September, 8–16, p. 8.

19. The Constitution Project. (2012). *Recommendations for Fusion Centers: Preserving Privacy & Civil Liberties While Protecting Against Crime & Terrorism*. Washington, D.C.: The Constitution Project.

20. The Constitution Project. (2012). *Recommendations for fusion centers: Preserving privacy & civil liberties while protecting against crime & terrorism*. Washington, D.C.: The Constitution Project, p. 21; See also Rollins, J. (2008). *Fusion centers: Issues and options for congress*. Washington, D.C.: Congressional Research Service.

21. U.S. House of Representatives Committee on Homeland Security. (2013). *Majority staff report on the national network of fusion centers*. Washington, D.C.: U.S. House of Representatives, p. 16.

22. U.S. Senate Permanent Committee on Investigations. (2012). *Federal support for and involvement in state and local fusion centers*. Washington, D.C.: U.S. Senate.

23. Rollins, J. (2008). *Fusion centers: Issues and options for congress*. Washington, D.C.: Congressional Research Service.

24. Rollins, J. (2008). *Fusion centers: Issues and options for congress*. Washington, D.C.: Congressional Research Service.

25. Rollins, J. (2008). *Fusion centers: Issues and options for congress.* Washington, D.C.: Congressional Research Service.

26. Kanable, R. (2011). Fusion centers grow up. *Law Enforcement Technology, September,* 8–16, p. 8.

27. U.S. General Accountability Office. (2010). *Information sharing: Federal agencies are helping fusion centers build and sustain capabilities and protect privacy, but could better measure results.* Washington, D.C.: U.S GAO.

28. U.S. Department of Justice, Global Justice Information Sharing Initiative. (2008). *Baseline capabilities for state and major urban area fusion centers: A supplement to the fusion center guidelines.* Washington, D.C.: Bureau of Justice Assistance.

29. U.S. Department of Justice, Global Justice Information Sharing Initiative. (2006). *Fusion center guidelines; Developing and sharing information and intelligence in a new era.* Washington, D.C.: Bureau of Justice Assistance; U.S. Department of Justice, Global Justice Information Sharing Initiative. (2008). *Baseline capabilities for state and major urban area fusion centers: A supplement to the fusion center guidelines.* Washington, D.C.: Bureau of Justice Assistance.

30. U.S. Department of Justice, Global Justice Information Sharing Initiative. (2013). *DHS/DOJ fusion process: Technical assistance programs and services, 7th edition.* Washington, D.C.: Bureau of Justice Assistance; U.S. Department of Justice. (2012). *2012 national network of fusion centers: Final report.* Washington, D.C.: Bureau of Justice Assistance.

31. Abold, J.L., Guidetti, R., & Keyer, D. (2012). "Strengthening the value of the national network of fusion centers by leveraging specialization: Defining 'centers of analytical excellence.'" *Homeland Security Affairs, 8,* 1–28, p. 5.

32. U.S. House of Representatives Committee on Homeland Security. (2013). *Majority staff report on the national network of fusion centers.* Washington, D.C.: U.S. House of Representatives.

33. U.S. General Accountability Office. (2010). *Information sharing: Federal agencies are helping fusion centers build and sustain capabilities and protect privacy, but could better measure results.* Washington, D.C.: U.S GAO.

34. U.S. General Accountability Office. (2010). *Information sharing: Federal agencies are helping fusion centers build and sustain capabilities and protect privacy, but could better measure results.* Washington, D.C.: U.S GAO.

35. German, M. & Stanley, J. (2007). *What's wrong with fusion centers?* Washington, D.C.: American Civil Liberties Union; Rollins, J. (2008). *Fusion centers: Issues and options for congress.* Washington, D.C.: Congressional Research Service.

36. National Fusion Center Association. (2014). *Homepage.* Retrieved online at https://nfcausa.org/.

37. Kanable, R. (2011). Fusion centers grow up. *Law Enforcement Technology, September,* 8–16, p. 11.

38. U.S. General Accountability Office. (2010). *Information sharing: Federal agencies are helping fusion centers build and sustain capabilities and protect privacy, but could better measure results.* Washington, D.C.: U.S GAO.

39. Monahan, T. (2010). The future of security? Surveillance operations at homeland security fusion centers. *Social Justice, 37,* 84–98; U.S. Senate Permanent Committee on Investigations. (2012). *Federal support for and involvement in state and local fusion centers.* Washington, D.C.: U.S. Senate.

40. Balko, R. (2013). *Rise of the warrior cop: The militarization of America's police forces.* New York, NY: Public Affairs.

41. Rollins, J. (2008). *Fusion centers: Issues and options for congress.* Washington, D.C.: Congressional Research Service; U.S. Department of Justice, Global Justice Information Sharing Initiative. (2008). *Baseline capabilities for state and major urban area fusion centers: A supplement to the fusion center guidelines.* Washington, D.C.: Bureau of Justice Assistance; U.S. General Accountability Office. (2010). *Information sharing: Federal agencies are helping fusion centers build and sustain capabilities and protect privacy, but could better measure results.* Washington, D.C.: U.S GAO.

42. Carter, D.L. & Carter, J.G. (2009). The intelligence fusion process for state, local, and tribal law enforcement. *Criminal Justice and Behavior, 36,* 1323–1339; U.S. General Accountability Office. (2010). *Information sharing: Federal agencies are helping fusion centers build and sustain capabilities and protect privacy, but could better measure results.* Washington, D.C.: U.S GAO.

43. Chermak, S., Carter, J., Carter, D., McGarrell, E.F. & Drew, J. (2013). Law enforcement's information sharing infrastructure: A national assessment. *Police Quarterly, 16,* 211–244.

44. Taylor, R.W. & Russell, A.L. (2012). The failure of police 'fusion' centers and the concept of a national intelligence sharing plan. *Police Practice and Research 13,* 184–200, p. 188.

45. U.S. Senate Permanent Committee on Investigations. (2012). *Federal support for and involvement in state and local fusion centers.* Washington, D.C.: U.S. Senate.

46. Cilluffo, F.J., Clark, J.R., Downing, M.P., & Squires, K.D. (2012). *Counterterrorism intelligence: Fusion center perspectives.* Washington, D.C.: Homeland Security Policy Institute, p. 13.

47. Cilluffo, F.J., Clark, J.R., Downing, M.P., & Squires, K.D. (2012). *Counterterrorism intelligence: Fusion center perspectives.* Washington, D.C.: Homeland Security Policy Institute, p. 16.

48. Cilluffo, F.J., Clark, J.R., Downing, M.P., & Squires, K.D. (2012). *Counterterrorism intelligence: Fusion center perspectives.* Washington, D.C.: Homeland Security Policy Institute, p. 29.

49. German, M. & Stanley, J. (2007). *What's wrong with fusion centers?* Washington, D.C.: American Civil Liberties Union, p. 6.

50. Monahan, T. (2009). The murky world of 'fusion centres.' *Centre for Crime and Justice Studies, 75,* 20–21; Monahan, T. (2010). The future of security? Surveillance operations at homeland security fusion centers. *Social Justice, 37,* 84–98; Monahan, T. & Palmer, N.A. (2009). The emerging politics of DHS fusion centers. *Security Dialogue, 40,* 617–636; Taylor, R.W. & Russell, A.L. (2012). The failure of police 'fusion' centers and the concept of a national intelligence sharing plan. *Police Practice and Research 13,* 184–200.

51. The Constitution Project. (2012). *Recommendations for fusion centers: Preserving privacy & civil liberties while protecting against crime & terrorism.* Washington, D.C.: The Constitution Project, p. 19.

52. Department of Homeland Security Office of Operations, Coordination and Planning. (2010, Nov. 15). 003 operations, collecting, planning, coordination, reporting, analysis, and fusion system of records. *Federal Register, 75,* 69, 689.

53. U.S. General Accountability Office. (2010). *Information sharing: Federal agencies are helping fusion centers build and sustain capabilities and protect privacy, but could better measure results.* Washington, D.C.: U.S GAO, p. 1.

54. The Constitution Project. (2012). *Recommendations for fusion centers: Preserving privacy & civil liberties while protecting against crime & terrorism.* Washington, D.C.: The Con-

stitution Project; Rosenbach, E. & Peritz, A.J. (2009). *Confrontation or collaboration? Congress and the intelligence Community: State and Local Fusion Centers.* Boston, MA: Harvard Kennedy School of Government; U.S. Senate Permanent Committee on Investigations. (2012). *Federal support for and involvement in state and local fusion centers.* Washington, D.C.: U.S. Senate.

55. U.S. Senate Permanent Committee on Investigations. (2012). *Federal support for and involvement in state and local fusion centers.* Washington, D.C.: U.S. Senate, p. 7.

56. Rollins, J. (2008). *Fusion centers: Issues and options for congress.* Washington, D.C.: Congressional Research Service, p. 15.

57. Rosenbach, E. & Peritz, A.J. (2009). *Confrontation or collaboration? Congress and the intelligence Community: State and Local Fusion Centers.* Boston, MA: Harvard Kennedy School of Government, p. 4.

58. Rollins, J. (2008). *Fusion centers: Issues and options for congress.* Washington, D.C.: Congressional Research Service; Rosenbach, E. & Peritz, A.J. (2009). *Confrontation or collaboration? Congress and the intelligence Community: State and Local Fusion Centers.* Boston, MA: Harvard Kennedy School of Government.

59. Cilluffo, F.J., Clark, J.R., Downing, M.P., & Squires, K.D. (2012). *Counterterrorism intelligence: Fusion center perspectives.* Washington, D.C.: Homeland Security Policy Institute, p. 18.

60. Rollins, J. (2008). *Fusion centers: Issues and options for congress.* Washington, D.C.: Congressional Research Service.

61. German, M. & Stanley, J. (2007). *What's wrong with fusion centers?* Washington, D.C.: American Civil Liberties Union, p. 21.

62. Monahan, T. (2009). The murky world of 'fusion centres.' *Centre for Crime and Justice Studies, 75,* 20–21; Rosenbach, E. & Peritz, A.J. (2009). *Confrontation or collaboration? Congress and the intelligence Community: State and Local Fusion Centers.* Boston, MA: Harvard Kennedy School of Government; Taylor, R.W. & Russell, A.L. (2012). The failure of police 'fusion' centers and the concept of a national intelligence sharing plan. *Police Practice and Research 13,* 184–200.

63. The Constitution Project. (2012). *Recommendations for fusion centers: Preserving privacy & civil liberties while protecting against crime & terrorism.* Washington, D.C.: The Constitution Project.

64. Harris, S. (2007). Issues and ideas—Fusion centers raise a fuss. *National Journal, 39,* 50–56, p. 50.

65. German, M. & Stanley, J. (2007). *What's wrong with fusion centers?* Washington, D.C.: American Civil Liberties Union.

66. German, M. & Stanley, J. (2007). *What's wrong with fusion centers?* Washington, D.C.: American Civil Liberties Union, p. 9.

67. U.S. Senate Permanent Committee on Investigations. (2012). *Federal support for and involvement in state and local fusion centers.* Washington, D.C.: U.S. Senate, p. 1.

68. Hylton, H. (2009). Fusion centers: Giving cops too much information? *Time.* Retrieved online at *http://content.time.com/time/nation/article/0,8599,1883101,00.html*; Monahan, T. (2010). The future of security? Surveillance operations at homeland security fusion centers. *Social Justice, 37,* 84–98.

69. Monahan, T. & Regan, P.M. (2012). Zones of opacity: Data fusion in post-9/11 security organizations. *Canadian Journal of Law & Society, 3,* 301–317.

70. Newkirk, A.B. (2010). The rise of the fusion-intelligence complex: A critique of political surveillance after 9/11. *Surveillance & Society, 8,* 43–60.

71. German, M. & Stanley, J. (2007). *What's wrong with fusion centers?* Washington, D.C.: American Civil Liberties Union, p. 10.

72. Monahan, T. & Regan, P.M. (2012). Zones of opacity: Data fusion in post-9/11 security organizations. *Canadian Journal of Law & Society, 3*, 301–317.

73. See The Guardian. (2014). *NSA files: Decoded, what the revelations mean for you.* Retrieved online at http://www.theguardian.com/world/interactive/2013/nov/01/snowden-nsa-files-surveillance-revelations-decoded.

74. The Constitution Project. (2012). *Recommendations for fusion centers: Preserving privacy & civil liberties while protecting against crime & terrorism.* Washington, D.C.: The Constitution Project.

75. German, M. & Stanley, J. (2007). *What's wrong with fusion centers?* Washington, D.C.: American Civil Liberties Union; See also Carter, D.L. & Carter, J.G. (2009). The intelligence fusion process for state, local, and tribal law enforcement. *Criminal Justice and Behavior, 36*, 1323–1339.

76. German, M. & Stanley, J. (2007). *What's wrong with fusion centers?* Washington, D.C.: American Civil Liberties Union.

77. Anderson, R. (2010). Watching the protestors: These spies may have known too much. *Seattle News Weekly.* Retrieved online at http://www.seattleweekly.com/2010-06-09/news/watching-the-protesters/; Monahan, T. (2010). The future of security? Surveillance operations at homeland security fusion centers. *Social Justice, 37*, 84–98.

78. German, M. & Stanley, J. (2007). *What's wrong with fusion centers?* Washington, D.C.: American Civil Liberties Union, p. 16.

79. German, M. & Stanley, J. (2007). *What's wrong with fusion centers?* Washington, D.C.: American Civil Liberties Union, p. 16.

80. Monahan, T. (2010). The future of security? Surveillance operations at homeland security fusion centers. *Social Justice, 37*, 84–98.

81. Monahan, T. (2010). The future of security? Surveillance operations at homeland security fusion centers. *Social Justice, 37*, 84–98.

82. The Constitution Project. (2012). *Recommendations for fusion centers: Preserving privacy & civil liberties while protecting against crime & terrorism.* Washington, D.C.: The Constitution Project.

83. The Constitution Project. (2012). *Recommendations for fusion centers: Preserving privacy & civil liberties while protecting against crime & terrorism.* Washington, D.C.: The Constitution Project; Monahan, T. (2010). The future of security? Surveillance operations at homeland security fusion centers. *Social Justice, 37*, 84–98.

84. The Constitution Project. (2012). *Recommendations for fusion centers: Preserving privacy & civil liberties while protecting against crime & terrorism.* Washington, D.C.: The Constitution Project; Monahan, T. (2010). The future of security? Surveillance operations at homeland security fusion centers. *Social Justice, 37*, 84–98.

85. Monahan, T. (2010). The future of security? Surveillance operations at homeland security fusion centers. *Social Justice, 37*, 84–98.

86. U.S. Senate Permanent Committee on Investigations. (2012). *Federal support for and involvement in state and local fusion centers.* Washington, D.C.: U.S. Senate.

87. Lambert, D. (2010). Intelligence-led policing in a fusion center. *FBI Law Enforcement Bulletin, December,* 1–6.

88. U.S. General Accountability Office. (2010). *Information sharing: Federal agencies are helping fusion centers build and sustain capabilities and protect privacy, but could better meas-

ure results. Washington, D.C.: U.S GAO; U.S. House of Representatives Committee on Homeland Security. (2013). *Majority staff report on the national network of fusion centers.* Washington, D.C.: U.S. House of Representatives.

89. German, M. & Stanley, J. (2007). *What's wrong with fusion centers?* Washington, D.C.: American Civil Liberties Union.

90. Lichtblau, E. (2004). U.S. holds Virginia man after taping at Marylands bridge. *The Washington Post.* Retrieved online at http://www.nytimes.com/2004/08/25/politics/25hamas.html.

91. Carter, D.L. & Carter, J.G. (2009). The intelligence fusion process for state, local, and tribal law enforcement. *Criminal Justice and Behavior, 36,* 1323–1339.

92. Taylor, R.W. & Russell, A.L. (2012). The failure of police 'fusion' centers and the concept of a national intelligence sharing plan. *Police Practice and Research 13,* 184–200, pp. 187–188; U.S. Senate Permanent Committee on Investigations. (2012). *Federal support for and involvement in state and local fusion centers.* Washington, D.C.: U.S. Senate.

93. U.S. Senate Permanent Committee on Investigations. (2012). *Federal support for and involvement in state and local fusion centers.* Washington, D.C.: U.S. Senate, p. 32.

94. U.S. Senate Permanent Committee on Investigations. (2012). *Federal support for and involvement in state and local fusion centers.* Washington, D.C.: U.S. Senate, p. 2.

95. Taylor, R.W. & Russell, A.L. (2012). The failure of police 'fusion' centers and the concept of a national intelligence sharing plan. *Police Practice and Research 13,* 184–200, pp. 187–188.

Chapter 4

Has DHS Federal Law Enforcement Grown out of Control?

Introduction

In his testimony before the US Congress in March of 2014, Secretary of Homeland Security Jeh Johnson stated that "the basic missions of the Department of Homeland Security are, and should continue to be, preventing terrorism and enhancing security; securing and managing our borders; enforcing and administering our immigration laws; safeguarding cyberspace; safeguarding critical infrastructure; and strengthening national preparedness and resilience."[1] He then used this as a justification for an increased budget for 2015 by specifically mentioning the need for security and enhancing security multiple times. In addition, he employed the words safeguarding and strengthening, emphasizing those same words over and over again. His testimony focused on the need to protect American against terrorism and that the way to achieve that end was to continue growing the Department of Homeland Security. More specifically, much of the budgetary increase was aimed at raising the number of federal law enforcement agents within the Department of Homeland Security.

The Department of Homeland Security (DHS), created in 2002, pulled together and reorganized many federal government agencies. The largest aspect of this reorganization was in regard to federal law enforcement personnel. The Border Patrol and Immigrations Enforcement became the US Customs and Border Protection (CBP) and the US Immigration and Customs Enforcement (ICE), and both saw the numbers of agents increase. Under ICE, they also added another organization known as Homeland Security Investigations (HSI), which acts as a bureau of investigation for Homeland Security. In addition, the Transportation Security Administration (TSA), which had only just recently come into existence, was brought under DHS and it saw its numbers increase annually as well.

Another agency that few knew even existed, the Government Services Administration Police were brought under DHS and made the Federal Protective Service (FPS) which is responsible for guarding federal government facilities throughout the US. Another agency, the Federal Air Marshals, which on 9/11 only had 37 agents, has increased to well over 2,000 agents, although the actual number is classified. Moreover, two other agencies were brought under the Department of Homeland Security, the US Coast Guard and the US Secret Service, and again, both of these agencies have also seen their numbers grow.

One example of the dramatic growth of these organizations since 9/11 is evidenced by the US Border Patrol, now Customs Border Protection (CBP). When it was the US Border Patrol in 1992, there were 4,139 agents working for the agency, covering America's borders with both Mexico and Canada.[2] Throughout the next decade, the number of Border Patrol agents doubled so that in 2001, there were approximately 9,000 agents. In the ten years following the terrorist attack on 9/11, the number more than doubled again to 21,934. Secretary Johnson has called for the hiring of 2,000 more agents.[3] The automatic response of Secretary Johnson and all of the secretaries before him has been a repetitive call for more federal law enforcement agents.

When the US was founded, there was only two federal law enforcement agencies based upon the implied powers of the US Congress within the US Constitution.[4] These two agencies were the US Marshals Service and the US Postal Inspectors. Even as late as the end of the nineteenth century, only one other agency had been added: the US Secret Service. The increase in federal law enforcement has largely been a late twentieth century phenomenon, and one that has increased exponentially since 9/11. At some point, one has to step back and question whether or not the growth of federal law enforcement, especially within the Department of Homeland Security, is justified and necessary or is it, at the very least, wasteful spending, or at worst, the defacto creation of a federal police force.

This chapter will first look at the history of federal law enforcement in the US, from its founding to the terrorist attack of 9/11. It will detail the creation and growth of federal law enforcement within the Department of Homeland Security in the post-9/11 era. It will then raise many of the issues and controversies surrounding these federal law enforcement agencies in order to wrestle with the question of whether this growth has been beneficial in making American free by securing it against terrorism, or has it contributed to a loss of freedom because in the name of security, this growth of federal law enforcement has had a detrimental effect upon America's civil liberties. It will ask the question: has the Department of Homeland Security's federal law enforcement grown too big?

History of Federal Law Enforcement

When the Founding Fathers met in Philadelphia, Pennsylvania, in the long, hot summer of 1787, they spent most of their time debating and crafting what the government of the US should look like. They ultimately settled upon a constitutional republic that was a federalist system of government allowing for both a centralized national government and decentralized state governments. In some cases, the national government would have powers vested in them in which the states would not be allowed to engage, such as the creation of a military and entering into trade agreements with other countries. There were other policy areas left unmentioned that would either allow the national and state governments to share power or those not delegated to the national government would be left to the states. This was further encapsulated in the US Constitution with the passage of the Bill of Rights, specifically under the 10th Amendment.

During the debates for how government would be structured, there was never any discussion about creating a national police force. The Founding Fathers knew this would be anathema to the states, as well as to the people, especially after having dealt with the issue under British rule. This is not to say that they did not discuss the issue of internal conflicts and the need for some mechanism to defend itself. In fact, that very issue came up that summer in the form of Shays' Rebellion.

Shays' Rebellion, named for its reluctant leader, Daniel Shays, was derived from a number of economic conditions placed upon the American people in the aftermath of the Revolutionary War.[5] The states had incurred a lot of debt and the state governments were attempting to find a means of paying down their debt. Higher taxes imposed upon local farmers, especially at a time when there were several years of bad harvests, caused the people to begin to wonder if they had simply replaced one oppressive government with another. Several confrontations ensued, with the most serious being the farmers attempt to capture the Springfield (MA) federal arsenal. The rebellion was eventually broken up, but it raised the question of whether states would be able to deal with and manage domestic violence. The debate at no time made the argument that there should be a federal police to quell such disturbances, but rather, the Founders' incorporated a solution into the US Constitution.

Under Article 4, Section 4, of the US Constitution, it explicitly states that "The United States shall guarantee to every state in this Union a Republican Form of Government, and shall protect each of them against Invasion; and on Application of the Legislature, or of the Executive (when the Legislature cannot be convened) against domestic Violence."[6] In other words, any problems with violence are left to the state to deal with until such time as they become too overwhelming for that state's resources. Then, and only then, could the national government intervene. Yet, in order to allow the national government to intervene, the state legislature had to make a formal request, or if the legislature was not in session and could not convene, then the governor of the state could make the formal request. Until then, the national government would have no authority to intervene in state affairs.

After the summer of 1787, with a new Constitution written, the document still needed to be ratified by the states to become the law of the land. Fearing there would not be enough states supporting ratification, John Jay, Alexander Hamilton, and James Madison took to writing under the pen name *Publius* in an attempt to convince the citizens of various states, especially New York, to ratify the Constitution. The most prolific of these authors of what came to be known as the *Federalist Papers* was Alexander Hamilton. In Federalist Paper #17, Hamilton addressed this issue of law enforcement, or as he put it: the administration of justice, when he wrote:

> There is one transcendent advantage belonging to the province of the state governments, which alone suffices to place the matter in a clear and satisfactory light,—I mean the ordinary administration of criminal and civil justice. This, of all others, is the most powerful, most universal, and most attractive source of popular obedience and attachment. It is that which, being the immediate and visible guardian of life and property, having its benefits and its terrors in constant activity before the public eye, regulating all those personal interests and familiar concerns to which the sensibility of individuals is more immediately awake, contributes, more than any other circumstance, to impressing upon the minds of the people, affection, esteem, and reverence towards the government. This great cement of society, which will diffuse itself almost wholly through the channels of the particular governments, independent of all other causes of influence, would insure them so decided an empire over their respective citizens as to render them at all times a complete counterpoise, and, not unfrequently, dangerous rivals to the power of the Union.[7]

What Hamilton articulated was that one reason for the people to support the passage of the US Constitution was for the fact policing and the administration of justice would remain in the hands of the state and local governments. And because the state and local governments retained the power of the police, in the extreme, it was the national government that had to fear the power of the local police, not the people fearing a powerful, and highly centralized national police force. And, thus, the US Constitution was passed.

Once the Constitution was ratified and the new government formed, it was critical to begin putting the infrastructure of government into place. The first act (Senate Bill Number 1 of the 1st US Congress) was to propose and pass the Judiciary Act of 1789. There were heated debates over the act, but it passed on September 24. Included in the act was the position of US Marshal. Each federal district and circuit court would be authorized to establish a US Marshal and Deputy Marshals who would be assigned to the court to serve primarily as a bailiff, providing court room security, moving prisoners, etc. President Washington wasted no time in appointing the first thirteen US Marshals, and thus was born the US Marshal Service. And that was it, the only federal law enforcement agency in existence. There was no large federal law enforcement agency; there were no federal police.

Over the next hundred years, a few additional agencies would be added. The first, in a sense had pre-dated the Constitution itself. Under the colonial government, Benjamin Franklin had been given the task of regulating the post offices and in 1772, he created the position of Surveyor. The job of the Surveyor was to audit the post offices. This position continued after the passage of the US Constitution because in that document it gave the power to Congress "to establish Post Offices and post Roads." In 1801, the Surveyor title was changed to Special Agent, and this formed the basis for the US Postal Inspectors Service, a police force in charge of protecting the US mail. The only other agency that came into existence in the 1800s was the US Secret Service, in the wake of the Civil War, in order to deal with the problems of counterfeiters, mostly from the South. Once again, the US Constitution gave the federal legislature the power "to provide for the Punishment of counterfeiting the Securities and current Coin of the United States," it made sense to have a law enforcement agency to enforce these laws and protect America's currency, and by right, it's economy.

The growth of federal law enforcement agencies, today numbering approximately 100, is largely a twentieth century phenomenon. The Federal Bureau of Investigation was created in 1908, after a contentious fight between President Theodore Roosevelt and the US Congress. Also, in 1919, because President Roosevelt and Congress has established the National Park System, a US Park Police agency was created. Then came the passage of the 18th Amendment, Prohibition, and a new federal law enforcement agency came into being to enforce those laws—the Bureau of Prohibition. When Prohibition was repealed and the federal government began targeting drugs, this agency became part of the Bureau of Dangerous Drugs and Narcotics, and later, combined with several agencies in 1973, to become the Drug Enforcement Administration. Also, added in the late twentieth century, were the US Customs, Border

Patrol, Air Marshals, and the Bureau of Alcohol, Tobacco, and Firearms. Each of these traces an interesting history, but they are all largely twentieth-century creations.

In addition, many federal police departments were created in the late twentieth century to police federal locations that were once policed by local officers. In Washington, D.C., where the Metropolitan Police Department was once responsible, the US Capitol Police, the Supreme Court Police, the Library of Congress Police, and even the National Zoo Police were formed. Outside of Washington, D.C., locations such as Hoover Dam, the Veteran's Administration, and the General Services Administration (responsible for federal office buildings), created their own federal police departments. So, the number of agencies continued to grow and the personnel continued to increase a little from time to time, until the 1990s, when the numbers increased dramatically, as government began to expand more widely. Nothing, however, can compare with the significant increases in the number of federal law enforcement personnel in the aftermath of 9/11.

Department of Homeland Security and the Growth of Federal Law Enforcement

On September 11, 2001, 19 radical Islamist terrorists hijacked four commercial airliners and used them as missiles to attack America.[8] Two of the airplanes flew into the World Trade Center buildings in New York City, and two were believed to be heading to Washington, D.C., to target the nation's capital. One of the plane's hijackers were taken over by the passengers on board and in their heroic efforts the plane crashed in a field in Pennsylvania. The other plane made it to Washington, D.C., but it is believed that, unable to control the plane, it went for a secondary target and crashed into the Pentagon. America was instantly at war with the terrorist group behind the attack, al-Qaeda.

While the US military mobilized for war and engaged the al-Qaeda-backed Taliban in Afghanistan, at home there was a call for changes in the way America protects itself; there was a sudden call for homeland security. The term itself had been already used among the political elite, but now it was employed to describe changes in domestic organizations tasked with protecting America. One of the first changes that came about was to cease having airlines and airports hire private security to screen passengers and, rather, create a large federal bureaucracy charged with that same mission. This is how the Transportation Security Administration came into being.

The more comprehensive step, however, was first the creation of the Office of Homeland Security within the White House, which served as the precursor to the development of a new federal Cabinet-level agency, the Department of Homeland Security (DHS).[9] In 2002, the US Congress passed the Homeland Security Act and President George W. Bush signed it into law. By the next year, the DHS was beginning to form and various parts of former agencies and whole agencies were absorbed into what would become the second largest federal bureaucracy, second only to the US Department of Defense. Numerous agencies were brought under the umbrella of Homeland Security and many of these were federal law enforcement agencies.

US Immigrations and Naturalization Service, which used to oversee both the administrative duties of naturalizing citizens and providing border protection, were brought into DHS, but they were split into two separate entities. The federal law enforcement agency, the former border patrol, was now the Customs Border Protection (CBP). It combined members of the US Customs agency that had previously existed, primarily those that had worked along the borders. The other federal law enforcement agents from US Customs, who were focused on investigations and intelligence, became the Immigration and Customs Enforcement (ICE). While the splitting of all of these agencies reduced each agency's number of personnel, very quickly the ranks of these federal law enforcement agencies began to grow. The CBP developed various offices, including one for Border Patrol, one for Field Operations, and one for Air and Marine. ICE developed four entities within its organization, including Enforcement Removal Operations (to deport illegal aliens), Homeland Security Investigations (an additional investigative unit with the overall federal investigative powers of ICE agents), the office of Intelligence and an Office of Professional Responsibility.

The DHS also created the National Protection and Programs Directorate, which oversees the Federal Protective Service (FPS). This organization was created in 1971, and oversees the properties administered by the General Services Administration (GSA). Prior to 9/11, they served more as building security for federal government buildings and facilities (non-military) across the US. The FPS under DHS quickly began to grow and became more focused on police duties than building security, turning over building security to contractual guards.

Another agency that was brought under the DHS was the aforementioned Transportation Security Administration (TSA). In order to fully staff airports across the US, it had to increase its number of personnel as well. Eventually, the Federal Air Marshal Service (FAMS) was also brought under the TSA's control because of the strong relationship regarding airline security, and its numbers grew exponentially. On 9/11 there were only 37 agents; it soon grew to over 2,000. Other agencies were brought into DHS in their entirety including the US Coast Guard, the US Secret Service, and the Federal Law Enforcement Training Center (FLETC).[10]

Since 9/11, there has been a steady growth in the Department of Homeland Security overall. Estimates were that in 2003, approximately 170,000 personnel were brought into the new department.[11] By 2010, the number had grown to 191,197 personnel, and today it stands at approximately 240,000. The number of federal law enforcement agents within DHS in every one of the agencies described has seen their number of personnel increased. As previously described, Customs and Border Protection has increased from 9,000 to 22,000 and the Federal Air Marshals has increased from 37 personnel to an estimated 2,000 (the actual number is classified).[12] The US Secret Service has gone from approximately 2,800 special agents in 2001 to 3,200 today, with another 1,300 Uniformed Division officers who are charged with protecting the White House. The Federal Protective Service has also increase its number of federal police officers, growing from less than 500 to over 900 today. All of this growth has been in some cases very rapid (e.g., TSA, FAMS), while all others have been steadily climbing, but it continues to increase. The reality, however, is that the increase in the number of federal law enforcement agents in DHS has not been without its problems, which is the subject of the next section.

Growth Issues

As the US Secret Service has grown it has been the subject of much debate for every time the president now moves, more Secret Service agents are deployed and more state and local assets are tapped to protect the president. Reports of roads, airports, and businesses being shut down, with the Secret Service not tolerating anyone's civil liberties have long been staples of complaints, which have only grown worse since 9/11 because of added protections for the president.[13] Since 2012, reports of Secret Service agent misconduct have also become more problematic.[14] The misconduct began with reports of Secret Service agents being intoxicated on duty and engaging with prostitutes in Cartegna, Columbia. Reports then surfaced that similar activity had occurred in a presidential trip to El Salvador. As the allegations became more widespread, congressional hearings into the scandal were held, and evidence continued to be presented stating that this behavior was common and that supervisors turned a blind eye.[15] The Secret Service eventually released data regarding allegations of misconduct going back to 2004, and the information eventually led to the Director of the Secret Service's retirement. Then, in 2013, despite additional allegations, the Secret Service's Office of Inspector General issued a report that cited no widespread misconduct in the agency, which seemed to contradict the many reports and congressional testimony.[16] Despite the report which cited no systemic problems, just three months later, Secret Service agents on an advance assignment in Amsterdam were recalled because of similar misconduct.[17]

There have also been allegations against the Immigration and Customs Enforcement (ICE) abusing its powers. One difficulty of assessing misconduct on the part of ICE is for the fact it deals with the very gray area of immigration policy and enforcement, which has become even more muddled with presidential executive orders that counter existing laws.[18] Even this has become problematic because it has been estimated that the number of ICE deportations has been rapidly plummeting since 2011, while the number of ICE agents continues to rise.[19] And, while there have been many reports that ICE agents have entered homes and businesses without warrants while engaging in immigration enforcement, because ICE is not an open organization, it is difficult to discern the validity of these allegations.[20] Research by the Vera Institute of Justice and other independent researchers, however, have found evidence that in many instances, ICE agents are ignoring the rule of law and detaining and deporting US citizens.[21] Still further, there have been 107 in detention deaths since 2003, and there is evidence that ICE officials worked to cover up immigrant deaths in jails.[22]

The agency that has come under more serious scrutiny since 9/11, however, has been the Customs Border Protection.[23] The growth of border patrol agents has placed more agents on the southern US border, yet, there are estimates that 30 to 40 percent of these agents are working not on the US-Mexican border, but further inland.[24] More at issue, however, has been the number of shootings along the border, often of unarmed individuals and many who were cross border (individuals on the Mexican side of the Rio Grande River, while agents were on the US side).[25] A Government Accountability Office report shows that the number of people killed by border agents rose from 241 in 1995 to 472 in 2005.[26] So many excessive use of force allegations have been made against CBP that they have undergone numerous investigations and have had their use of force policy curtailed.[27] Still further, there have been numerous CBP officers who have been found to be engaging in corrupt behavior along the border, including making false documents, giving false statements, extorting money, and helping to smuggle illegal aliens into the US[28]

The Federal Protective Service, a little known police force that has grown under the Department of Homeland Security has also come under closer scrutiny for some of its actions and behaviors. One aspect of the Federal Protective Service that has come under scrutiny is their use of private contracts where the security personnel who were hired by the contractors were derelict in their duties and found to be engaging in misconduct. In this case, it was not the FPS officers, but rather the lack of supervision over the private contractors and for the fact that many of these private contractors were found to have been felons.[29] This was further highlighted after the Washington, D.C., Navy Yard shooting when twelve people were killed in September of 2013, for it was FPS contractors providing the security for the military installation. The FPS has also found that the agency overall is rife with inner turmoil that has created problems in its own rights.[30] More recently, the Department of Homeland Security used the FPS police to monitor Tea Party protests over the Internal Revenue Services' abuse of targeting conservative and Tea Party members through selective audits.[31] While the protests were in front of IRS facilities which are protected by the FPS, the strong presence of FPS police officers created a stir. This ultimately led to requests regarding the activities of FPS officers and through Freedom of Information Act requests it was discovered that as far back as 2006, FPS police have been used to monitor certain political protest groups.

Perhaps the agency with the most number of complaints, allegations of misconduct, corruption, and a negative image is the Transportation Security Administration (TSA). There have been so many reported abuses by TSA officers that whole websites have developed that list the crimes and abuses.[32] In addition, investigations into the TSA have been conducted repeatedly by both government agencies and private research organizations.[33] Further, TSA agent abuse is often the focus of much of the congressional testimony and ever present is the issue of how best to reform the agency.[34] Many of the recommendations have been to move away from TSA being a public agency and returning their duties to the private sector.[35] Even former TSA agents have begun to speak out on the abuses of fellow TSA agents on American citizens, including the one by Jason Harrington titled, "Dear America, I Saw You Naked."[36] Americans have become so dissatisfied that it has become common for them to use their cellphones and post TSA abuse on YouTube. For a sampling, go to YouTube and type in "TSA abuse." While documenting the abuses of TSA would easily take another book to detail, everyone agrees that this national police agency (and it is a police agency) has become too powerful and too abusive of American civil liberties.[37]

The one agency that has moved around within DHS, but finally settled under the TSA is the Federal Air Marshals Service. This organization, like its parent agency has been filled with allegations of misconduct, discrimination, retaliation, and criminal employees.[38] Many FAMS officers have been found to have criminal records, psychological problems, and many have abused their positions of authority, including some who were running drugs while serving on duty as air marshals.

Another area where allegations of abuse have surfaced is in the expenditures of the Department of Homeland Security itself. One recent controversial area of expenditure has been in each of the DHS agencies, including Offices of Inspector General, making wide purchases of ammunition which they claim is for training. Recent analysis by government agencies have essentially agreed that the numbers have actually either been declining or are relatively stable.[39] This, in turn, has led many to point out that there has been no independent verification and that the evidence they are not stockpiling is biased.

Another debate that has arisen is the increased funding by homeland security for surveillance equipment.[40] The Department of Homeland Security has been instrumental in providing funding to state and local police agencies for the purchase of license plate readers, devices that can scan license plates, read them, and then check the plate identification numbers through existing database. Other grants have funded local police agencies to purchase Stingray devices which are devices that allow the police the ability to track individual cell phones as long as they are turned on and connected to a cell tower, which almost all of them are. These devices have the ability to track phones geographically and know their location at any given moment, and they can store information based on date, time, and location. Still further, DHS has provided grants for state and local police agencies to purchase city-wide surveillance cameras, those that can not only record digital film footage, but those that can record biometric features and have facial recognition software. Still further, there are grants for local agencies to purchase drones, which have the capabilities of monitoring people through video cameras that have infrared, heat sensors, and night-vision capabilities. Thus, the argument is that DHS is turning America into a surveillance state.[41]

Finally, many have argued that what much of this growth has led to is mission creep.[42] That what the Department of Homeland Security was created for and originally intended to address, protecting America's homeland against terrorists, has grown and expanded to encompass everything from terrorism to local crimes and that DHS federal law enforcement investigations are not only taking on cases that would have once been left to the Federal Bureau of Investigation, but cases that are best suited for local police. In part, the mission creep has occurred because there exists no specific definition of the term homeland security itself, which means it can mean anything and everything to anyone within DHS.[43] Moreover, there has been so little oversight of the DHS and its federal law enforcement agencies that they have been given free rein to expand their reach, authority, and investigations.[44] Still further, because the agency is so large, it is difficult to have adequate leadership to properly direct the organization and thus each agency is left to its own devices to do as they see fit. And, while DHS will state that there are many layers of bureaucracy and many forms of oversight over DHS, this promotes ambiguity, rather than alleviating it, thus making it unclear as to who has the right to investigate allegations of abuse.

Has DHS Federal Law Enforcement Grown Too Large?

Since the terrorist attacks on 9/11 and the creation of the Department of Homeland Security in 2002, the organization has seen nothing but rapid expansion. The agency has grown from 170,000 personnel in 2003 to over 240,000 by 2014, and its budget has increased from $29 billion in 2003 to $61 billion in 2014. And Secretary Johnson has asked for another increase in the budget so that DHS can continue to focus on its mission, which is left rather vague and all encompassing. More importantly, the area that has seen the largest growth is in the area of federal law enforcement personnel. For a country that was founded on nearly no federal law enforcement personnel because it envisioned that power to rest in the hands of local governments, this nation has seen a dramatic growth, especially in the past 15 years, of federal law enforcement, what may be called a national police force.

To date, very few have questioned the validity of this rapid and continued growth. Growth for the mere sake of growth is never a good idea and in this case, the growth of federal law enforcement, America runs the risk of allowing for the growth of a police state, one that may in the name of security, deny the very freedoms it is supposedly trying to protect. So, it is important to step back and debate the merits of continually growing the Department of Homeland Security and its federal law enforcement assets.

The one primary argument for continuing to grow federal law enforcement is in the name of security. There are threats not only from international terrorists, but the argument is that we also face many threats from domestic terrorists. In addition, there are dangerous cartels working within the US that are foreign in nature, ranging from the various international drug cartels to the Russian mafia. Still further, state and local law enforcement often do not have the personnel, the budget, or the necessary jurisdiction to investigate these types of crimes, and the joint task force concept can be cumbersome and slow. In order to be more effective and more efficient in conducting these types of investigations, federal law enforcement has many advantages. This is also why there is a strong need for many of the federal government agencies, especially in the Department of Homeland Security, to have their own police force, because those agencies are best at knowing the policy area they are investigating. Still further, many argue (often wrongly) that crime is rising, disorder is rising, and both the number of terroristic threats and attacks on America are rising. In order for America to remain safe, it is imperative that federal law enforcement have the necessary personnel, budgets, and equipment to keep America safe.

There are many arguments against the increase in the number of federal law enforcement agents as well. One common argument is that government spending dedicated to increasing federal law enforcement, takes away money from other domestic spending on children, health care, and roads. Another argument is that the problems associated with DHS federal law enforcement, ranging from low morale to criminal behavior, have come as a result of growing too fast, not having enough oversight, and providing inadequate training. So many of the agencies grew at such an incredibly rapid rate (e.g., Air Marshals and the Border Patrol), that they were unable to properly screen those they hired and trained, or that they now supervise, and monitor in the field. As a result, agents become disgruntled and complacent, and at worst, corrupt.

Further arguments have centered on the fact that when federal law enforcement agents are unsupervised, there is an increased risk that they will violate civil liberties. Even when doing their job and doing as they are ordered, federal law enforcement still stands in the possible position of violating citizen's civil liberties, just as the local police may do. The difference is, however, that there is more control over local police departments by the local community than there is over federal law enforcement agencies. Citizen complaints can move police departments to change unacceptable policies and procedures, whereas citizen complaints to federal law enforcement agencies or the DHS will be filed and lost in a large federal bureaucracy and it is doubtful citizens will be able to affect change. When it comes to federal law enforcement, there is little ability on the part of the public to control behavior. This leads to hubris which can lead to violations of civil liberties and further abuse of power.

Conclusion

The Founding Fathers had the opportunity to structure the national government so that it had built into its foundation the ability to protect itself through the creation of a national police force. It did not do so, even when a case of domestic insurrection (Shays' Rebellion) was occurring at the same time as they were deliberating. Rather, they chose to leave the power of law enforcement and the administration in the hands of state and local governments and create a situation where the only way the national government could intervene in domestic matters, was when the state legislature (or governor) made a formal request to Congress (or the president).[45] The writers of the Constitution knew that in order to balance civil liberties with security, this was the proper thing to do.

Over the course of American history, very slowly at first, and more rapidly over the past 25 years, the national government has continued to grow its federal law enforcement industry and it is clear through DHS Secretary Johnson's testimony before Congress, they intend to keep growing it in the future.[46] It is time we step back and ask is the current and future growth of federal law enforcement truly necessary for our security or has it become a threat to our civil liberties? In the name of fighting a war on terror, have we traded our freedoms for a sense of security? One way to frame the conflict between security and civil liberties, and how federal police in the name of the former can violate the latter, even when doing their job, is to watch a simple cell phone video. Go to YouTube and watch the video of the little three-year-old girl confined to a wheelchair who was on her way to Disney World only to be pulled aside by the Transportation Security Administration and searched, then ask yourself: Are we winning the war on terror?[47]

Endnotes

1. Johnson, J. (2014). Secretary Johnson announces fiscal years 2015 budget request. Retrieved online at http://www.dhs.gov/news/2014/03/04/secretary-johnson-announces-fiscal-year-2015-budget-request.

2. See U.S. Customs and Border Protection. (2014). Border Patrol Overview—Nationwide Staffing 1992–2013. Retrieved online at http://www.cbp.gov/border-security/along-us-borders/overview.

3. Johnson, J. (2014). Secretary Johnson announces fiscal years 2015 budget request. Retrieved online at http://www.dhs.gov/news/2014/03/04/secretary-johnson-announces-fiscal-year-2015-budget-request.

4. Marion, N.E. & Oliver, W.M. (forthcoming). *Federal Law Enforcement Agencies*. Frederick, MD: Wolters Kluwer.

5. Richards, L.L. (2002). *Shays's rebellion: The American revolution's final battle*. Philadelphia, PA: University of Pennsylvania Press.

6. United States Constitution.

7. Hamilton, A. (1787). The Federalist No. 17: The Insufficiency of the Present Confederation to Preserve the Union. Retrieved online at http://thomas.loc.gov/home/histdox/fed_17.html.

8. National Commission on Terrorist Attacks Upon the United States. (2004). *The 9/11 commission report: Final report of the national commission on terrorist attacks upon the United States*. New York, NY: Norton & Company, Inc.

9. Oliver, W.M., Marion, N.E., & Hill, J.B. (2015). *Introduction to homeland security: Policy, organization, and administration.* Burlington, MA: Jones & Bartlett Learning.

10. Department of Homeland Security. (2014). Who joined DHS. Retrieved from http://www.dhs.gov/who-joined-dhs.

11. Copeland, C.W. (2011). The federal workforce: Characteristics and trends. *Congressional Research Service.* Retrieved from http://assets.opencrs.com/rpts/RL34685_20110419.pdf; United States Department of Homeland Security. (2014). Official website of the department of homeland security. Retrieved from http://www.dhs.gov/"

12. Haddal, C.C. (2010). Border security: Key agencies and their missions. *Congressional Research Service.* Retrieved from http://fas.org/sgp/crs/homesec/RS21899.pdf; Politifact.com. (2011). Obama says border patrol has double the number of agents since 2004. *Politifact.* Retrieved from http://www.politifact.com/truth-o-meter/statements/2011/may/10/barack-obama/obama-says-border-patrol-has-doubled-number-agents/; U.S. Customs and Border Protection. (2014). Border Patrol Overview—Nationwide Staffing 1992–2013. Retrieved online at http://www.cbp.gov/border-security/along-us-borders/overview.

13. Reese, S. (2013). The U.S. secret service: An examination and analysis of its evolving missions. *Congressional Research Service.* Retrieved from http://fas.org/sgp/crs/homesec/RL34603.pdf.

14. National Public Radio. (2014). Stories about secret service scandal. Retrieved from http://www.npr.org/tags/151268592/secret-service-scandal.

15. National Public Radio. (2014). Stories about secret service scandal. Retrieved from http://www.npr.org/tags/151268592/secret-service-scandal.

16. Department of Homeland Security Office of Inspector General. (2013). Adequacy of USSS efforts to identify, mitigate, and address instances of misconduct and inappropriate behavior. Washington, D.C.: Department of Homeland Security.

17. National Public Radio. (2014). Stories about secret service scandal. Retrieved from http://www.npr.org/tags/151268592/secret-service-scandal.

18. Franke-Ruta, G. (2014). Obama's game changer on young illegal immigrants. *The Atlantic.* Retrieved from http://www.theatlantic.com/politics/archive/2012/06/obamas-game-changer-on-young-illegal-immigrants/258550/.

19. Vaughan, J.M. (2013). Deportation numbers unwrapped: Raw statistics reveal the real story of ICE enforcement in decline. *Center for Immigration Studies.* Washington, D.C.: Center for Immigration Studies.

20. See for instance American Civil Liberties Union. (2014). Immigration and Customs Enforcement. Retrieved from https://www.aclu.org/blog/tag/immigration-and-customs-enforcement.

21. Stevens, J. (2011). Detaining and deporting U.S. citizens as aliens. *Virginia Journal of Social Policy & the Law, 18,* 607–720; Taylor, M. (2008). Immigration officials detaining, deporting American citizens. *McClatchyDC.* Retrieved from http://www.mcclatchydc.com/2008/01/24/25392/immigration-officials-detaining.html.

22. Bernstein, N. (2014). In-custody deaths. *The New York Times.* Retrieved from http://topics.nytimes.com/top/reference/timestopics/subjects/i/immigration_detention_us/incustody_deaths/index.html.

23. Haddal, C. C. (2010). Border security: The role of the U.S. border patrol. *Congressional Research Service.* Washington, D.C.: CRS.

24. Finland, R. (2013). Why adding 21,000 border patrol is a dysfunctional plant that will

waste billions. *Forbes Magazine*. Retrieved from http://www.forbes.com/sites/richardfinger/2013/07/21/why-adding-21000-border-patrol-is-a-dysfunctional-plan-that-will-waste-billions/.

25. Police Executive Research Forum. (2013). *U.S. customs and border protection: Use of force review: cases and policies*. Washington D.C., PERF; Rosenblum, M.R. (2012). Border security: Immigration enforcement between ports of entry. *Congressional Research Service*. Retrieved from http://fpc.state.gov/documents/organization/180681.pdf.

26. U.S. Government Accountability Office. (2005). *Illegal immigration: Border-Crossing deaths have doubled since 1995, border patrol's efforts to prevent deaths have not been fully evaluated*. Washington, D.C.: U.S. Government Accountability Office.

27. U.S. Customs and Border Protection. (2014). CBP releases use of force policy handbook and police executive research forum report. Retrieved from http://www.cbp.gov/newsroom/national-media-release/2014-05-30-000000/cbp-releases-use-force-policy-handbook-and-police.

28. Center for Investigative Reporting. (2014). Crossing the line: Corruption at the border. Retrieved from http://bordercorruption.apps.cironline.org/; U.S. Government Accountability Office. (2012). *Border security: Additional actions needed to strengthen CBP efforts to mitigate risk of employee corruption and misconduct*. Retrieved from http://www.gao.gov/assets/660/650505.pdf.

29. Federal Register. (2009). Prohibition on federal protective service guard services contracts with business owned, controlled, or operated by an individual convicted of a felony. *Federal Register*. Retrieved from http://www.gpo.gov/fdsys/pkg/FR-2009-11-16/html/E9-27330.htm

30. U.S. General Accountability Office. (2014). *The federal protective serve report to congressional requesters*. Washington, D.C.: U.S. GAO.; U.S. General Accountability Office. (2013). *Challenges associated with federal protective service's contract guards and risk assessments at federal facilities*. Washington, D.C.: U.S. GAO.; U.S. General Accountability Office.

31. The Partnership for Civil Justice. (2013). New documents reveal: DHS spying on peaceful demonstrations and activists. Retrieved from http://www.justiceonline.org/commentary/new-documents-reveal-dhs.html.

32. See for instance: The master list of TSA crimes and abuses at http://tsanewsblog.com/master-list-of-tsa-abuses-and-crimes/; TSA goons at http://www.tsagoons.com/; or Shiny badge: Tracking TSA abuses at http://shinybadge.com/.

33. See for instance Edwards, C. (2013). Privatizing the transportation security administration. *Cato Institute*. Washington, D.C.: Cato Institute; U.S. Government Accountability Office. (2013). Transportation Security: TSA could strengthen monitoring of allegations of employee misconduct. Washington, D.C.: US GAO.

34. Transportation Security Administration. (2014). Testimony. Retrieved from http://www.tsa.gov/press/releases/2014/06/24/testimony.

35. Edwards, C. (2013). Privatizing the transportation security administration. *Cato Institute*. Washington, D.C.: Cato Institute.

36. Harrington, J.E. (2014). Dear America, I saw you naked. *PoliticoMagazine*. Retrieved from http://www.politico.com/magazine/story/2014/01/tsa-screener-confession-102912.html#.U6xVwfkVp8E.

37. Edwards, C. (2013). Privatizing the transportation security administration. *Policy Analysis, Cato Institute*. Retrieved from http://object.cato.org/sites/cato.org/files/pubs/pdf/pa742_web_1.pdf; Moore, C. (2012). Is the TSA protecting homeland security or protecting federal employees. *My Heritage*. Retrieved from http://www.myheritage.org/news/is-the-tsa-protecting-homeland-security-or-protecting-federal-employees/.

38. Department of Homeland Security office of Inspector General. (2012). Allegations of misconduct and illegal discrimination and retaliation in the federal air marshal service.

Washington, D.C.: US DHS; USA Today. (2008). Crimes by air marshals raise questions about hiring. *USA Today*, November 17.

39. Congressional Research Service. (2013*). Recent department of homeland security ammunition solicitations, contracts and purchases.* Washington, D.C.: Congressional Research Service; U.S. Government Accountability Office. (2014). *Ammunition purchases have declined since 2009.* Washington, D.C.: US GAO.

40. Timm, T. (2014). The US government doesn't want you to know how the cops are tracking you. *The Guardian.* Retrieved from http://www.theguardian.com/commentisfree/2014/jun/14/cops-tracking-calls-stingray-surveillance; Whitehead, J.W. (2014). Has the department of homeland security become America's standing army? *The Rutherford Institute.* Retrieved from https://www.rutherford.org/publications_resources/john_whiteheads_commentary/has_the_dept_of_homeland_security_become_americas_standing_army; Wolverton, J. (2013). Seattle latest city to install DHS surveillance equipment. *The New American.* Retrieved from http://www.thenewamerican.com/usnews/constitution/item/16930-seattle-latest-city-to-install-dhs-surveillance-equipment.

41. Blako, R. (2013). *Rise of the warrior cop: The militarization of America's police forces.* New York, NY: Public Affairs.

42. Balko, R. (2014). DHS: A wasteful, growing, fear-mongering beast. *The Washington Post.* Retrieved from http://www.washingtonpost.com/news/the-watch/wp/2014/05/07/dhs-a-wasteful-growing-fear-mongering-beast/; Coleman, M. (2014). Mission creep: Homeland security a 'runaway train.' The Albuquerque Journal. Retrieved from http://www.abqjournal.com/390438/news/homeland-security-a-runaway-train.html; Darby, B. (2013). Mission creep in law enforcement: Expanding federal fiefdoms. *Breitbart.* Retrieved from http://www.breitbart.com/Big-Government/2013/12/24/Mission-Creep-in-Federal-Law-Enforcement-Agencies-Perpetuating-Their-Fiefdoms-And-Damaging-States-Abilities.

43. Coleman, M. (2014). Mission creep: Homeland security a 'runaway train.' The Albuquerque Journal. Retrieved from http://www.abqjournal.com/390438/news/homeland-security-a-runaway-train.html.

44. Balko, R. (2014). DHS: A wasteful, growing, fear-mongering beast. *The Washington Post.* Retrieved from http://www.washingtonpost.com/news/the-watch/wp/2014/05/07/dhs-a-wasteful-growing-fear-mongering-beast/.

45. U.S. Constitution, Article 4, Section 4.

46. Johnson, J. (2014). Secretary Johnson announces fiscal years 2015 budget request. Retrieved online at http://www.dhs.gov/news/2014/03/04/secretary-johnson-announces-fiscal-year-2015-budget-request.

47. See for instance ABC News: https://www.youtube.com/watch?v=s_TAoMUVeVg.

Chapter 5

Is Intelligence-Led Policing a Proper Role for Local Police?

Introduction

The police received a tip from a concerned citizen who noticed that his neighbor and some friends had been up all night working in the garage, then left together in a van with blacked out windows that he had never seen before. Asked for the license plate, he could only remember a part of it. He was also hesitant to tell them that the neighbor and his friends were of Middle-Eastern descent. The police thanked the citizen and sent the information over to the Intelligence-Led Policing (ILP) unit.

The ILP officer called up the Division of Motor Vehicles database and entered the partial tag, and while the computer was searching, he then accessed a personal property database and found the name of the individual who had only recently purchased the house. Switching back to the motor vehicle check, it took no time to find the home owner's name in the license plate list, and now with the full tag information, called up the driver's license information of the owner. A quick credit check found the individual had a spotless record, but that all transactions only dated back 18 months. He then began a criminal background check on the individual as well as a check through the SARs (Suspicious Activity Report) database. The individual suspect had no criminal record, but a number of SARs hits, all of which alluded to suspicious activity, particularly taking pictures of the main metro station downtown. This raised some eyebrows with the ILP officer.

He decided his next course of action was to access the License Plate Reader database to locate the current position of the vehicle, when he received a hit. The location was half the distance between the home and the metro station. He notified his team about the situation and they accessed traffic cameras in advance of the last known location of the van and found it still heading toward the metro station. Pictures from the traffic cameras were quickly downloaded and the images expanded, pixilation issues were fixed with imaging software, and clear photos of the driver (the homeowner) and another passenger were obtained. The team immediately saw the explosive vests the two were wearing.

The Counter-Terrorism team was summoned, and other police assets were notified, including the metro transit police. Satellites were now put into use to track the vehicle. The counter-terrorism team's snipers were then in place when the van pulled up and before the buttons could be pushed to explode the vests and the additional explosives in the van, the two were shot between the eyes, head shots so as to stop all motor reflexes from pushing the button.

The scenario you just read was not real. It is the kind of scenario that people often see on television shows such as *24*. The reality is, television shows like *24* are fictitious, but they are often what people envision when they hear the term Intelligence-Led Policing—the process of collecting vast amounts of information and analyzing that information in real time in order to create actionable intelligence. Consider, however, the vast amount of data the imagined ILP officer in the scenario above had at his disposal. The officer accessed numerous databases in which average Americans, who have committed no crime and for which there was no reason to suspect they were engaged in any crime, had their information reviewed by the police. Still further, imagine if the owner of the house had no suicide vest, had stayed up all night with some friends fixing the van, and was then driving them to the metro station. Just innocent citizens going about their daily lives.

Prior to 9/11, the police conducted criminal investigations, accessing information about people only when there was a reasonable suspicion that they were committing a crime (In the scenario, was there anything that amounted to reasonable suspicion that a crime was taking place?). Intelligence was kept separate from criminal investigations. Now, the line is becoming more blurred and the so-called wall between these two has fallen. The controversy in this case is whether or not Intelligence-Led Policing is a proper role for local police or is it too great a threat to Americans' civil liberties?

History of Police Intelligence

Modern American policing began in the nineteenth century, when the Boston (MA) Police Department established its full time police department in 1838.[1] Throughout the century, policing was inherently part of the American political landscape which was dominated by political machines that were more interested in protecting the power of the political party in office rather than policing the streets to "serve and protect."[2] Policing was wholly corrupt and very often brutal.[3] As part of this corruption, certain police departments and individuals within policing often gathered intelligence as a means of political control and then used that intelligence for personal gain. One of the most infamous of these individuals was Inspector Thomas F. Byrnes of the New York Police Department who, during the Lexow Committee investigations into police corruption in 1894 and 1895, was exposed for high levels of graft, much of which was collected through intelligence gathering.[4]

Policing in the early twentieth century was focused on reforming policing, to sever its ties with politics, to become more professional, and to focus its attention on crime control and police investigations. As a result of this emphasis, especially the emphasis on the reduction of political ties, police departments for the most part abandoned the gathering of police intelligence and maintaining files on citizens. There was, however, one very important exception to this, and that was the collection of police intelligence on not only citizens, but politicians, movie stars, etc., by the Federal Bureau of Investigation's Director, J. Edgar Hoover.[5]

Hoover had been a part of the FBI's administrative staff in 1917 when Russia's Bolshevik Revolution turned the world's attention toward the threat of Communism. Hoover played an instrumental role in the collection of police intelligence that was targeted toward members of the American Communist Party and those involved in the Industrial Workers of the World (IWW) that had staged labor strikes that were against American big business and capitalism. In addition, a number of attacks occurred that were either associated, loosely associated, or at least suspected to be tied to these groups, including the famous Wall Street Bombing which occurred on September 16, 1920.[6]

All of this turmoil led US Attorney General Alexander Mitchell Palmer to conduct what became known as the "Palmer Raids," roundups of those the US Department of Justice and Federal Bureau of Investigation had been keeping dossiers on and who were considered threats to American security. Mass arrests were made and the majority of these individuals were then deported back to their country of origin. The actions of Palmer were criticized and found to have violated the US Constitution. Palmer's career ended and the first Red Scare (1919–1921) faded into history. J. Edgar Hoover, however, became the new director of the Federal Bureau of Investigation and learned a number of lessons from the fall-out of the first Red Scare.[7]

Hoover had amassed an enormous amount of police intelligence on many Americans throughout the 1930s, and especially during World War II, when the FBI took on the role of providing security for America through intelligence gathering. In the 1950s, Hoover continued the collection of intelligence on suspected Communists and Socialists, but it was the activities of Senator Joe McCarthy who launched the second Red Scare (1947–1954). Although most police departments did not have intelligence units, it was becoming clear that many were keeping dossiers on people, whether they were suspected of a crime or not. It was through these, and especially the FBI's files, that certain individuals were being targeted as Communists and were subsequently being blacklisted. Despite this, it was not until the 1960s that challenges to the police collection of intelligence became to surface.[8]

The 1960s was a time of social upheaval, and many movements (the civil rights movement, women's movement, anti-Vietnam War protests, and campus unrest), brought American citizens into conflict with the police. It was soon discovered that the police were maintaining files on American citizens, many who had committed no crime, nor were under any investigation, but the intelligence was being collected because they *might* commit a crime and they *might* be a threat, so dossiers were developed in advance of something that *might* happen.[9] Many of those targeted began to fight back, demanding to see what intelligence the police were collecting about them and to challenge the constitutionality of these dossiers in court.[10]

Police departments typically would not release the files, but legal challenges and court orders eventually forced their hands. The resulting effect was that those citizens who were targeted could now expose this police practice to the rest of the American people.[11] This also forced the US Senate to begin investigating what type of intelligence the federal government was keeping on American citizens. The US Senate Select Committee to Study Government Operations was established, and led by Senator Frank Church (D-Idaho), it became known as the Church Committee. One of the most sensational aspects of government intelligence being collected came with the exposure of the FBI's Counter Intelligence Program (COINTELPRO) that was run by J. Edgar Hoover from 1959 to 1971, when Hoover ended it because of the investigation.[12] Although later it was learned that while COINTELPRO was shut down, the FBI continued the practices of tracking Americans.

Hoover was never held accountable for these illegal practices, for he died in 1972, before the Church Committee released its final report. That report concluded:

> Too many people have been spied upon by too many Government agencies and too much information has been illegally collected. The Government has often undertaken the secret surveillance of citizens on the basis of their political beliefs, even when those beliefs posed no threat of violence or illegal acts on behalf of a hostile foreign power. The Government, operating primarily through secret and bias informants, but also using other intrusive techniques such as wiretaps, microphone

"bugs", surreptitious mail opening, and break-ins, has swept in vast amounts of information about the personal lives, views, and associations of American citizens. Investigations of groups deemed potentially dangerous—and even of groups suspected of associating with potentially dangerous organizations—have continued for decades, despite the fact that those groups did not engage in unlawful activity.[13]

It then noted that "[g]overnmental officials—including those whose principal duty is to enforce the law—have violated or ignored the law over long periods of time and have advocated and defended their right to break the law."[14]

The fallout from the Church Committee reports was that many police departments found themselves facing lawsuits and both city and states began passing laws to curtail the gathering of police intelligence and dossiers on American citizens unless they were under investigation for a crime. It effectively ended nearly every police intelligence unit in the nation. As the Rand Corporation's analysis of the fallout stated, "[P]olice commissions and police chiefs felt that intelligence operations only brought lawsuits."[15] Any police intelligence gathering had become relegated to police investigations of criminal matters.

At the federal level, Congress wrestled with how to respond to the Church Committee's report. What they ultimately passed was the Foreign Intelligence Surveillance Act (FISA). FISA was primarily focused on the requirements for the federal government, such as the Central Intelligence Agency or the Federal Bureau of Investigation conducting surveillance and gathering intelligence. It was not focused on local law enforcement. However, it did have implications for law enforcement because it created what became known as "the wall," a prohibition against intelligence agencies and law enforcement agencies sharing information.[16] Intelligence and law enforcement had to be kept separate in order to protect people's civil liberties.

On September 11, 2001, when nineteen Islamists hijacked four American passenger planes and flew two of them into the World Trade Center buildings in New York City, one into the Pentagon in Arlington, Virginia, and the last crashed in a field in Pennsylvania after passengers overtook the hijackers, everything changed. In the name of security, national security, and homeland security, the concept of police collecting intelligence on terrorists was not even second guessed. Vast amounts of intelligence began to be collected, lists and dossiers maintained, and something that had been either illegal or virtually taboo out of civil rights concerns, returned without question. The so-called "wall" had fallen. Police intelligence gathering was deemed a worthy cause in the war on terror, and what came in vogue and was soon being adopted by police departments across the US, was Intelligence-Led Policing (ILP).

Intelligence-Led Policing (ILP)

The exact origin of Intelligence-Led Policing is somewhat questionable, for it appears in the 1990s in England as a concept or idea that was discussed.[17] Some have stated that it developed when the Kent Constabulary was faced with an increase in property crimes, and a budget that had been drastically cut.[18] Others have stated that it was a 1993 Audit Commission Report on public safety in England that began the development of Intelligence-Led Policing.[19] This eventually led to the publication of Her Majesty's Inspectorate of Constabulary's publication titled, *Policing with Intelligence* which was published in 1997.[20] By the late 1990s, England and Australia were engaging in Intelligence-Led Policing.[21]

In the US, it has been said that Mark Reibling was the originator of the concept. In his book, *Wedge— The Secret War between the FBI and CIA,* published in 1994, he discussed the conflicts between these two organizations, exposing the problems of attempting to keep intelligence and criminal investigation information separate.[22] In other words, the wall referred to earlier was creating turf wars between these two bureaucracies. Reibling saw the benefits of the two working together and that through the sharing of intelligence with the police, they might have actionable intelligence that could launch or assist in criminal investigations. The goal was information sharing, not separation.

ILP was also discussed in policing circles in the 1990s, especially amongst those engaged in Compstat such as the NYPD, due, in part, to some of the similarities, or applications of ILP to Compstat or Compstat to ILP.[23] Compstat had been a method implemented during the Guiliani Administration under Police Commissioner William Bratton that sought to hold precinct commanders accountable for crime in their jurisdictions and demanding crime reduction through information, analysis, and innovative methods of police deployment.[24] ILP crossed over to information gathering and analysis in order to develop what was called "actionable intelligence," intelligence that would be useful to the police to launch a criminal investigation, redeploy police personnel, or identify problems.[25]

It was not until the tragic events of September 11, 2001, that the wall was removed between intelligence and criminal investigations and Intelligence-Led Policing quickly advanced.[26] By 2004, the US Department of Justice had published a guide for state, local and tribal law enforcement agencies on the collection of intelligence by police agencies, and the Bureau of Justice Assistance published a document that called ILP *The New Intelligence Architecture.*[27] Very soon it was commonly talked about in policing circles and within the academic community.[28] And then books began to appear, fleshing out the concept even more.[29] Despite all of the publications, understanding the specifics of Intelligence-Led Policing has been somewhat vague as the concept has seen widespread, but highly varied development. Early considerations of ILP tended to associate it with Community Policing, but this was in large part because early publications were funded by the US Department of Justice's Office of Community Oriented Policing Services, and things had to be tied to community policing in order to receive grant funding.[30] More recently, ILP has been closely tied to the development of Fusion Centers, but it is difficult to say whether this is the final form of ILP or if it is but one variant of the overall concept (see Chapter 3).

In order to best understand Intelligence-Led Policing as a concept, it makes most sense to define it; however, even this runs into problems for there is no one commonly held definition. Most articles on ILP tend to default to the definition provided by Carter & Carter (2009) when they wrote of ILP as:

> The collection and analysis of information related to crime and conditions that contribute to crime, resulting in an actionable intelligence product intended to aid law enforcement in developing tactical responses to threats and/or strategic planning related to emerging or changing threats.[31]

While the definition is sound for the concept of taking information and converting it to actionable intelligence, what is left is an assumption that the concept of intelligence itself is understood. Yet, as Peterson (2005) notes, "[B]ecause of misuse, the word 'intelligence' means different things to different people."[32] Hence, she calls for a clarification as to what is meant by the word that is so critical to the concept of Intelligence-Led Policing.

Peterson first distinguishes the difference between information and intelligence. Information is the raw data that is collected from various sources. More formally, it has been defined as, "pieces of raw, unanalyzed data that identifies persons, evidence, events, or illustrates processes that indicate the incidence of a criminal event or witnesses or evidence of a criminal event."[33] Information is thus the vast amounts of data collected that can later be analyzed. This may include for police purposes: surveillance logs, travel records, credit card statements, banking transactions, wiretaps, trash collection ("dumpster diving"), location of vehicles through license plate readers, and tracking of cell phones.

Intelligence is the product that occurs after information has been analyzed. More formally, the definition of intelligence is "the collection and analysis of information to produce an intelligence end product designed to inform law enforcement decision making at both the tactical and strategic level."[34] For instance, a photo may be information, but when it is analyzed, it may reveal a crime in progress (this has actually happened multiple times with Google taking photos for its street-view on Google Maps[35]), a license plate number of the vehicle, a photo of the person driving, and hence the intelligence that a certain identified person, committed a specific crime. With evidence of a crime in hand and a suspect identified, this is actionable intelligence. This yields that formula which states: "information plus analysis equals intelligence."[36]

The formula, while helpful, then makes another assumption. It assumes we understand what analysis is and how it takes place.[37] Many believe that computers perform analysis by linking various disparate pieces of information together. This may be, for computers have the capacity to move through large databases at incredibly fast speeds and then make connections between databases. So, searches through credit card files to find a specific name and track the credit card's usage is easy, along with the location, date, and time it was used. It can then search the motor vehicle files for the vehicle the person owns, along with their license plate. Then, it can explore license plate reader databases to find the location, date, and time where that vehicle has been, and from there, check traffic monitor cameras for visual evidence to corroborate the license plate readers, etc. All of this can be done and interconnected, as long as the police analysts has access to all of these databases.

Computers are good for making specific linkages with data that exists in numbers and letters, such as names, dates, license plate numbers, etc. They are not good, however, at exploring such details as a picture and then being able to identify what is occurring in that picture. Human analysts are then necessary to make sense of nuances such as body language, circumstances, environment, etc. For instance, two photos of a person holding a gun may raise eyebrows, but if one is in a field, where the gunman is hiding behind a haystack, the gun has an orange tip, and the sign on the fence in the background says "paintball," the analysts can most likely dismiss this as non-criminal. However, the other photo of a gunman hiding behind a car, where the car has several holes in it, and there is a person fleeing down the street, may suggest a crime is occurring. Humans are needed for their ability to identify nuances and make sense of raw data. This also, then, yields intelligence.

It should also be noted that many additional terms get added to these definitions of intelligence, such as tactical intelligence or strategic intelligence. Tactical intelligence is that intelligence which can be acted upon for it "directs immediate action."[38] Strategic intelligence, however, is focused on the larger picture and only "evolves over time and explores long-term, large-scope solutions."[39] Then, of course, there is also the term "police intelligence" which is ultimately what Intelligence-Led Policing is seeking. "In the law enforcement/

national security business," according to FBI Deputy Assistance Director of the Office of Intelligence, this type of intelligence "is information about those who would do us harm in the form of terrorist acts or other crimes, be they property crimes or violent crimes."[40]

Despite all of the definitions about what Intelligence-Led Policing is supposed to be, what it really is and does is more important for understanding the concept. Carter (2005) described what it should look like in a guide for law enforcement agencies, which detailed it as the creation of an intelligence unit within a police department that would then be responsible for the collection of information through various networks and systems, followed by its analysis. He then discussed the staffing issues, how to analyze data in light of the intelligence requirements and threat assessments. Then there was a discussion about how best to disseminate the information and sharing it with other agencies. This guide, like so many other resources, however, was vague on the specifics of how data was actually analyzed and what the final intelligence product would actually look like. In part, this is because of the case-by-case nature of each event, thus specifics cannot be covered for every situation, data, and circumstances will dictate. This, however, has left the police, when creating Intelligence-Led Policing units, to employ trial and error methods when attempting to determine how exactly to analyze data and what intelligence end products should look like.

In the years immediately after 9/11, many police departments attempted to develop their own Intelligence-Led Policing units. New York City Police Department was one of the first to adopt the creation of an intelligence unit, specifically creating the Intelligence Division & Counter-Terrorism Bureau and employing intelligence analysts with the agency (although it should be noted that the analyst positions themselves are staffed by civilians, not police officers), although New York is the exception and not the rule.[41] According to the Law Enforcement Management and Administrative Statistics (LEMAS) study conducted in 2007, "about 4,000 full-time sworn personnel in local police departments were employed in intelligence positions with primary duties related to terrorist activities."[42] Most of these tended to be in police departments serving a population of 500,000 or more (90 percent), and most "used computers in an analytic capacity related to intelligence gathering, crime analysis, analyzing community problems, and crime mapping."[43] In fact, it was noted that only 40 percent of departments used computers for intelligence gathering, and nearly all of the intelligence units were not solely focused on the issue of terrorism.

In the 2007 LEMAS study, there was no collection of information regarding police departments and their use of Fusion Centers (see Chapter 3), and that was because the idea was just beginning to take shape at that time. This was because many police departments wanting an Intelligence-Led Policing unit could not afford their own, for they did not have the resources to fund it, staff it, or operate one. The idea of combining resources to create regional Intelligence-Led Policing units, the Fusion Centers, took hold at about this time and they began to flourish. However, as chapter 3 noted, they have developed into something similar to ILP, but have not been all together successful. The question then for Intelligence-Led Policing is: has it been successful?

Several studies that have looked at Intelligence-Led Policing have not necessarily addressed this particular question directly. One study, looking at the implementation of Intelligence-Led Policing in state law enforcement agencies, found that the more these agencies engaged in homeland security, the more they interacted with federal agencies.[44] Yet, increased communication, engagement, and even information/intelligence sharing, may not necessarily mean the Intelligence-Led Policing is successful in its core intent. Others studies have primarily looked at Fusion Centers as the embodiment of Intelligence-Led Policing, but even these are not necessarily helpful in understanding if ILP has been successful for they have asked the opinions of those leading the Fusion Centers if they think it has been successful, the very people who have a vested interest in assuring everyone that their job is important.[45]

Several publications that have come from the US Department of Justice have attempted to provide success stories of Intelligence-Led Policing. One, published in 2009, provided some vignettes, but were vague on agency specifics, so verifying the accuracy was limited.[46] The success stories highlighted were also primarily focused on what is known as "hot spot" policing, and police departments have been deploying these methods without intelligence units since the early 1990s.[47]

Another publication that year, *Reducing Crime though Intelligence-Led Policing,* provides ten examples, and while these case studies are high on agency specifics, they tend to be low on details regarding the actual success.[48] For example, a case study detailing Austin's adoption of a combination Compstat, community policing, crime prevention through environmental design, rapid response teams, and Intelligence-Led Policing, Austin was able to "identify the 20 percent of the population that causes 80 percent of the crime problem."[49] While identification is important, the question should be: did it result in actionable intelligence that had an impact? The case study notes this qualification, "The Austin Police Department project is still being refined," but then goes on to say "successes have been achieved in reducing violent crime as well as burglaries and other repetitive offenses."[50] These last three statements are rather vague. It then only adds that "for example, there was a 15 percent reduction in burglary of vehicles in 2010."[51] Yet, it does not say that the reduction in burglary of vehicles was directly attributed to Intelligence-Led Policing. All of these case studies are similar in that nearly all of them are vague in the exact nature of the Intelligence-Led Policing aspects (they are usually combined with something else) and the actual specifics of the success are questionable as to whether or not they can be tied directly back to ILP. Most of these appear to be police departments engaging in police operations and then calling any data analysis Intelligence-Led Policing.

So, has Intelligence-Led Policing been successful? There is no evidence to date that demonstrates it has been successful. There is, conversely, no evidence to suggest it has been a failure either. The only success is that those engaged in ILP (and Fusion Centers) think highly of it, but that may simply be because they like their job and would like to keep them. This all raises many questions about Intelligence-Led Policing and the many controversies surrounding its adoption by the local police, the topic to which this chapter now turns.

Is Intelligence-Led Policing a Proper Role for Local Police?

In order to assess the efficacy of police departments engaging in Intelligence-Led Policing, it would help to have some empirical studies that assess this very matter. Unfortunately, to date, there have been no empirical studies that have made any attempt at determining if ILP works or not.[52] Lacking this type of evidence, it is difficult to assess whether or not ILP is worth the police engaging in, especially at the risk of violating the civil liberties of American citizens. While we do not know if it is truly successful, we also do not know if it has been unsuccessful. However, history can sometimes be a good indicator as to whether or not a program such as this is successful or problematic.

History has shown us that the police collection of information, the creation of dossiers, and the use of intelligence, is fraught with problems. This type of intelligence gathering in the past, has led the police to violate people's civil rights, despite the fact that certain measures were put in place to protect against such things happening. The Church Committee revealed numerous civil rights violations against innocent American citizens all in the name of security. In fact, there were so many violations, this is what led to the wall being created between intelligence gathering and criminal investigations. It prevented the police from collecting and maintaining intelligence on American citizens unless there was first, reasonable suspicion to believe a crime had been committed, and only for the purposes of gathering enough evidence to support probable cause in order to secure a search warrant, and arrest warrant, or both.

A Senate Committee on Homeland Security and Governmental Affairs, receiving testimony regarding the police collection of intelligence, primarily related to the Fusion Centers, found that the collection of intelligence by the police had offered no success stories as it related to countering terrorism and that the information gathering in many instances had violated the civil rights of American citizens.[53] In other words, despite all of the safety measures taken to prevent the police from violating people's constitutional rights, the use of police to gather intelligence still managed to violate citizen's civil rights. This was very reminiscent of the Church Committee's findings in the 1970s.[54] Now the wall has fallen and the difference between intelligence gathering and criminal investigations have been blurred, but the people are told that there are better safeguards in place to prevent civil rights violations. It is absolute hubris to suggest that policymakers today are better at protecting civil rights violations than were their predecessors and that no violations will occur in the future. We are already seeing violations as evidenced by the information released by Edward Snowden from the National Security Agency and the Internal Revenue Service's targeting of conservatives and Tea Party members. And, if history is any guide, we should absolutely expect to see more in the future.

Perhaps the greatest controversy surrounding Intelligence-Led Policing pertains to the fall of that wall between intelligence gathering and criminal investigation. After 9/11, in the name of security, the wall simply fell. There was no discussion of the larger implications regarding this. The movement to Intelligence-Led Policing began out of a sense of need to provide security and because the capacity for intelligence gathering was readily available with the growth of databases and the ability to search through them. Just because the police can track people through security cameras, motor vehicle databases, credit reports, bank statements, credit card and debit card usage, license plate readers, library activity, google searches and a whole host of other data available, that does not necessarily mean that they should. The question that never appears to have been asked, discussed, or debated was should police be involved in intelligence gathering? Perhaps it is time we had this debate.

There is also somewhat of a controversy that underlies the police movement to Intelligence-Led Policing, and that is what are they actually doing? If the success stories touted by the Bureau of Justice Assistance are any indication, police departments engaging in Intelligence-Led Policing, may not really be engaging in intelligence, but rather good old fashion policing (criminal investigations). The reality may be that policing is really continuing with its traditional role of criminal investigations and the use of the term ILP may be wrongly applied. The ten scenarios highlighted as successful ILP, were really using such things as problem solving policing, hot spot policing, or crime analysis, not intelligence analysis. Yet, while there may be little concern now for ILP becoming problematic, there is always the issue of mission creep, where programs such as this begin simple and with a narrow focus, but over time find new uses and broaden its scope, at which time it becomes more problematic, more intrusive, and more likely to violate civil rights.

The violation of civil rights is, in the end, the true controversy. There is a delicate balance between protecting people against terrorists and criminals (security) and protecting them against an intrusive government (civil rights). Whenever we demand more security from government, it has to come at the expense of civil liberties.[55] The controversy then is: have we, in the name of national security, given local police too much power through Intelligence-Led Policing?

Conclusion

The movement of local police departments to adopt Intelligence-Led Policing in the post-9/11 era, has never been adequately addressed as whether or not this is a proper role and function of local police in America. In the name of homeland security, it developed as a means of making America more secure. The wall between intelligence and criminal investigation just simply fell. The requirement that was in place to protect citizens from the police that mandated the police had to have a reasonable suspicion that a person was involved in a crime before they could begin collecting information and intelligence on that individual simply fell. Now, police can collect and analyze vast amounts of data regarding average American citizens and sift through that data to develop police intelligence without necessarily having either reasonable suspicion or probable cause because they are engaging in Intelligence-Led Policing. Is this a proper role for the local police in our democratic society?

Endnotes

1. Lane, R. (1967). *Policing the city: Boston, 1822–1885.* New York, NY: Atheneum.

2. Lane, R. (1967). *Policing the city: Boston, 1822–1885.* New York, NY: Atheneum; Monkkonen, E.H. (1981). *Police in urban America, 1860–1920.* New York, NY: Cambridge University Press.

3. Walker, S. (1977). *Critical history of police reform: The emergence of professionalism.* Lanham, MD: Lexington Books.

4. Conway, J. N. (2010). *The big policeman: The rise and fall of America's first, most*

ruthless, and greatest detective. Guildford, CT: Lyons Press; Goodwin, D.K. (2013). *The bully pulpit: Theodore Roosevelt, William Howard Taft, and the golden age of journalism.* New York, NY: Simon & Schuster; Morris, E. (2001). *The rise of Theodore Roosevelt.* New York, NY: Modern Library.

5. Ackerman, K.D. (2011). *Young J. Edgar: Hoover and the red scare, 1919–1920.* Falls Church, CA: Viral History Press.

6. Gage, B. (2010). *The day Wall Street exploded: A story of America in its first age of terror.* New York, NY: Oxford University Press.

7. Ackerman, K.D. (2011). *Young J. Edgar: Hoover and the red scare, 1919–1920.* Falls Church, CA: Viral History Press; Hoyt, E.P. (1969). *The Palmer Raids, 1919–1920.* New York, NY: The Seabury Press.

8. Carter, D.L. (2005). Brief history of law enforcement intelligence: Past practice and recommendations for change. *Trends in Organized Crime, 8,* 51–62; Carter, D.L. (2004). *Law enforcement intelligence: A guide for state, local and tribal law enforcement agencies.* Washington, D.C.: U.S. Department of Justice Office of Community Oriented Policing Services.

9. Carter, D.L. (2005). Brief history of law enforcement intelligence: Past practice and recommendations for change. *Trends in Organized Crime, 8,* 51–62; Carter, D.L. (2004). *Law enforcement intelligence: A guide for state, local and tribal law enforcement agencies.* Washington, D.C.: U.S. Department of Justice Office of Community Oriented Policing Services.

10. Jenkins, B.M., Wildhorn, S., & Lavin, M.M. (1982). *Intelligence constraints of the 1970s and domestic terrorism.* Washington, D.C.: Rand Corporation (U.S. Department of Justice).

11. American Friends Service Committee. (1979). *The police threat to political liberty.* Philadelphia, PA: AFSC; Donner, F.J. (1991). *Protectors of privilege.* Berkeley, CA: The University of California Press.

12. Johnson, L. (1985). *A season of inquiry: The senate intelligence investigation.* Lexington, KY: The University Press of Kentucky.

13. U.S. Senate Select Committee to Study Governmental Operations with Respect to Intelligence Activities. (1976). *Intelligence activities and the rights of Americans—Book II.* Washington, D.C.: U.S. GPO.

14. U.S. Senate Select Committee to Study Governmental Operations with Respect to Intelligence Activities. (1976). *Intelligence activities and the rights of Americans—Book II.* Washington, D.C.: U.S. GPO.

15. Jenkins, B.M., Wildhorn, S., & Lavin, M.M. ( ). *Intelligence constraints of the 1970s and domestic terrorism.* Washington, D.C.: Rand Corporation (U.S. Department of Justice), p. 12.

16. McAdmas, J.G. III. (n.d.). Foreign intelligence surveillance act (fisa): An overview. *Federal Law Enforcement Training Center.* Retrieved from http://www.fletc.gov/training/programs/legal-division/downloads-articles-and-faqs/research-by-subject/miscellaneous/ForeignIntelligenceSurveillanceAct.pdf.

17. Carter, D.L. & Carter, J.G. (2009). Intelligence-led policing: Conceptual and functional considerations for public policy. *Criminal Justice Policy Review, 20,* 310–325.

18. Peterson, M. (2005). *Intelligence led policing: The new intelligence architecture.* Washington, D.C.: Bureau of Justice Assistance.

19. Heaton, E. (2000). The prospects for intelligence-led policing: Some historical and quantitative considerations. *Policing and Society: An International Journal of Research and Policy, 9,* 337–355; Ratcliffe, J.H. (2003). Intelligence-led policing. *Trends & Issues in Crime and Criminal Justice,* April, 1–6.

20. Her Majesty's Inspectorate Constabulary (HMIC). (1997). *Policing with Intelligence.* London, England: Her Majesty's Inspectorate Constabulary.

21. Ratcliffe, J.H. (2003). Intelligence-led policing. *Trends & Issues in Crime and Criminal Justice*, April, 1–6.

22. Riebling, M. (1994). *Wedge—The secret war between the FBI and CIA*. New York, NY: Alfred A. Knopf.

23. Henry, V. E. (2002). *The compstat paradigm: Management accountability in policing, business and private sector*. Flushing, NY: Looseleaf Law Publications, Inc.; Silverman, E. B. (1999). *NYPD battles crime: Innovative strategies in policing*. Boston, MA: Northeastern.

24. Bratton, W. with Knobler, P. (1998). *Turnaround: How America's top cop reversed the crime epidemic*. New York, NY: Random House.

25. Carter, D.L. & Carter, J.G. (2009). Intelligence-led policing: Conceptual and functional considerations for public policy. *Criminal Justice Policy Review, 20,* 310–325.

26. Chermak, S., Carter, J., Carter, D., McGarrell, E.F., & Drew, J. (2013). Law enforcement's information sharing infrastructure: A national assessment. *Police Quarterly, 16,* 211–244.

27. Carter, D.L. (2004). *Law enforcement intelligence: A guide of state, local, and tribal law enforcement agencies*. Washington, D.C.: U.S. Department of Justice Office of Community Oriented Policing Services; Peterson, M. (2005). *Intelligence led policing: The new intelligence architecture*. Washington, D.C.: Bureau of Justice Assistance.

28. For the policing circles, see for instance: Guidetti, R. & Martinelli, T.J. (2009). Intelligence led policing—A strategic framework. *The Police Chief*. Retrieved from http://www.policechiefmagazine.org/magazine/index.cfm?fuseaction=display&article_id=1918&issue_id=102009; Martinelli, T., & Carter, D.L. (2013). Ethical defensibility: Using the intelligence-led policing template to avoid the appearance of unconstitutional policing. *The Police Chief, 80,* 52–56; For the academic, see for instance: Jackson, A.L. & Brown, M. (2007). Ensuring efficiency, interagency cooperation, and protection of civil liberties: Shifting from a traditional model of policing to an intelligence-led policing (ilp) paradigm. *Criminal Justice Studies, 20,* 111–129; Carter, J. G. & Phillips, S.W. (2013). Intelligence-led policing and forces of organisational change in the USA. *Policing and Society*. Retrieved from http://www.tandfonline.com/doi/full/10.1080/10439463.2013.865738#tabModule; McGarrell, E.F., Freilich, J.D., & Chermak, S. (2007). Intelligence led policing as a framework for responding to terrorism. *Journal of Contemporary Criminal Justice, 23,* 142–158.

29. See for instance: Baker, T. (2009). *Intelligence-led policing: Leadership, strategies and tactics*. New York, NY: Looseleaf; Ratcliffe, J.H. (2008). *Intelligence led policing*. Cullompton, England: Willan Publishing.

30. Carter, D.L. (2004). *Law enforcement intelligence: A guide of state, local, and tribal law enforcement agencies*. Washington, D.C.: U.S. Department of Justice Office of Community Oriented Policing Services.

31. Carter, D.L. & Carter, J.G. (2009). Intelligence led policing: Conceptual considerations for public policy. *Criminal Justice Policy Review, 20,* 310–325, at p. 317.

32. Peterson, M. (2005). *Intelligence led policing: The new intelligence architecture*. Washington, D.C.: Bureau of Justice Assistance, p. 3.

33. Carter, D.L. (2004). *Law enforcement intelligence: A guide of state, local, and tribal law enforcement agencies*. Washington, D.C.: U.S. Department of Justice Office of Community Oriented Policing Services; p. 9; Global Intelligence Working Group. (2004). *Criminal intelligence for the chief executive*. Washington, D.C.: Office of Justice Programs, p. 5.

34. Carter, D.L. (2004). *Law enforcement intelligence: A guide of state, local, and tribal

law enforcement agencies. Washington, D.C.: U.S. Department of Justice Office of Community Oriented Policing Services; p. 11; Global Intelligence Working Group. (2004). *Criminal intelligence for the chief executive.* Washington, D.C.: Office of Justice Programs, p. 6.

35. See for instance Criminal Justice Schools. (2014). 20 crimes caught on Google street view. Retrieved from http://www.criminaljusticeschools.com/blog/20-crimes-caught-on-google-street-view/.

36. Peterson, M. (2005). *Intelligence led policing: The new intelligence architecture.* Washington, D.C.: Bureau of Justice Assistance, p. 3.

37. Cope, N. (2004). 'Intelligence led policing or policing led intelligence?' Integrating volume crime analysis into policing. *British Journal of Criminology, 44,* 188–203; Smith, A. (ed). (1997). *Intelligence led policing.* Richmond, VA: International Association of Law Enforcement Intelligence Analysts, Inc.

38. Peterson, M. (2005). *Intelligence led policing: The new intelligence architecture.* Washington, D.C.: Bureau of Justice Assistance, p. 3.

39. Peterson, M. (2005). *Intelligence led policing: The new intelligence architecture.* Washington, D.C.: Bureau of Justice Assistance, p. 3.

40. Carter, D.L. (2004). *Law enforcement intelligence: A guide of state, local, and tribal law enforcement agencies.* Washington, D.C.: U.S. Department of Justice Office of Community Oriented Policing Services; p. 13.

41. Deflem, M. (2010). *The policing of terrorism: Organizational and global perspectives.* New York, NY: Routledge.

42. Reaves, B.A. (2010). *Local police departments, 2007.* Washington, D.C.: Bureau of Justice Statistics, p. 7.

43. Reaves, B.A. (2010). *Local police departments, 2007.* Washington, D.C.: Bureau of Justice Statistics, p. 22.

44. Ratcliffe, J. H. & Guidetti, R. (2008). State police investigative structure and the adoption of intelligence-led policing. *Policing: An International Journal of Police Strategies & Management, 31,* 109–128; Schaible, L.M. & Sheffield, J. (2012). Intelligence-led policing and change in state law enforcement agencies. *Policing: An International Journal of Police Strategies & Management, 35,* 761–784.

45. Chermak, S., Carter, J., Carter, D., McGarrell, E.F., & Drew, J. (2013). Law enforcement's information sharing infrastructure: A national assessment. *Police Quarterly, 16,* 211–244.

46. Global Justice Information Sharing Initiative. (2009). *Navigating your agency's path to intelligence-led policing.* Washington, D.C.: Bureau of Justice Assistance.

47. Braga, A. A. & Weisburd, D.L. (2010). *Policing problem places: Crime hot spots and effective prevention.* New York, NY: Oxford University Press.

48. Bureau of Justice Assistance. (2008). *Reducing crime through intelligence-led policing.* Washington, D.C.: Bureau of Justice Assistance.

49. Bureau of Justice Assistance. (2008). *Reducing crime through intelligence-led policing.* Washington, D.C.: Bureau of Justice Assistance, p. 9.

50. Bureau of Justice Assistance. (2008). *Reducing crime through intelligence-led policing.* Washington, D.C.: Bureau of Justice Assistance, p. 9.

51. Bureau of Justice Assistance. (2008). *Reducing crime through intelligence-led policing.* Washington, D.C.: Bureau of Justice Assistance, p. 9.

52. Chermak, S., Carter, J., Carter, D., McGarrell, E.F., & Drew, J. (2013). Law enforcement's information sharing infrastructure: A national assessment. *Police Quarterly, 16,*

211–244; Taylor, R.W. & Russell, A.L. (2012). The failure of police "fusion" centers and the concept of a national intelligence sharing plan. *Police Practice and Research, 13,* 184–200.

53. U.S. Senate. (2012). *Federal support for and involvement in state and local fusion centers.* Washington, D.C.: Permanent Subcommittee on Investigations.

54. U.S. Senate Select Committee to Study Governmental Operations with Respect to Intelligence Activities. (1976). *Intelligence activities and the rights of Americans—Book II.* Washington, D.C.: U.S. GPO.

55. Price, M. (2013). *National security and local police.* New York, NY: Brennan Center for Justice.

Chapter 6

Is the Threat of Terrorism on the Rise?

Introduction

On Christmas Day, 2009, a passenger by the name of Umar Farouk Abdul-mutallab boarded a plane in Amsterdam headed for Detroit, Michigan. He was on a suicide mission for al-Qaeda and managed to smuggle a homemade bomb, sewn into his underwear, past airport security at two stops. It was on his second flight that he attempted to detonate the bomb.

Just like Richard Reid during his shoe bombing plot in 2001, Abdulmutal-lab was positioned perfectly—next to a window and over the fuel tank. Passengers on board the flight reported hearing a loud pop, like a firecracker, and saw smoke rising from Abdulmutallab's seat. According to reports, the 22-year-old Nigerian's underwear contained 80 grams of Pentaerytritol tetranitrate (PETN), which was more than enough to blow a hole in the airliner. He attempted to detonate the bomb with acid in a syringe. Instead, the acid melted the syringe and caused a fire.[1]

Hours later, with Flight 253 over the North Atlantic, an analyst at Customs and Border Protection at its National Targeting Center would piece together that Abdulmutallab was a risk and arranged for him to be met on arrival in Detroit. In 2012, he was jailed for life without parole.

The foiled attempt of the underwear bomber on Christmas Day 2009 is an example of the significant progress the Department of Homeland Security (DHS) and its many partners have made in fulfilling specific recommendations by the 9/11 Commission to make our nation stronger, safer, and more resilient.[2] Despite progress made through our counterterrorism efforts, is the threat of terrorism in the US on the rise? Are we smarter about the kinds of threats we face? How does the "See Something, Say Something™" campaign help in the fight against terrorism? This chapter examines terrorism hazards and the new threat environment in the US.

The Terrorist Threat: An Overview

The word "terrorism" is difficult to define. Not unlike the concept of homeland security, defining terrorism continues to be a much debated topic. A 2011 report from the Council of Foreign Relations finds several definitions of terrorism that exist within the federal government.[3] While some incidents are easily identified as terror—such as the 9/11 attacks—it becomes harder to distinguish with events such as the 2009 Fort Hood shooting. According to the report, lone-wolf violence is on the rise, but "it is difficult to determine whether such an act of violence falls under the legal definition of 'domestic terrorism.'"[4] Terrorism is defined in the US Code as "international terrorism" and "domestic terrorism" for purposes of Chapter 113B of the Code, entitled "Terrorism" (see Table 6.1).

Some scholars have argued that restricting the definition of terrorism lessens the larger meaning. This is partially due to the fact that terrorism has not remained static but rather has evolved over the years.[5]

Table 6.1. Definitions of Terrorism in the US Code

"**International Terrorism**" means activities with the following three characteristics:

- Involve violent acts or acts dangerous to human life that violate federal or state law;
- Appear to be intended (i) to intimidate or coerce a civilian population; (ii) to influence the policy of a government by intimidation or coercion; or (iii) to affect the conduct of a government by mass destruction, assassination, or kidnapping; and,
- Occur primarily outside the territorial jurisdiction of the US, or transcend national boundaries in terms of the means by which they are accomplished, the persons they appear intended to intimidate or coerce, or the locale in which their perpetrators operate or seek asylum.

"**Domestic Terrorism**" means activities with the following three characteristics:

- Involve acts dangerous to human life that violate federal or state law;
- Appear intended (i) to intimidate or coerce a civilian population; (ii) to influence the policy of a government by intimidation or coercion; or (iii) to affect the conduct of a government by mass destruction, assassination, or kidnapping; and,
- Occur primarily within the territorial jurisdiction of the US.

18 U.S.C. § 2332b defines the term "federal crime of terrorism" as an offense that:

- Is calculated to influence or affect the conduct of government by intimidation or coercion, or to retaliate against government conduct; and
- Is a violation of one of several listed statutes, including § 930(c) (relating to killing or attempted killing during an attack on a federal facility with a dangerous weapon); and § 1114 (relating to killing or attempted killing of officers and employees of the US).

Source: Federal Bureau of Investigation—Terrorism Definition http://www.fbi.gov/about-us/investigate/terrorism/terrorism-definition.

Whether it is called "violent extremism" or "domestic terrorism," the idea of terrorism is not a new form of violence. Recorded historical evidence supports terrorism's origins at about 2,000 years with the emergence of violent Jewish fanatical groups such as the Sicari; however, the term "terrorism" itself was not coined until 1793–1794, during the French Revolution.[6] During this time newly defined notions of nationalism and citizenship also saw the emergence of a new predominately secular terrorism. Political ideologies such as Marxism also created a fertile sense of unrest at the existing order, with terrorism offering a means for change.[7] Before the twentieth century, terrorism made its way to American soil. Not only were anarchists active in America throughout the 1880s, but the first terrorist organization was formed in 1867—the white supremacist organization called the Ku Klux Klan (KKK).

A reoccurring theme in the homeland security literature is that America was "sleeping" before 9/11. For instance, August 7, 1998, does not strike the average American as a day of infamy but in counterterrorism circles it is known as the day that al-Qaeda attacked not one but two American embassies in East Africa.[8] Two years later, the US Navy destroyer the USS *Cole* sustained a suicide bomb attack. The terrorist organization al-Qaeda claimed responsibility for the attack that took the lives of seventeen Navy sailors and injured thirty-nine more.[9] While these events made headlines, terrorism at that time was usually considered a backwater issue that would burst onto the scene every few years and then fade while other national security issues took priority.[10]

Earlier events on American soil were also troubling, yet not defining by 9/11 standards. The following list chronicles some of these events.

1978–1995: The Unabomber

Between the years of 1978 and 1995, the Unabomber (Ted Kaczynski) sent sixteen bombs through the mail to targets including universities and airlines. A Harvard graduate, Kaczynski became a recluse and was ideologically opposed to technological progress. His reign of terror began on May 28, 1978, when a bomb exploded at the University of Illinois at Chicago. One person was injured. Over the next seventeen years Ted Kaczynski would target universities and airlines thus earning him the nickname "Unabomber"—code name for UNiversity and Airline BOMbing targets.[11] Kaczynski was not affiliated with any organized terror group and hunting him down proved to be the FBI's longest-running domestic terrorism investigation. A tip from his brother aided in his capture in April 1996. By then he had killed three and injured more than twenty-three individuals. He pled guilty in January of 1998 and was sentenced to life in prison.

1993: The First World Trade Center Bombing

On February 23, 1993, a massive explosion occurred in the basement parking lot of the World Trade Center in New York City. The act was in retaliation against the US' support of Israel and intervention in the Middle East. Two men, one identified as Jordanian Eyad Ismoil and the other Kuwaiti Ramzi Yousef, drove a truck loaded with 1,300-pound nitrate-hydrogen gas stuffed with cyanide into the parking garage below Tower One. Yousef lit a 20-foot fuse, and the two fled before the blast unleashed.[12] The intention was to bring down the building but instead it killed six adults, one unborn child and injured 1,042.[13] The blast caused extensive damage to seven of the building's floors and created a large crater 130 feet in width and 150 feet in length.[14] Along with Ismoil and Ramzi, five other men were convicted of the attack. One of the plotters behind the attack was Yousef Ramzi's uncle—Khalid Sheikh Mohammed—who later claimed to be the mastermind of the 9/11 attacks which ultimately brought the Twin Towers down. Mohammed gave Yousef advice, tips, and cash in preparation for the 1993 bombing.[15] This incident resulted in increased efforts to address the terrorist threat and is often referred to as the first contemporary terrorist attack on US soil.

1995: Oklahoma City Bombing

One of the most notable examples of domestic terrorism occurred on April 19, 1995, in Oklahoma City when Timothy McVeigh and Terry Nichols parked a Ryder truck loaded with a powerful bomb in front of the Alfred P. Murrah Federal Building. The bomb, made up of agricultural fertilizer, diesel fuel, and other chemicals, exploded at 9:02 a.m., killing 168 people, including nineteen children attending a daycare program.[16] McVeigh wanted revenge over the way the government handled the Branch Davidian standoff in Waco, Texas, exactly two years earlier and thought the destruction of one federal building could spark a revolution.[17] On August 19, 1995, he was indicted on eleven federal counts, including conspiracy to use a weapon of mass destruction. He was convicted and later put to death by lethal injection in 2001. The Oklahoma City bombing was the worst act of homegrown terrorism in our nation's history.[18]

1996: Centennial Olympic Park Bombing

Eric Robert Rudolph was 29 years old when he planted pipe bombs and shrapnel underneath benches in the main square of the Olympic grounds during the 1996 Summer Olympics in Atlanta, Georgia. The blast killed two spectators and wounded another 111. Rudolph was also responsible for a series of anti-abortion and anti-gay bombings around the US between 1996 and 1998. His motivation for the Centennial Olympic Park bombing was to "anger and embarrass the government in the eyes of the world for its abominable sanctioning of abortion on demand."[19] Rudolph became a fugitive and was on the FBI's Ten Most Wanted list for several years. He was captured unexpectedly in May 2003, when a patrol officer found him digging for food in a dumpster. In 2005, he accepted a plea deal and was sentenced to five consecutive life sentences for all of the attacks. He is currently serving his time in the US Penitentiary Administrative Maximum Facility (ADX) located near Florence, Colorado. Dubbed the "Alcatraz of the Rockies," ADX Florence is the same supermax facility where other domestic and international terrorists have been held.[20]

2001: 9/11 Attacks on the World Trade Center, the Pentagon, and Shanksville, Pa.

On September 11, 2001, terrorists hijacked four planes and crashed them into the twin towers of the World Trade Center in New York City, the Pentagon in Washington, D.C., and a field in Shanksville, Pennsylvania. These actions resulted in the collapse of the Twin Towers, the destruction of a section of the Pentagon, and the crash of a domestic airliner that resulted in 2,974 deaths.[21] It was the deadliest terrorist attack in US history. The terrorist group al-Qaeda took responsibility for the attacks, led by mastermind Osama bin Laden.

In the immediate aftermath, the Department of Homeland Security (DHS) was created and a flurry of legislation and presidential directives were enacted. The most controversial was the USA PATRIOT Act of 2001 (Public Law 107–56) which aimed "to deter and punish terrorist acts in the US and around the world, to enhance law enforcement investigatory tools, and for other purposes."[22] In addition, the 9/11 Commission was established by President Bush to study the events leading up to the September 11 attacks and the actions that were taken immediately following the attack. A major finding of the 9/11 Commission's report was that there were government failures in policy, capabilities, and management.[23] The intelligence community, the CIA, and the FBI were highly criticized and Congress was admonished for its failure to financially support counterterrorism programs. The final report was issued on July 22, 2004, with a specific set of recommendations in the following categories:

- Attack terrorists and their organizations;
- Prevent the continued growth of Islamist terrorism;
- Protect against and prepare for terrorist attacks;
- Establish a National Counterterrorism Center;
- Appoint a National Intelligence Director, and
- Encourage the sharing of information among government agencies and with state and local officials.[24]

The events of September 11, 2001, forever changed the way the nation and the world views security. With implementation of the 9/11 Commission recommendations, major steps have been taken to make certain that another terrorist attack on US soil does not take place. Despite these efforts, the fact remains that there have been roughly 60 Islamist-inspired terrorist plots against the homeland since 9/11.[25] According to a 2013 Heritage Foundation study, about fifty-three of these plots were thwarted long before the public was even in danger, due in large part to the efforts of US law enforcement and the intelligence community.[26] While there has not been an attack on the scale of 9/11, there have been four significant attacks on America in the past thirteen years:

1. The intentional driving of an SUV into a crowd of students at the University of North Carolina-Chapel Hill in 2006;
2. The shooting at an army-recruitment office in Little Rock, Arkansas, in 2009;
3. The shooting by US Army Major Nidal Hasan at Fort Hood, also in 2009; and,
4. The Boston Marathon bombings in 2013.[27]

It is important to note that forty-nine of the sixty plots could be considered homegrown terrorism, meaning that one or more of the actors were American citizens, legal permanent residents, or visitors radicalized mostly in the US.[28] The targets in each of the sixty plots fell into three categories: military facilities, targets in New York City, or mass gatherings. While four plots were successful, and three foiled merely by luck or the swift action of private citizens, the rest were thwarted in their early stages by US, and occasionally international, law enforcement.[29] The following are some of the foiled terrorist plots that have occurred since 9/11:

2001: The Shoe Bomber

Richard Reid, a British citizen with ties to al-Qaeda, attempted to blow up a plane with hidden explosives implanted in his shoes. During the flight from Paris to Miami, Reid tried to light a fuse to ignite the explosives and was subdued by passengers and flight attendants. The plane made an emergency landing at Boston's Logan International Airport where Reid was taken into custody.[30]

2003: Plot to Collapse the Brooklyn Bridge

Iyman Faris, a naturalized US citizen originally from Kashmir who lived in Columbus, Ohio, was arrested for conspiring to use blowtorches to collapse the Brooklyn Bridge. The plot was devised after meetings with al-Qaeda leadership, including Khalid Sheihk Mohammed. The New York City Police Department learned of the plot and increased police surveillance around the bridge. Faris and his superiors eventually called off the attack.[31]

2006: Plot to Blow up the Sears Tower in Chicago

Narseal Batiste and six others plotted to blow up the Sears Tower in Chicago, FBI offices, and other government buildings around the country. Batiste, a former Chicago deliveryman, and his accomplices were arrested in June 2006 after an FBI informant uncovered their scheme. At trial, Batiste testified that he invented the fake plot in order to con money out of a man who claimed to be an operative of al-Qaeda.[32] In November, 2009, five of the seven men were sentenced to prison terms ranging from six to 13.5 years. Batiste received the longest sentence.[33]

2009: Synagogue Terror Plot

In May 2009, four men were arrested by the New York City Police Department for plotting to blow up New York-area Jewish centers and shoot down planes at a nearby Air National Guard Base. James Cromitie, David Williams, Onta Williams, and Laguerre Payen attempted to gain access to Stinger missiles and were caught in the act of placing bombs in the buildings and in a car. Ultimately the bombs were duds because undercover agents sold the defendants fake explosives as part of an ongoing sting operation. All four were convicted.[34]

2012: AQAP Bomb Plot

The Yemen-based al-Qaeda in the Arabian Peninsula (AQAP) planned to blow up a US-bound airliner on the first anniversary of Osama bin Laden's death in May 2012. The would-be bomb was an upgraded version of the explosive used in the foiled 2009 Christmas Day underwear bomb attempt. According to officials, the improvements made to the bomb included the use of high-grade military explosives, the potential inability to be detected by full-body scanners at airports, and the capability of destroying the aircraft.[35] The plot was prevented by a CIA double agent posing as a member of the organization with direct access to the leadership. This infiltration of the AQAP network allowed the US to launch a successful drone strike, which killed Fahd al-Quso, who was wanted for the bombing of the USS *Cole* in Yemen in 2000.[36]

Weakening of Al-Qaeda Central?

Since 9/11, the killing of dozens of high-level al-Qaeda militants has dealt a serious blow to al-Qaeda's core leadership. The most significant among them was the capture and subsequent killing of Osama bin Laden on May 2, 2011. The US intelligence community, led by the CIA, spent almost ten years hunting down the al-Qaeda leader. While some would argue that this has not minimized the terror threat, others agree that it was significant enough to defeat al-Qaeda central and diminish their ability to carry out an attack in the US.[37] Concerns that bin Laden's death would provoke a rash of attacks in the West have not happened. Since President Obama has taken office, roughly 33 key al-Qaeda leaders have been killed by drone strikes in Pakistan and the leaders have been forced to focus on survival.[38] Ayman al-Zawahiri, an eye surgeon who helped found the Egyptian militant group Islamic Jihad, was named the new leader of al-Qaeda a few weeks after bin Laden's death. Since that time, Zawahiri has tried to assert his control over al-Qaeda affiliated groups, even intervening in a dispute between Jabhat al-Nusra and al-Qaeda in Iraq (AQI), which has since organized into the terrorist group ISIS—the Islamic State of Iraq and Syria. The chaotic conditions in the Middle East continue to be a challenge for al-Qaeda and Zawahiri. But despite repeated claims that al-Qaeda Central is weakened and "on the run," the global war on jihadi terrorism continues to flourish.[39]

A New Threat Environment

Today, the US faces a more diverse and complex threat than it did on September 11, 2001. An evolving threat from al-Qaeda, the birth of the global jihadist movement, the rise of affiliates, and an increasing threat from homegrown violent extremists all present increasingly difficult challenges to securing the homeland. Authorities in the US can no longer prioritize al-Qaeda threats over those emanating from affiliate groups; they now must cover them all.[40]

International Threats

The 2013 report, *Jihadist Terrorism: A Threat Assessment* concluded that the US faces a different terrorist threat than it did on September 11, 2001. The borders between domestic and international terrorism have blurred, and the US' adversaries are not only organizations, but also individuals.[41]

As discussed above, the al-Qaeda terror network has become so decentralized that its affiliates now pose a greater direct threat to the US. Al-Qaeda's expanding global network continues to be a major concern for us here at home. According to Seth Jones, associate director of the RAND Corporation's International Security and Defense Policy Center, the number of jihadists groups and fighters have increased especially in Tunisia, Algeria, Mali, Libya, Egypt, Lebanon, and "especially in Syria, where jihadists have been flocking to engage in jihad, gain combat experience, and to train for future battles elsewhere around the globe.[42] Recently, the civil war in Syria has become a magnet for al-Qaeda and other global Islamist jihadi ideologues which are using the battlefield as a recruitment ground to train future terrorists. In all likelihood, the plan is to use these recruits to set up terrorist cells throughout the world.[43]

The rise of the Islamic State of Iraq and Syria (ISIS)—a brutal al-Qaeda faction grown out of the ongoing civil war in Syria—quickly has become the new face of terror. ISIS is now one of the largest, richest terrorist organizations in history. With an apocalyptic, end of day vision, ISIS controls territory in ways that al-Qaeda never did. Al-Qaeda was "hosted" by the Taliban in Afghanistan and did not operate with complete freedom. ISIS, on the other hand, has taken control of hundreds of square miles in two countries (Iraq and Syria) and has a presence all the way from Syria's Mediterranean coast to the south of Baghdad—similar in size to the state of Indiana.[44] The aim of ISIS is to create an Islamic State across Sunni areas of Iraq and in Syria. The ranks of ISIS are filled with thousands of radicals holding Western passports, including British citizens and some Americans.

On August 28, 2014, Prime Minister David Cameron raised the threat level in the UK to "severe"—the second highest level. His decision was based on developments in the Middle East, including the brutal beheading of American Journalist James Foley and concerns that terror plots were likely to involve fighters who travelled from the UK and Europe to join the ISIS cause.[45] It has been estimated that some 12,000 foreign fighters have gone to Syria to fight with ISIS—approximately 100 Americans and roughly 1,000 or so from Europe and the UK. Some of the most extreme terrorist militants are carrying British passports. Supported by tribes in Eastern Syria and the Sunni middle class, ISIS has proven to be highly capable and extremely vicious. Secretary of Homeland Security Jeh Johnson warned that Syria has become "a matter of homeland security" because extremists there "are actively trying to recruit Westerners, indoctrinate them, and see them return to their home countries with an extremist mission."[46] Returning foreign fighters are a ticking time bomb. They require nothing more than a plane ticket to travel to US cities.[47]

Another international concern is the June 2014 release of the "Taliban Five." In a prisoner exchange for Taliban-held American solider Bowe Bergdahl, five top Taliban detainees were released from the Guantanamo Bay Detention Center. Considered to be the most extreme and dangerous, they include: Khair Ull Said Wali Khairkhwa (a direct associate of Bin Laden), Mullah Mohammad Fazl (partially responsible for the massacre of thousands of Afghan Shiites during the Taliban's rule), Abdul Haq Wasiq (former deputy chief of the Taliban government's intelligence service), Mohammed Nabi Omari (former chief of communications in the Taliban government), and Mullah Norullah Noori (a senior Taliban military commander).[48] These individuals were released to the custody of Qatar on the condition they be held under house arrest for one year. Experts in the intelligence community are convinced that these men will return to the religiously mandated jihad against America and will be welcomed back—as heroes.[49] Some experts argue that their roles will not be that significant should they return to the jihad given their time away and the changes to the organization. However, the fact still remains that all five are extremely valuable to the movement and will be an asset to al-Qaeda/Taliban anti-American efforts. [50]

Homegrown Threats

The FBI defines Homegrown Violent Extermism as a person of any citizenship who has mostly lived in the US and who engages in terrorist activity to advance an ideology.[51] Recent violence in the US such as the Boston Marathon Bombings and the deadly shooting at Fort Hood have raised the radar of the

FBI and have made HVE a top priority. This presents a broader challenge of preventing terrorist attacks that originate with citizen and residents of the US rather than foreign adversaries. The shift to plotting by individual and pairs who lack ties to foreign groups poses a distinct type of threat—they are more difficult to detect.[52] The Congressional Research Service (CRS) estimates that there have been sixty-three homegrown violent jihadist plots or attacks in the US since September 11, 2001.[53] Between May 2009 and December 2012, arrests were made for forty-two "homegrown," jihadist-inspired terrorist plots by American citizens or legal permanent residents of the US. While most of the 2009—2012 homegrown plots likely reflect a trend in jihadist terrorist activity away from schemes directed by core members of significant terrorist groups like al-Qaeda, recent events suggest that ideologies supporting violent jihad continues to influence some Americans.[54]

Many regard the term "violent extremism" the same as "violent jihadist" and "jihadist terrorism."[55] In this sense it is believed that when someone moves from believing in jihad to illegally pursuing it via violent methods—he or she becomes a terrorist.[56] This move from belief to violence is individualized, thus no clear cut path has been identified. However, the following have been cited as playing key roles in the radicalization process: (1) intermediaries, charismatic individuals who often help persuade previously law-abiding citizens to radicalize or even become violent jihadists; and (2) social networks, which support and reinforce the decisions individuals make as they embrace violent jihad.

Categorizing types of homegrown jihadist plots is no easy task. At present, there is no workable general profile of a domestic violent jihadist. An analysis by the Congressional Research Service identified four broad themes which have emerged in the quest for this profile: endgames, suicide or martyrdom, lone wolves, and divergent capabilities (see Table 6.2).

Of the four themes, lone wolf terrorism is especially disturbing. Lone wolf terrorism involves violent acts by self-radicalized individuals designed to promote a cause or belief.[57] Lone wolves have demonstrated that they can be as dangerous as terrorist groups and are increasingly found among right-wing reactionaries and religiously radicalized jihadists.[58] Difficult to track and almost impossible to prevent, this emerging type of terrorism is becoming a top priority for the FBI. These attacks have become more common as individuals have gained the ability to strike without the training and funding of terrorist groups. All these individuals need is access to the internet where they can find everything from how to make a bomb to maps and diagrams of potential targets.[59] The Unabomber, Oklahoma City bomber, Fort Hood shooter, and Oslo assailants are examples of this new form of terrorist.[60]

Table 6.2. Four Broad Themes of Homegrown Jihadist Plots since 9/11

Endgames	Plots included a variety of endgames such as individuals who were exclusively interested in becoming foreign fighters in conflict zones involving jihad abroad; the intent to use explosives or incendiary devices; and other schemes which from the start only intended to fund or materially support the activities of other jihadists.
Suicide or Martyrdom	Only twelve plots included individuals who were interested in killing themselves and engaging in violent jihad.
Lone Wolves	All four successful homegrown attacks since 9/11 were conducted by lone wolves.
Divergent Capabilities	The operational capabilities of participants in the homegrown plots since 9/11 varied. Some used bomb-making skills—others were less experienced.

Source: Bjelopera, J.P. (2013). *American Jihadist Terrorism: Combating a Combating a Complex Threat*. (CRS-R41416). Washington DC: Library of Congress. Retrieved from http://fas.org/sgp/crs/terror/R41416.pdf.

While lone wolf terrorists are self-radicalized, political or religious motivation may not always be the reason for their actions. Rather, they might be motivated by personal agendas in response to some real or perceived organizational or institutional event. Single-issue protest groups such as the Animal Liberation Front (ALF) or anti-abortion activists have also produced a number of lone wolf terrorist attacks.[61] Since a terrorist acting alone is highly unlikely to tell others what he or she is planning, the authorities have a difficult time determining who is actually prepared to commit a terrorist attack to advance a cause.[62] Acting outside of a terrorist group, a lone wolf may choose to kill a single person or a small group of targets but may also be responsible for a major terrorist incident.[63] For example, John Allen Muhammad, the Washington, D.C., sniper, created fear and panic while going on a shooting spree in October of 2002. In a span of three weeks, the sniper terrorized more than five million people in the D.C. metropolitan area—shooting thirteen people and killing ten.

Finally, an aspect of the homegrown extremist threat that is especially troubling is the continued ability of jihadist groups to organize networks in the US that direct funds and personnel abroad.[64] Between 2011 and 2013, forty-four individuals were indicted on terrorism related offenses. Twenty-four of those individuals where charged not because they were involved in plots against the

US, but because they provided "material support" to terrorist groups overseas or attempted to fight abroad with these groups.[65]

"If You See Something, Say Something™"

"If You See Something, Say Something™," the homeland security equivalent to Nike's "Just Do It" advertisement, has become a global catchphrase.[66] First introduced in 2002 for the Metropolitan Transit Authority, the slogan was aimed at making travelers more aware of potential terrorist threats. The line was created by Allen Kay, chairman for a Manhattan ad agency, Korey Kay & Partners. Kay wanted to prevent another disaster and to make a positive change in the aftermath of the 9/11 attacks. By January 2003, the slogan was plastered across subways and buses as part of MTA's security-awareness campaign. MTA obtained a trademark for the slogan in 2007, and by 2008 the phrase went viral. It reverberated beyond New York, being seen everywhere from mass transit stations, to coffee houses, and the Super Bowl. Since its introduction in 2002, the tagline has been licensed by the MTA to 54 domestic and international transportation providers and government agencies to use in their own anti-terrorism campaigns.

In July 2010, the MTA licensed their slogan to the Department of Homeland Security (DHS) who then launched a national "If You See Something, Say Something™" campaign of their own. DHS has called their campaign a "simple and effective program to raise public awareness of indicators of terrorism and terrorism-related crime, and to emphasize the importance of reporting suspicious activity to the proper state and local law enforcement authorities.[67] DHS supports the concept that homeland security begins with hometown security and that an alert public plays a crucial role in keeping our nation safe."[68] Reporting suspicious activity includes: unattended packages in a public place, someone trying to break into a restricted area, or other types of suspicious behavior.

Is the Threat of Terrorism on the Rise?

The best way to protect the US from terrorism is to ensure a strong, capable domestic counterterrorism enterprise—and to understand the continuing nature of the terror threat.[69] We have made progress since the events of September 11, 2001, but are we smarter about the kinds of threats we now face? Is the threat of terrorism on the rise and what are we doing as a nation to address it? How does the "See Something, Say Something™" campaign help in the fight against terrorism?

Events in the Middle East have heightened concerns of terrorist threats both abroad and in the US. The civil war in Syria and the fighting in Iraq have become breeding grounds for a newer and deadlier terrorist group ISIS—a group "beyond anything we have seen" according to Defense Secretary Chuck Hagel.[70] While we are well-equipped with counterterrorism resources, the threat has increased. There is no longer a clear-cut line between domestic and international terrorism. Radicalized American citizens are fully capable of entering the US and committing atrocities. For example, an American jihadi from Florida was able to travel to Syria and back to the US undetected before his final suicide mission in May 2014.[71] In 2011, we were warned by the Russian government about problems with Boston Marathon bomber Tamerlan Tsarnaev—two years before he and his younger brother set off bombs at the finish line.[72] While the American jihadi from Florida chose to complete his suicide mission in Syria, the Tsarnaev brothers completed their attack on American soil. In both instances, these individuals fell through the cracks. The FBI cannot police everyone, and it is quite possible that if an individual stays off of social networking, he or she can probably fly under the radar and get away with an attack.

On the other hand, we have made many strides in security since the attacks of September 11, 2001. There has not been a significant attack by foreign terrorists since 9/11. Much of this is a result of our counterterrorism efforts. For example, the Department of Justice has significantly improved its ability to identify, penetrate, and dismantle terrorist plots as a result of a series of structural reforms, the development of new intelligence and law enforcement tools, and a new mindset that encourages information sharing.[73] Intelligence-sharing was a key weakness highlighted by the 9/11 Commission in its review of government operations prior to the 2001 terrorist attacks.[74] The following highlights key actions taken by the DOJ since 9/11 to enhance the nation's counter-terror efforts:

- **Protecting America through Investigation and Criminal Prosecution**— Federal prosecutors have successfully used the criminal justice system to identify, prosecute, and incarcerate terrorists and would-be terrorists. Some of the more significant international terrorism prosecutions in recent years are the New York Subway plotters, the Times Square bombers, and members of the al-Shabaab terror recruitment organization from the Minneapolis area.[75] Furthermore, an increased focus on countering homegrown violent extremism (HVE) has resulted in a number of charges brought against an increasing number of individuals, including US citizens and legal permanent residents, who were living in this country, became radicalized, and took steps to act on their extremist beliefs.

- **Structural Changes to Enhance Counter-Terrorism Efforts**—DOJ and its component agencies have restructured their operations to better address national security threats and prevent terrorist attacks. In 2006, the Justice Department National Security Division merged the various national security components into one division, thereby housing all aspects under one roof. The FBI has undertaken the most significant transformation in its history by restructuring its operations. Some of the major changes include: doubling the number of FBI intelligence analysts and tripling the number of linguists; creating the National Joint Terrorism Task Force (JTTF) at FBI headquarters, consisting of approximately forty-one member agencies; and establishing various units that have enhanced counterterrorism capabilities, including the 24/7 Counterterrorism Watch, which serves as the FBI's primary point of notification for all potential terrorist threats.[76]
- **Legal Changes to Enhance Counter-Terrorism Efforts**—Since 9/11 the DOJ has worked closely with Congress and other federal agencies to strengthen the nation's laws against terrorism. The USA PATRIOT Act of 2001 has aided in the disruption of many terrorist plots. Expiring provisions of the act were reauthorized by the USA PATROT Act Improvement and Reauthorization Act of 2005, and by subsequent legislation in 2009 and 2011. These legal changes have helped to tear down the so-called FISA "wall" that prevented effective information sharing between law enforcement and the intelligence communities. Additionally, it allowed federal agents to better track sophisticated terrorists, increased penalties for those who commit certain crimes, and added additional safeguards to protect privacy interests and civil liberties.[77]

New counterterrorism technologies have also helped us to make our nation more secure. Significant progress has been made in areas to assist with border control, visas, and airline security. The TSA has implemented better security scanners, facial recognition systems, and other systems to improve security at our nation's airports. These effective technologies have been upgraded several times since 9/11. At our border checkpoints, x-rays, body scanners, iris or digital scans, security cameras, and machine-readable travel documents are some of the tools authorities now have at their disposal. Furthermore, a vast government database, which houses raw intelligence and terrorist suspects, has doubled in recent years reaching over 1.1 million suspects.[78]

While there has not been a successful attack on America the size of 9/11, the bombings in Boston remind us that the threat of terrorism is real and we must remain vigilant to keep our country safe. One way to accomplish this is through the "See Something, Say Something™" campaign. But does the "See

Something, Say Something™" campaign help in our fight against terrorism hazards? According to a 2013 Gallup poll, less than half of Americans say they have heard of the anti-terrorism slogan.[79] Since obtaining the licensed use of the slogan in 2010, DHS has awarded millions of dollars in federal grants to promote the campaign with dozens of states, cities, sports teams, and other organizations.[80] Gallup found that despite DHS efforts, there are large differences in awareness across regions, specifically the East (64 percent) and the West (37 percent).[81] One explanation for the higher awareness in the East is that many recent terrorist activities have occurred in that region. Lower levels in the South (61 percent) are concerning since places such as Atlanta and Charlotte contain major transportation hubs. Overall, the poll reveals substantial gaps in awareness for millions of people in the South, West, and Midwest[82] (see Table 6.3).

Despite the results of this poll, there have been numerous instances where the "See Something, Say Something™" campaign has worked. For example, there is the 2010 attempted bombing of Times Square where two street vendors discovered smoke coming out of a car and alerted police. Passengers caught the Christmas Day underwear bomber in 2009, and in 2001 it was a passenger who pointed out the shoe bomber—Richard Reid—to a flight attendant over the Atlantic.[83]

Table 6.3. Americans' Awareness of "See Something, Say Something™"
% by Region

	East	Midwest	South	West
Yes, have heard slogan	64	44	39	37
No, have not heard slogan	35	55	61	61

Source: Gallup Poll December 17–18, 2013.

Conclusion

More than a decade after the Towers fell, the Pentagon burned, and a field in Pennsylvania was scarred, the fact remains that America has not eradicated the terrorism threat. While security has been improved and our counterterrorism efforts have increased, newer threats continue to challenge the homeland. However, we are arguably doing a much better job of countering the terrorist threat. Over 53 plots foiled since 9/11 is a notable number that illustrates progress being made. Despite this, as we have improved our counterterrorism efforts, the threat itself has changed. Newer threats in the form of homegrown violent extremism (HVE), and Americans joining jihadist movements in Syria and other places are creating a renewed sense of urgency. A major challenge for law enforcement is gauging how quickly and at what point individuals move from radicalized beliefs to violence so that a terrorist plot can be detected and disrupted. With lots of manpower, money, and military equipment, violent extremist groups like ISIS have also grown to be a formidable threat.

The US along with the rest of the world must meet the challenges of terrorism. We cannot stop all opportunities for terrorism to occur; however we can understand the causes of terrorism and the individuals or groups who are willing to commit these acts. It is likely in the years to come that the threat of terrorism will ebb and flow, much like many of our other national issues. Only time will tell if our counterterrorism efforts and policies are strong enough to stop the next attack.

Endnotes

1. Castagnera, J.O. (2013). Counterterrorism Issues: Case Studies in the Courtroom. CRC Press., p. 170.

2. Napolitano, J. (September 2011). "Progress Toward a More Secure and Resilient Nation." *Homeland Security Affairs* 7, 10 Years After: The 9/11 Essays, Retrieved from http://www.hsaj.org/?article=7.2.14.

3. Masters, J. (2011). Militant Extremists in the United States. *Council on Foreign Relations.* Retrieved from http://www.cfr.org/terrorist-organizations-and-networks/militant-extremists-united-states/p9236.

4. Resnick, B. (April 16, 2013). A brief history of terrorism in the United States. *The National Journal.* Retrieved from http://www.nationaljournal.com/nationalsecurity/a-brief-history-of-terrorism-in-the-united-states-20130416.

5. Burgess, M. (July 2, 2003). "A Brief History of Terrorism." Center for Defense Information, Retrieved from http://www.cdi.org/friendlyversion/printversion.cfm?documentID=1502.

6. Burgess, M. (July 2, 2003). "A Brief History of Terrorism." Center for Defense Information, Retrieved from http://www.cdi.org/friendlyversion/printversion.cfm?documentID=1502.

7. Burgess, M. (July 2, 2003). "A Brief History of Terrorism." Center for Defense Information, Retrieved from http://www.cdi.org/friendlyversion/printversion.cfm?documentID=1502.

8. Sheehan, M. A. (2008*) Crush the Cell: How to Defeat Terrorism Without Terrorizing Ourselves.* Three Rivers Press, New York.

9. Bullock, A., Haddow, G.D., Coppola, D.P. (2013) *Introduction to Homeland Security* 4th edition.

10. Sheehan, M.A. (2008). *Crush The Cell: How to Defeat Terrorism Without Terrorizing Ourselves*. Three Rivers Press, New York.

11. Federal Bureau of Investigation, Chicago Division (2014, August 6). *A Brief History*. Retrieved from http://www.fbi.gov/chicago/about-us/history.

12. Norman, J. (February 26, 2013) "The 1993 World Trade Center bombers: Where are they now?" CBS News. Retrieved from http://www.cbsnews.com/news/the-1993-world-trade-center-bombers-where-are-they-now/.

13. Resnick, B. (April 16, 2013) A brief history of terrorism in the United States. *The National Journal*. Retrieved from http://www.nationaljournal.com/nationalsecurity/a-brief-history-of-terrorism-in-the-united-states-20130416.

14. Bullock, A., Haddow, G.D., Coppola, D.P. (2013) *Introduction to Homeland Security* 4th edition.

15. Norman, J. (February 26, 2013) "The 1993 World Trade Center bombers: Where are they now?" CBS News. Retrieved from http://www.cbsnews.com/news/the-1993-world-trade-center-bombers-where-are-they-now/.

16. Bullock, A., Haddow, G.D., Coppola, D.P. (2013) *Introduction to Homeland Security* 4th edition.

17. Resnick, B. (April 16, 2013) A brief history of terrorism in the United States. *The National Journal*. Retrieved from http://www.nationaljournal.com/nationalsecurity/a-brief-history-of-terrorism-in-the-united-states-20130416.

18. Federal Bureau of Investigation (August 6, 2014) *Famous Cases and Criminals: Terror Hits Home: The Oklahoma City Bombing*. Retrieved from http://www.fbi.gov/about-us/history/famous-cases/oklahoma-city-bombing.

19. Resnick, B. (April 16, 2013). A brief history of terrorism in the United States. *The National Journal*. Retrieved from "http://www.nationaljournal.com/nationalsecurity/a-brief-history-of-terrorism-in-the-united-states-20130416.

20. Watson, L. (May 20, 2014). "Inside the Alcatraz of the Rockies." *The Daily Mail*. Retrieved from http://www.dailymail.co.uk/news/article-2633716/Inside-Alcatraz-Rockies-The-supermax-prison-Colorado-Abu-Hamza-spend-rest-life.html.

21. Bullock, A., Haddow, G.D., Coppola, D.P. (2013). *Introduction to Homeland Security* 4th edition.

22. Bullock, A., Haddow, G.D., Coppola, D.P. (2013). *Introduction to Homeland Security* 4th edition, p. 45.

23. Bullock, A., Haddow, G.D., Coppola, D.P. (2013). *Introduction to Homeland Security* 4th edition.

24. Bullock, A., Haddow, G.D., Coppola, D.P. (2013). *Introduction to Homeland Security* 4th edition, p. 50.

25. Zuckerman, J. Bucci, S.P., Carafano, J.J. (2013). *"60 Terrorist Plots Since 9/11: Continued Lesson in Domestic Counterterrorism,"* The Heritage Foundation *Special Report*, No. 137, July 22, 2013.

26. Zuckerman, J. Bucci, S.P., Carafano, J.J. (2013). *"60 Terrorist Plots Since 9/11: Continued Lesson in Domestic Counterterrorism,"* The Heritage Foundation *Special Report*, No. 137, July 22, 2013, p. 1.

27. Zuckerman, J. Bucci, S.P., Carafano, J.J. (2013). *"60 Terrorist Plots Since 9/11: Con-*

tinued Lesson in Domestic Counterterrorism," The Heritage Foundation *Special Report,* No. 137, July 22, 2013, p.2.

28. Zuckerman, J. Bucci, S.P., Carafano, J.J. (2013). *"60 Terrorist Plots Since 9/11: Continued Lesson in Domestic Counterterrorism,*" The Heritage Foundation *Special Report,* No. 137, July 22, 2013, p.2.

29. Zuckerman, J. Bucci, S.P., Carafano, J.J. (2013). *"60 Terrorist Plots Since 9/11: Continued Lesson in Domestic Counterterrorism,*" The Heritage Foundation *Special Report,* No. 137, July 22, 2013, p.2.

30. Resnick, B. (April 16, 2013). A brief history of terrorism in the United States. *The National Journal.* Retrieved from http://www.nationaljournal.com/nationalsecurity/a-brief-history-of-terrorism-in-the-united-states-20130416.

31. Zuckerman, J. Bucci, S.P., Carafano, J.J. (2013). *"60 Terrorist Plots Since 9/11: Continued Lesson in Domestic Counterterrorism,*" The Heritage Foundation *Special Report,* No. 137, July 22, 2013, p.4.

32. Chicago Tribune (November 21, 2007). Defense Rests in Trial of Sears Tower case. Retrieved from http://articles.chicagotribune.com/2007-11-21/news/0711210022_1_narseal-batiste-liberty-city-seven-plotting.

33. Zuckerman, J. Bucci, S.P., Carafano, J.J. (2013). *"60 Terrorist Plots Since 9/11: Continued Lesson in Domestic Counterterrorism,*" The Heritage Foundation *Special Report,* No. 137, July 22, 2013, p.6.

34. Zuckerman, J. Bucci, S.P., Carafano, J.J. (2013). *"60 Terrorist Plots Since 9/11: Continued Lesson in Domestic Counterterrorism,*" The Heritage Foundation *Special Report,* No. 137, July 22, 2013, p. 8.

35. Zuckerman, J. Bucci, S.P., Carafano, J.J. (2013). *"60 Terrorist Plots Since 9/11: Continued Lesson in Domestic Counterterrorism,*" The Heritage Foundation *Special Report,* No. 137, July 22, 2013, p.14.

36. Zuckerman, J. Bucci, S.P., Carafano, J.J. (2013). *"60 Terrorist Plots Since 9/11: Continued Lesson in Domestic Counterterrorism,*" The Heritage Foundation *Special Report,* No. 137, July 22, 2013, p.14.

37. Bergen, P., Hoffman B., Hurley, M., Southers, E. (2013). "Jihadist Terrorism: a threat assessment." Bipartisan Policy Center Homeland Security Project.

38. Bergen, P., Hoffman B., Hurley, M., Southers, E. (2013). "Jihadist Terrorism: a threat assessment." Bipartisan Policy Center Homeland Security Project, p. 23.

39. Charlaff, J. and Kimery, A. (2014). "The Traction of Al Qaeda." *Homeland Security Today.* April/May 2014. Vol. 11, No. 3.

40. O'Brien, L. B. (2011). "The Evolution of Terrorism Since 9/11" *FBI Law Enforcement Bulletin.* Retrieved from http://www.fbi.gov/stats-services/publications/law-enforcement-bulletin/september-2011.

41. Bergen, P., Hoffman B., Hurley, M., Southers, E. (2013). "Jihadist Terrorism: a threat assessment." Bipartisan Policy Center Homeland Security Project.

42. Charlaff, J. and Kimery, A. (2014). "The Traction of Al Qaeda." *Homeland Security Today.* April/May 2014. Vol. 11, No. 3, p. 29.

43. Charlaff, J. and Kimery, A. (2014). "The Traction of Al Qaeda." *Homeland Security Today.* April/May 2014. Vol. 11, No. 3, p. 30.

44. McCain, J. and Graham L. (2014). "Stop Dithering, Confront ISIS" in *The New York Times* August 31, 2014 op-ed.

45. Cowell, A. (2014) "ISIS Fears Prompt Britain to Raise Terror Threat Level." *The New York Times,* August 28, 2014.

46. Charlaff, J. and Kimery, A. (2014). "The Traction of Al Qaeda." *Homeland Security Today.* April/May 2014. Vol. 11, No. 3, p. 30.

47. McCain, J. and Graham L. (2014) "Stop Dithering, Confront ISIS" in *The New York Times* August 31, 2014 op-ed.

48. Garner, G. (2014). "Unleashing Terror: Disaster of releasing Taliban leaders is a foregone conclusion." *Homeland Security Today* June/July 2014. Vol. 11, No. 4.

49. Garner, G. (2014). "Unleashing Terror: Disaster of releasing Taliban leaders is a foregone conclusion." *Homeland Security Today* June/July 2014. Vol. 11, No. 4.

50. Garner, G. (2014). "Unleashing Terror: Disaster of releasing Taliban leaders is a foregone conclusion." *Homeland Security Today* June/July 2014. Vol. 11, No. 4, p. 4.

51. DHS (2011). "Implementing 911 Commission Recommendations Progress Report" 2011 Retrieved from http://www.dhs.gov/preventing-terrorism-and-enhancing-security.

52. Bergen, P., Hoffman B., Hurley, M., Southers, E. (2013). "Jihadist Terrorism: a threat assessment." Bipartisan Policy Center Homeland Security Project.

53. Bjelopera, J.P. (2013). *American Jihadist Terrorism: Combating a Combating a Complex Threat.* (CRS- R41416). Washington DC: Library of Congress. Retrieved from http://fas.org/sgp/crs/terror/R41416.pdf.

54. Bjelopera, J.P. (2013). *American Jihadist Terrorism: Combating a Combating a Complex Threat.* (CRS- R41416). Washington DC: Library of Congress, p. 1. Retrieved from http://fas.org/sgp/crs/terror/R41416.pdf.

55. Bjelopera, J.P. (2013). *American Jihadist Terrorism: Combating a Combating a Complex Threat.* (CRS- R41416). Washington DC: Library of Congress, p. 2. Retrieved from http://fas.org/sgp/crs/terror/R41416.pdf.

56. Bjelopera, J.P. (2013). *American Jihadist Terrorism: Combating a Combating a Complex Threat.* (CRS- R41416). Washington DC: Library of Congress. Retrieved from http://fas.org/sgp/crs/terror/R41416.pdf.

57. Bates, R. A. (2012). "Dancing With Wolves: Today's Lone Wolf Terrorists," *The Journal of Public and Professional Sociology:* Vol. 4: Iss, 1, Article 1.

58. Bates, R. A. (2012). "Dancing with Wolves: Today's Lone Wolf Terrorists," *The Journal of Public and Professional Sociology:* Vol. 4: Iss, 1, Article 1.

59. Simon, J.D. (2013). *Lone wolf terrorism: understanding the growing threat.* New York: Prometheus.

60. Bates, R. A. (2012). "Dancing with Wolves: Today's Lone Wolf Terrorists," *The Journal of Public and Professional Sociology:* Vol. 4: Iss, 1, Article 1.

61. Bates, R. A. (2012). "Dancing with Wolves: Today's Lone Wolf Terrorists," *The Journal of Public and Professional Sociology:* Vol. 4: Iss, 1, Article 1, p.3.

62. Combs, C. C. (2013). Terrorism in the Twenty-First Century. 7th edition Pearson.

63. Combs, C. C. (2013). Terrorism in the Twenty-First Century. 7th edition Pearson, p. 210.

64. Bergen, P., Hoffman B., Hurley, M., Southers, E. (2013). "Jihadist Terrorism: a threat assessment." Bipartisan Policy Center Homeland Security Project.

65. Bergen, P., Hoffman B., Hurley, M., Southers, E. (2013). "Jihadist Terrorism: a threat assessment." Bipartisan Policy Center Homeland Security Project, p. 19.

66. Duboff J. (2010, May 10) 'If You See Something, Say Something.': The Homeland Security Equivalent of 'Just Do It', *New York Magazine.*

67. DHS (2014) "If You See Something, Say Something. ™" Campaign. www.dhs.gov.

68. DHS (2014) "If You See Something, Say Something ™" Campaign. www.dhs.gov.

69. Zuckerman, J. Bucci, S.P., Carafano, J.J. (2013) *"60 Terrorist Plots Since 9/11: Continued Lesson in Domestic Counterterrorism,"* The Heritage Foundation *Special Report,* No. 137, July 22, 2013.

70. Carter, C.J. and Ansari, A. (2014). "Pentagon chief, 'ISIS beyond anything we have seen'" CNN World August 22, 2014. Retrieved online at http://www.cnn.com/2014/08/21/world/meast/iraq-crisis/index.html?iid=article_sidebar.

71. Schmidt M.S. & Mazzetti, M. (2014, July 30). "Suicide Bomber From U.S. Came Home Before Attack" *The New York Times.*

72. Shane, S., Schmidt, M.S. & Schmitt E (2013, April 25). "Russia's Warnings on Bombings Suspect Sets Off a Debate." *The New York Times.*

73. Department of Justice. (September 7, 2011). *Fact Sheet: Justice Department Counter-Terrorism Efforts Since 9/11.* Retrieved from http://www.justice.gov/opa/pr/2011/September/11-opa-1136.html.

74. Johnson, K. (2014, August 5). "U.S. terrorism database doubled in recent years" *USA TODAY.*

75. Department of Justice. (September 7, 2011). *Fact Sheet: Justice Department Counter-Terrorism Efforts Since 9/11.* Retrieved from http://www.justice.gov/opa/pr/2011/September/11-opa-1136.html.

76. Department of Justice. (September 7, 2011). *Fact Sheet: Justice Department Counter-Terrorism Efforts Since 9/11.* Retrieved from http://www.justice.gov/opa/pr/2011/September/11-opa-1136.html.

77. Department of Justice. (September 7, 2011) *Fact Sheet: Justice Department Counter-Terrorism Efforts Since 9/11.* Retrieved from http://www.justice.gov/opa/pr/2011/September/11-opa-1136.html.

78. Johnson, K. (2014, August 5) "U.S. terrorism database doubled in recent years." *USA TODAY.*

79. Ander, S. and Swift, A. (2013) "See Something, Say Something" Unfamiliar to Most Americans. Retrieved from http://www.gallup.com/poll/166622/something-say-something-unfamiliar-americans.aspx.

80. Ander, S. and Swift, A. (2013). "See Something, Say Something" Unfamiliar to Most Americans. Retrieved from http://www.gallup.com/poll/166622/something-say-something-unfamiliar-americans.aspx.

81. Ander, S. and Swift, A. (2013) "See Something, Say Something" Unfamiliar to Most Americans. Retrieved from http://www.gallup.com/poll/166622/something-say-something-unfamiliar-americans.aspx.

82. Ander, S. and Swift, A. (2013) "See Something, Say Something" Unfamiliar to Most Americans. Retrieved from http://www.gallup.com/poll/166622/something-say-something-unfamiliar-americans.aspx.

83. Mendte, L. (2010). "Lessons from Times Square, See Something, Say Something." *Philadelphia Magazine* Retrieved from http://www.phillymag.com/news/2010/05/03/lesson-from-times-square-see-something-say-something/.

Chapter 7

What Should Be the Role of Citizen Volunteers in Disaster Response?

Introduction

All disasters, regardless of size or type, natural (earthquakes or hurricanes) or man-made (fires, nuclear or transportation accidents), are local events first. Local responders are the people who are on the scene before any others to provide medical help, food, housing, to help locating missing relatives or loved ones, or provide evacuation assistance to those who need it. In some cases, help from "outsiders" may not appear for days or even weeks.

Because the emergency can be so massive and the need for assistance so great, many of those first responders will be trained volunteers, or those who jump in to provide assistance where it may be needed. When an emergency strikes an area, many residents have strong feelings of community and civic obligation and they have an emotional need to reach out and help others. One way they can help is to volunteer and provide assistance to their communities and their neighbors who need it.

The importance of having locally trained volunteers is essential in the event of a disaster on many levels. Sometimes, disaster response from federal groups can often be slow, as demonstrated after Hurricane Katrina.[1] Federal organizations can be unorganized and inadequate, or may be unable to reach the disaster site because of road blockages or other transportation issues. Moreover, first responders who provide fire and medical services cannot always meet the substantially increased demand for immediate services after a disaster. There may be an enormous number of victims in need of assistance. It is not uncommon for there to be a breakdown of communication systems so that others are unaware of specific needs for emergency services.

Those who choose to volunteer can play a critical role in providing assistance in all types of crises and can be an invaluable asset in an emergency.[2] Volunteers can provide and deliver important resources and services to the right place and the right time during a time of disaster. Tasks can get done more quickly when there are more people to help. Victims can be freed; food, water, and other supplies can be distributed; and medical care provided. Volunteers can expand the resources of state and local communities to help them become more resilient.[3]

Another benefit to volunteers is that they incur no cost—their services are free. In light of the continuing rising financial outlays for disaster preparation and recovery, there has been an increasing amount of attention paid to making disaster response more cost effective and cost efficient. Volunteers, who do not receive monetary compensation for their actions, can mean that there will be a comprehensive response that is economical at the same time.[4]

That being said, it is essential that volunteers are well-trained prior to an event. Large numbers of untrained volunteers can cause burdens for public managers and be an impediment to providing assistance. Untrained volunteers are more likely to be injured. They can even slow down response efforts and pose further risks to victims, other volunteers, and even the trained response personnel.[5] It is therefore imperative that volunteers receive training in providing assistance so that they will not be a danger to themselves or others or otherwise complicate the rescue efforts. When communities and volunteers are trained and ready to respond, it means that people and agencies in the area can begin the recovery process immediately.[6]

The training process should also include programs geared toward preparing members of the general public for any potential disaster. When the community members are prepared, the public is better able to cope with the short-term after-effects of an emergency and is more resilient in the long run. Research indicates local outreach is critical in educating the public about local hazards, local warning systems, and local response plans. Effective outreach, education, and training programs should be geared toward addressing specific needs of each family. Those families with children or with older adults will more than likely have different needs after disaster strikes.[7]

Trained volunteers and citizens play a critical role in helping communities meet their needs in preparing for and responding to disasters. But what should their exact role be, and to what extent should they be involved? What options exist for those who want to be prepared for a disaster, or who seek to volunteer in the case of a disaster? This chapter reviews the role of volunteers in disaster relief for both terrorist attacks and natural disasters.

FEMA

The Federal Emergency Management Agency, or FEMA, is the federal agency that is responsible for organizing and overseeing the federal response to a disaster or emergency (see Chapter 1). In addition to their many other tasks, FEMA personnel oversee multiple programs to help train volunteers so they can participate in disaster preparation or provide assistance during a disaster.

One FEMA program intended to get citizens and communities involved in preparedness training was the National Day of Action, or *PrepareAthon*. The first one occurred on April 30, 2014. The goal of the program was to increase preparedness for all emergencies by the use of hazard-specific drills, group discussions, and other exercises. This year, the *PrepareAthon* was focused around four specific hazards: tornadoes, wildfires, floods, and hurricanes. The overall goal was to help communities understand which disasters could happen in their community, what types of damage might they expect, and what actions might be needed after those disasters hit. That way, they could be more prepared in case that event occurred.[8]

Youth Disaster Preparedness and Education

Another initiative supported by FEMA for training volunteers focuses on preparing youth. This is because the youth are often the ones to help collect and organize the family's preparedness material, or who encourage families to pursue other activities such as preparing a family disaster plan. In 2008, Congress created the National Commission on Children and Disasters when it became apparent after Hurricanes Ike and Katrina that the needs of families with children during an emergency were largely ignored.[9] The commission released a report in October 2009 in which the committee members noted that many preparedness training programs are geared toward adults, with things like evacuation plans, plans for distributing supplies, and operating temporary shelter facilities. The commission members noted that it was necessary to establish training programs for youth to address the specific needs of the young people. They noted that youth disaster education programs can have an impact on children's perceptions of what to do during a disaster, and that many children can play a role in disaster preparedness education and training. Thus, they noted that it is important that preparedness programs be developed to target the youth population.

According to the commission, there are many benefits to having young people trained as disaster volunteers. They have sometimes endless energy that can be tapped. They are also savvy with technology that can be a useful means of communication. Teens have open minds and are eager to learn and assist others. They are open to creative thinking to find unique solutions to problems. All of these characteristics can save time and add value to a disaster services.

The committee members recommended that training and education programs for young people be graduated, beginning with basic messages, yet still incorporate all phases of emergency management: preparedness, mitigation, response, and recovery. Disaster preparedness education should be combined with other learning initiatives implemented in schools. Moreover, home discussions of family emergency plans should be encouraged that incorporate needs of the youth.[10]

National Preparedness Community

Another way FEMA supports preparing volunteers is through the National Preparedness Community, a project developed in FEMA's Community Preparedness Division. Here, FEMA partners with non-profit groups and federal departments that provide communities with different resources for educating and training the public. This involves education multiple groups: individuals (families), businesses, and communities.

Individuals/Families

FEMA understands that Individuals can make a major difference in their communities if they are prepared for an attack or crisis. While first responders are trained to carry out their specific tasks, their jobs would be easier if individuals and families were also trained and prepared. Families need to have emergency supplies (e.g., water, food, medical needs) on hand in case a disaster should strike. They also need to develop communication strategies and meeting plans. When families are prepared, everyone can contribute to the safety and security of communities.

Businesses

Businesses have a different role in preparedness than individuals. Developments in technology (e.g., the internet), along with the globalization of trade, communication and travel, provide business owners with a greater opportunity to expand their companies. However, these technological advances can also make businesses more vulnerable to attack. It is important that business owners have continuity plans that will help them prevent attacks, or, if one should happen, to rebuild quickly afterwards. If a business owner is trained to prevent a possible attack, mitigate the possible effects of an attack, and recover from an attack, there may be less disruption to the productivity of the company, the employees, and its profits, as well as the provision of services to clients.[11]

While most of today's business owners recognize the need to protect themselves from a possible attack, that does not always translate into action. While most business owners understand that their companies may be vulnerable, few business owners seem to have an actual plan to either mitigate or recover from an attack. Those companies that have prepared for an attack may not have prepared enough and may be unable to continue their full operations should a disaster occur. Moreover, many businesses that have created plans have not informed or trained their employees on those ideas, and many have not tested the arrangements to see if they will work.[12]

The Public

A trained public is critical if a community is to be resilient after a disaster. The public needs to be knowledgeable about relevant local risks and response plans, or how they can help in the case of a crisis. If they choose to volunteer their services, community members must also be adequately trained.

USA Freedom Corps/Citizen Corps

In 2002, not long after the terrorist attacks on the US, state and local governments realized the critical role that trained volunteers could play in protecting local communities. Officials also recognized the need to have more trained volunteers who could provide this invaluable assistance to first responders should an emergency occur. On April 8, 2002, President George W. Bush announced the creation of a new program he called the USA Freedom Corps, which quickly received the support of Congress.[13] This new organization was a way to provide opportunities for citizens to train for, and participate in, a variety of activities that would make their families and neighborhoods safer in the event that a disaster should strike. It is a way to strengthen and organize different numerous volunteer service organizations both in the US and abroad. President Bush described the program as one that would encourage citizens to volunteer and be part of preparing for and protecting the US from further attacks, and in the long run, increase a community's ability to respond to an emergency.

There are many components of the USA Freedom Corps program. One of those is Citizen Corps. As described by President Bush, Citizen Corps is "an opportunity to work with local officials to make the homeland security more prepared."[14]

Citizen Corps

Citizen Corps was designed to coordinate volunteer pursuits across the nation regarding national disasters. To help ensure the effectiveness of the Citizen Corps, it was housed within the Federal Emergency Management Agency (FEMA), within the Department of Homeland Security. Their mission statement reads, "to harness the power of every individual through education, training and volunteer service to make communities safer, stronger, and better prepared to respond to the threats of terrorism, crime, public health issues, and disasters of all kinds."[15]

The Citizen Corps supports training and educating volunteers at all levels so that communities will be more prepared to respond to emergencies. The premise of their goal is that citizens who are better prepared to take care of themselves and others in times of crisis will enhance both preparedness and response. Citizen Corps creates volunteer opportunities for those citizens who want to participate in the case of an event. In the end, the Citizen Corps seeks to produce a network of community volunteers who are trained to respond in emergency situations to help their communities.

Another key component of Citizen Corps is the development of collaborative efforts between government officials and community leaders regarding preparedness, planning, mitigation, response, and recovery plans. FEMA officials work with other federal groups, state and local government officials, first responders and emergency managers, and the volunteer community. Representatives from federal agencies work alongside officials from local communities so that everyone is included in the same training programs and has a similar knowledge base, making communication easier if needed.

As part of their mission, Citizen Corps reaches out to the general public and asks them to be prepared for an emergency.[16] The agency estimates that only half of Americans have an emergency Personal Preparedness Kit.[17] Citizen Corps wants residents to prepare themselves, their families and their communities with these kits that will contain plans and supplies to aid in the case of a disaster. Another way they work with citizens is through training, which may involve taking part in classes related to emergency preparedness, response actions, CPR training or other first aid, and even procedures for search and rescue.

Citizen Corps has identified a different theme for each month of the year that can be the basis of programs to enhance public safety, preparedness, resilience, and volunteerism and to encourage civic participation. The monthly themes for 2014 were Winter Fire Safety, Winter Storm Preparation (January); Earthquake Awareness (February); Severe Weather Preparedness (March); Financial Preparedness (April); Heat Awareness and Wildfire Prevention (May); Hurricane Preparedness and Rip Current Awareness (June); Heat and Drought Preparedness/ Firework and Park Safety (July); Workplace Preparedness (August); Wildfire Awareness/ Campus Fire Safety (September); Fire Prevention, Safe Schools (October); Critical Infrastructure Preparedness (November); Winter Storm Awareness, Holiday Preparedness (December).[18]

Citizen Corp Councils

Citizen Corps activities at the local level are overseen by Citizen Corp Councils, which are managed through local governments. One of the core missions of the councils is to engage the entire community to support preparedness in all phases of emergency management. Thus, most councils work to create and/ or revise their community's response plans, including their Community Vulnerability/Risk Assessments, Mitigation Plans, Alert and Warning Systems, Evacuation Plans, or Shelter Plans.[19] These plans are specific to the needs of that community. The councils rely on the different strengths within each community as a way to prepare the volunteers in all-hazards approach to their preparedness and response plan. Citizen Corps Councils provide participating communities with educational information and training courses that target key populations in that area. They also address local risks and develop plans specific to that location.[20]

Each local Citizen Corps Council cooperates with other organizations (federal, state, and local) and local businesses to organize first responders and volunteers for an efficient response to an event so that efforts and resources are not wasted by being duplicated. The councils provide training for volunteers so they are able to assist in disaster response or recovery. Trained volunteers are then made part of local plans. They can then respond to disasters that may occur in their local jurisdiction or outside of their jurisdiction if there are mutual aid agreements with neighboring communities.

Many Citizen Corps Councils offer volunteers with skill-centered training as a way to develop more specified or technical skills. About half of the Citizen Corps Councils indicate that they offer Emergency Management training as one specialized area in which volunteers can choose to hone their skills.

Others offer first aid/CPR/AED training, or Preparedness Education/Outreach skills. On the average, councils reported that they offer three or four specialized areas in which volunteers can participate.

The councils provide training to residents in a variety of ways. They reach out to schools, workplaces, and even places of worship as a way to have contact with a large number of residents. They provide training on local alert and warning systems, local shelters, evacuation methods, family emergency planning, or local drills. The councils report that on average, they support four or five types of outreach as a way to increase personal and family preparedness, including community events, web-based information, messages from community leaders, use of social media, and printed materials.[21]

Most Citizen Corps Councils are comprised of members from both government and private organizations, as well as from the community and volunteer organizations. Some have representation from youth-based organizations, and many have representation from various types of community or faith based organizations, schools, or hospitals.[22] They also include emergency management leaders and first responders from the area. It is important that the councils include representatives and resources from all sectors of the community so that when a response plan is created, it will ensure that the needs of the entire community will be addressed. This includes residents who may have physical or mental disabilities or other needs, children, individuals with limited English proficiency, and even pets and service animals.[23]

If a community seeks to be affiliated with Citizen Corps, local officials must first meet with officials from the FEMA Community Preparedness Division to discuss the details of a partnership and different opportunities with Citizen Corps. They must agree to support the mission of citizen participation in making America safer. They then submit a complete application package to FEMA. FEMA's Office of General Counsel reviews the application. If it is approved, representatives from Citizen Corps and the local community sign a "Statement of Affiliation" which includes an agreement that includes a statement whereby the community agrees to recognize the purpose and mission of Citizen Corps. The community organization must agree to acknowledge the relationship by establishing things such as website links, co-logos on publications, and references to Community Corps in printed materials that may be distributed during training sessions. Community organizations must agree to coordinate activities so that the resources for Citizen Corps are used effectively. They also must agree to communicate with FEMA and keep them informed of those activities that are conducted to support Citizen Corps. They must also provide an annual report summarizing those activities and submit it to FEMA.[24]

Starting in January 2011, FEMA's Individual and Community Prepared-ness Division (ICPD) initiated a new web-based registration process that re-quires all Citizen Corps Councils to submit detailed information on their organization and activities as a condition for state approval to become regis-tered Councils.[25]

The number of Citizen Corps Councils registered with DHS/FEMA grew rapidly after 2002. As of 2011, there were 1,083 Citizen Corps Councils lo-cated across the country, representing over 178 million citizens (58 percent of the population in the country). This gives Citizen Corps nationwide coverage, with trained volunteers who are ready to assist in the event of an emergency to carry out national preparedness goals and local plans.[26] Nationally, Citizen Corps Councils reported that over three million hours (3,057,248 hours) were contributed by 176,699 volunteers in council supported activities in 2010. This can be translated to an economic value of over $65 million for the year. Fur-ther, the majority of councils have trained volunteers for disaster response and recovery roles (93 percent) and have used their trained volunteers to respond to disasters in their area (76 percent).[27]

Local Citizen Corps Councils are created, administered, and receive fund-ing through a variety of methods. Most have created formal documents such as bylaws and charters. In their annual budgets, most councils indicate mul-tiple funding sources. About half indicate that their funding is not dependent on allocations from the federal government, whereas about half of established councils report budgets comprised of over half of their budgets coming from FEMA. FEMA promotes multiple funding sources to support the councils and the programs.[28] Some councils reported that they seek funding for their pro-grams from outside sources. About 15 percent of councils reported that they have status as a 501(c)(3) organization that permits them to seek and receive funding as a nonprofit organization.[29] From fiscal year 2002 through fiscal year 2011, the Homeland Security Grant Program included a Citizen Corps Program (CCP) funding stream that was dedicated to supporting both individual and community preparedness. Each state is responsible for administering Citizen Corps and HSGP grant funds.[30] CCP was not funded in the FY 2012 budget.[31]

Five Citizen Corp Partner Programs

There are five Citizen Corps Partner Programs that give citizens the op-portunity volunteer in their communities if a disaster were to strike. These five federally sponsored programs help build the potential capacity for first re-sponders by the using skilled volunteers. This allows for communities to use the resources and materials that are available to them more efficiently and respond more effectively in the case of a disaster.

Over 40 percent of Citizen Corps Councils report they have a relationship with three or more Partner Programs. More than 90 percent of Community Corp Councils indicate that they have formed partnerships with local CERT programs and almost half report that they partner with and support MRC (46 percent) and Neighborhood Watch (46 percent).[32]

These programs are all part of the AmericaCorps program initiated by President Bush. In announcing the programs, Bush described each of them. He said,

"And here—there are ways to help. We need volunteers who are trained in emergency preparedness and response to participate in what we call Community Emergency Response Team programs. They first started in Los Angeles, Mayor Hahn was telling me. All the cities represented here on this stage have now got CERT programs. It gives people a chance to be a part of an emergency-response mechanism, both urban and rural, in America. If you're interested in helping, dial up the phone and the web site I'm about to give you, so that you can be a part of emergency preparedness in your communities.

We need volunteers on the Neighborhood Watch programs. Neighborhood Watch—I hope you're familiar with it—is a way for communities to be—citizens to become involved with making each neighborhood more secure. Neighborhood Watch is a structure which already exists. We want to expand it in America. We want more folks to be a part of the Neighborhood Watch program, to make our communities more prepared.

Operation—what's called—we call it terrorism information program; it's a tip program. This is a program where truckers can report anything that might be suspicious to local authorities. One of the most innovative tip programs in the country took place in Maine. Governor King, in working with the local FBI, signed up a lot of lobstermen, so when they're out there pulling their pots to get the lobsters, if they see something suspicious taking place along the Maine coast, that they share information with the local jurisdictions, local law enforcement jurisdictions. If people see anything suspicious, utility workers, you ought to report it. This is a way to organize that which already happens in our communities on a daily basis and a way to make the homeland more secure and more prepared.

We've got what's called the VIP program, VIPS, and that's Volunteers in Police. And that's what we've talked about today here in

Knoxville. I don't know if you know this or not, but I would say the vast majority of police departments need volunteer labor to help make their departments function. The chief here in Knoxville was telling me that he could not live without the fact that we've got a lot of volunteers right from your community, probably your neighbors, that go down there on a daily basis, to help make the police department function more smoothly. This is a good way to help in your community, if you're interested in helping.

And then we have what's called the Medical Reserve Corps. This is a chance for active and retired doctors and nurses to lend a hand in preparing any community for an emergency. It makes a lot of sense to say to a retired doc or a retired nurse, 'You know, you've still got your skills. You still care about people. Here's a good way for you to serve the community.' We need this participation from our citizenry. It's not only good for each community; it's good for the citizens to know that they're helping to serve a great nation by serving their community."[33]

Each of these programs are described below.

CERT

In 1985, officials from Los Angeles adapted a community program based out of Tokyo which tested citizen skills and responses during and after an earthquake. This program that was adapted to fit into the Los Angeles area so that officials could educate and involve citizens in responding to disasters. This program became the impetus for the national CERT program, which stands for Community Emergency Response Team. In 1993, the CERT program was adopted by FEMA, which then standardized the program throughout the nation and increased the validity of citizen training. Since then, the CERT program has grown and become very popular throughout the nation.[34]

CERT program officials educate individuals about disaster preparedness. Officials educate citizens in the importance of being prepared for a disaster and give people basic disaster response skills. Once trained, CERT members can support first responders and provide immediate assistance to affected individuals in their neighborhoods or workplaces until professional responders arrive on the scene. They can also help to organize other volunteers at a disaster site. Moreover, CERT members can help with non-emergency preparedness projects that improve the safety of their community.[35] Those trained by CERT officials may perform residential/neighborhood checks, traffic/crowd management, Emergency Operation Center staffing, shelter staffing, and community relations/distribution of emergency information to the public. Other functions that CERT volunteers perform include basic search and rescue, sandbagging, debris removal, managing/processing supplies or donations, general evacuation, fire safety, initial damage assessment, special needs evacuation, and medical interventions.[36]

The CERT program is administered by the Federal Emergency Management Agency (FEMA) but is usually managed by local government officials who include the CERT team members into the local emergency response plans.

Those individuals with CERT training are better prepared to respond to emergencies in their communities. When disaster strikes, CERT trained individuals can provide immediate assistance to their families and neighbors, collect critical information that may be needed by first responders. CERT graduates also assist with many non-emergency projects to help improve safety and disaster preparedness in their communities.

Medical Reserve Corps (MRC)

Established in July 2002, the Medical Reserve Corps (MRC) Program was a way to tap the skills of both active and retired medical and mental health professionals (e.g., nurses, dentists, pharmacists, and even veterinarians) who sought to volunteer their skills during local emergencies and throughout the year. MRC volunteers coordinate with local emergency response teams to provide medical assistance as needed. During non-emergency times, the MRC have programs to advance public health initiatives in the community, such as immunization programs and blood drives. The MRC program is administered by the Department of Health and Human Services but is based in the community and function locally.

As part of the MRC program, non-medical volunteers are also trained and can be used in support or administrative roles such as paperwork, interpreters, etc. The Office of the Civilian Volunteer Medical Reserve Corps is found in the Office of the US Surgeon General (part of the Department of Health and Human Services). It serves as a clearinghouse for information that can help communities establish, implement, and maintain MRC units.

USAOnWatch/Neighborhood Watch

The USAOnWatch/Neighborhood Watch Program that provides information, training, and resources to citizens and law enforcement agencies throughout the country. For many years, Neighborhood Watch programs have involved local residents who patrol the streets in their neighborhoods watching for unusual (mostly criminal) behavior. If such activity is observed, the activity is reported to law enforcement who can then respond. While most well-known for reporting criminal behavior, these groups also helped assist those who were ill or in need of medical attention. These programs have expanded in recent years, particularly after September 11, 2001, beyond their traditional crime prevention role. Now, they help neighborhoods focus on disaster preparedness, emergency response, and terrorism awareness. While patrolling neighborhoods, volunteers look for suspicious behavior that could be related to terrorist acts. USAonWatch/Neighborhood Watch is administered by the National Sheriffs' Association alongside the Bureau of Justice Assistance, US Department of Justice.

Volunteers in Public Service (VIPS)

After 9/11, state and local law enforcement have seen their roles and responsibilities increase. There are now more safety concerns at public events or entertainment venues that demand the attention of law enforcement. The VIP program provides trained volunteers with the skills needed to assist state and local law enforcement in carrying out these and other tasks. Volunteers can perform tasks such as clerical responsibilities which will allow law enforcement to focus on their frontline duties. In the case of an emergency, the volunteers could provide non-law enforcement assistance to police. In that case they may assist with search and rescue activities or assist victims or others needing assistance. The VIPS programs is funded by the Department of Justice, but managed and implemented by the International Association of Chiefs of Police.

Fire Corps

Fire Corps was first launched in December 2004 to train community members so they can volunteer their time to their local fire/EMS departments in non-emergency situations. This allows departments to focus on emergency response and to increase the medical and fire services they provide. Fire Corps programs provide trained citizens who can carry out simple tasks, thus enhancing the capacity of fire and rescue departments. Trained volunteers can help local fire departments in a variety of activities including fire safety outreach and education, youth programs, and administrative support (bookkeeping or data entry). Fire Corps can also teach citizens about the emergency services offered. In the long run, Fire Corps will help to make communities safer and better prepared to respond to an emergency, should it occur. Fire Corps is funded through DHS and is managed and implemented through a partnership between the National Volunteer Fire Council, the International Association of Fire Fighters, and the International Association of Fire Chiefs. Those communities with a Fire Corps programs may be eligible for grant opportunities through the Citizen Corps Council and through the DHS Assistance to Firefighters Grant Program.

The Fire Corps National Advisory Committee provides valuable input and feedback for the program. It assists in directing the program's strategic direction. Members of the NAC include: the Congressional Fire Services Institute, the Fire Department Safety Officers Association, the International Association of Arson Investigators, the International Association of Black Professional Fire Fighters, the International Association of Fire Chiefs, the International Association of Fire Fighters, the International Association of Women in Fire and Emergency Services, the International Fire Service Training Association, the International Society of Fire Service Instructors, the National Association of Hispanic Firefighters, the National Association of State Fire Marshals, the National Fire Protection Association, the National Volunteer Fire Council, the North American Fire Training Directors, and the Volunteers in Police Service.[37]

What Should Be the Role of Citizen Volunteers in Disaster Response?

While most communities currently rely on volunteers from their neighborhoods to bolster their ability to respond to emergencies, the questions soon become, should we rely on volunteers to respond to disasters? Are volunteers a valid resource that should be relied on for disaster relief? Should the role of volunteers be limited to helping only in certain situations? What should be the role of volunteers in assisting victims?

There are many obvious reasons to encourage the use of volunteers and promote activities by those who want to help to take an active role in assisting first responders. Often, these unpaid workers are able to arrive at an emergency site prior to first responders and can begin providing assistance to victims immediately. Volunteers can be on the scene within seconds or minutes after a disaster, whereas it may take much longer before firetrucks, ambulances, and personnel arrive, especially if roads are blocked or not travelable because of the disaster. Of course, that immediate response can be critical for saving lives.

When first responders arrive at a scene, the volunteers can provide additional assistance to ensure the safety of victims and ensure that they receive any needed care. Since most first responders do not have extensive medical training, those volunteers with that expertise, such as doctors and nurses, will be able to provide additional aid. Even those volunteers without extensive medical training can assist in providing minor medical services to those in shock or unable to think clearly, or have some other minor medical need. The bottom line is that volunteers are able to provide an extra "set of hands" to help victims or carry out tasks that are necessary.

For these reasons, volunteers should be trained in multiple aspects of disaster relief and should be encouraged to take an active role should an emergency occur. With this perspective, volunteers can provide essential medical care and other assistance alongside first responders. This means that volunteers should be an essential part of a community's response plan.

On the other hand, there are many reasons that volunteer activities should be limited. One reason for this is that volunteers must be continually trained to guarantee their skills are honed, and this can be very costly to local governments. Those who choose to help out in disasters, it is argued, should not be forced to pay for their training. Instead, because they provide a service to the community, the training should be free for them. This forces a community government, police force, or medical agency to pay for the cost related to training materials and support. Moreover, there is really no way to force these volunteers to obtain the necessary training. If an emergency occurs, there will be no one checking identification to determine if that volunteer is trained.

If not trained well, volunteers may become a hindrance and actually impede the work of first responders and make their jobs more complicated, especially in an emergency situation. Volunteers may "get in the way" and prevent professionals from carrying out necessary tasks. Moreover, because volunteers may not have the necessary equipment to perform tasks, they may get injured, in which case the first responders and medical teams will have additional victims to treat.

In some cases, volunteers cannot be relied upon to be at a site when needed. Because they are volunteers, they cannot be required to appear immediately after an event, or even show up at all. They may choose not to help, or may be unable to do so, because of other obligations. There is no way to "control" what a volunteer does. In some cases, volunteers may overreach their authority, thinking that they are trained to do something they are not, causing further harm or injury.

This perspective would support the idea that volunteers should play only a minor role in disaster response, relying instead on official first responders to step in when needed. In this case, the role of volunteers would be limited to things such as preparing their families for a disaster and ensuring that they have a "personal preparedness kit" or a family plan for communicating with each other in the period immediately after an emergency.

Conclusion

Clearly, federal, state, and local governments support the use of citizen volunteers in disaster relief. They rely on the extra assistance to help victims after a disaster. Agencies at all levels of the government provide training to those who seek to be prepared and play a role in disaster relief. However, the reliance on volunteers poses other difficulties. The role that volunteers should play, if any, needs to be defined and reassessed to resolve the question of citizen participation in providing assistance to disaster victims.

Endnotes

1. "The Federal Response to Hurricane Katrina: Lessons Learned." (February 2006). Washington, D.C.: Government Printing Office. Retrieved from http://georgewbush-whitehouse.archives.gov/reports/katrina-lessons-learned/.

2. Witesman, Eva M. (June/July 2009). "Planning for Emergency Response Volunteers" *PA Times*, pg. 6–7.

3. Witesman, Eva M. (June/July 2009). "Planning for Emergency Response Volunteers" *PA Times*, pg. 6–7.

4. Flint, Courtney G. and Joanne Stevenson. (2010). "Building Community Disaster Preparedness with Volunteers: Community Emergency Response Teams in Illinois." *Natural Hazards Review* p. 118–124; King, D. (2007). "Organizations in Disaster." *Natural Hazards* 40, 657–665.

5. Witesman, Eva M. (June/July 2009). "Planning for Emergency Response Volunteers" *PA Times*, pg. 6–7.

6. Flint, Courtney G. and Joanne Stevenson. (2010). "Building Community Disaster Preparedness with Volunteers: Community Emergency Response Teams in Illinois." *Natural Hazards Review* p. 118–124; D. King 2007. "Organizations in Disaster." *Natural Hazards* 40, 657–665.

7. FEMA. (September 2012). "Citizen Corps Councils Registration and Profile Data." Retrieved from http://www.fema.gov/media-library-data/20130726-1854-25045-2121/citizen_corps_councils_final_report_9_27_2012.pdf.

8. FEMA, "America's PrepareAthon" Retrieved from http://community.fema.gov/connect.ti/AmericasPrepareathon;/view?objectID=217843&exp.

9. FEMA (2010). "Bringing Youth Preparedness Education to the Forefront: A Literature Review and Recommendations" Citizen Preparedness Review, Issue 6. Retrieved from https://www.signup4.net/Upload/AMER11A/FEMA192E/Youth%20Preparedness%20Education.pdf; "What About the Children?" (October 14, 2008). WP Opinions, *The Washington Post*. Retrieved from http://www.washingtonpost.com/wp-dyn/content/article/2008/10/13/AR2008101302279.html.

10. FEMA, (2010). "Bringing Youth Preparedness Education to the Forefront: A Literature Review and Recommendations" Citizen Preparedness Review, Issue 6. Retrieved from https://www.signup4.net/Upload/AMER11A/FEMA192E/Youth%20Preparedness%20Education.pdf.

11. FEMA. (2011). "Business Continuity and Disaster Preparedness Planning Patterns and Findings from Current Research: Citizen Preparedness Review, Issue 7. Retrieved from

http://www.fema.gov/media-library-data/20130726-1854-25045-5729/citizen_prep_
review_issue_5.pdf.
    12. FEMA. (2011). "Business Continuity and Disaster Preparedness Planning Patterns
and Findings from Current Research: Citizen Preparedness Review, Issue 7. Retrieved from
http://www.fema.gov/media-library-data/20130726-1854-25045-5729/citizen_prep_
review_issue_5.pdf.
    13. George W. Bush: "Remarks on the Citizens Corps in Knoxville." (April 8, 2002).
Online by Gerhard Peters and John T. Woolley, *The American Presidency Project*. Retrieved
from http://www.presidency.ucsb.edu/ws/?pid=62742.
    14. George W. Bush: "Remarks on the Citizens Corps in Knoxville," (April 8, 2002).
Online by Gerhard Peters and John T. Woolley, *The American Presidency Project*. Retrieved
from http://www.presidency.ucsb.edu/ws/?pid=62742.
    15. FEMA, "Citizen Corps" Volunteer Opportunities. Retrieved from http://
www.ready.gov/citizens-corps.
    16. FEMA, "About Citizen Corps." Retrieved from Ready.gov; http://www.ready.gov/
about-citizen-corps.
    17. FEMA, Citizen Corps, Individual and Community Preparedness Division. (2007). "Cit-
izen Preparedness Review" Issue 5; Retrieved from http://www.fema.gov/media-library-data/
20130726-1854-25045-5729/citizen_prep_review_issue_5.pdf.
    18. Ready.gov. (2014). "Citizen Corps: Monthly Themes 2014." Retrieved from http://
www.ready.gov/citizen-corps-monthly-themes-2014.
    19. FEMA. (September 2012). "Citizen Corps Councils Registration and Profile Data."
Retrieved from http://www.fema.gov/media-library-data/20130726-1854-25045-2121/
citizen_corps_councils_final_report_9_27_2012.pdf.
    20. FEMA. (September 2012). "Citizen Corps Councils Registration and Profile Data."
http://www.fema.gov/media-library-data/20130726-1854-25045-2121/citizen_corps_
councils_final_report_9_27_2012.pdf.
    21. FEMA. (September 2012). "Citizen Corps Councils Registration and Profile Data."
Retrieved from http://www.fema.gov/media-library-data/20130726-1854-25045-2121/
citizen_corps_councils_final_report_9_27_2012.pdf.
    22. FEMA (September 2012). "Citizen Corps Councils Registration and Profile Data."
Retrieved from http://www.fema.gov/media-library-data/20130726-1854-25045-2121/
citizen_corps_councils_final_report_9_27_2012.pdf.
    23. FEMA/. (September 2012). "Citizen Corps Councils Registration and Profile Data."
Retrieved from http://www.fema.gov/media-library-data/20130726-1854-25045-2121/
citizen_corps_councils_final_report_9_27_2012.pdf.
    24. "Terms and Conditions for Citizen Corps Affiliation" Ready.gov. Retrieved from
http://www.ready.gov/citizan-corps-affiliate-programs/terms-and-conditions-citizen-corps.
    25. FEMA. (September 2012). "Citizen Corps Councils Registration and Profile Data."
Retrieved from http://www.fema.gov/media-library-data/20130726-1854-25045-2121/
citizen_corps_councils_final_report_9_27_2012.pdf
    26. FEMA. (September 2012). "Citizen Corps Councils Registration and Profile Data."
Retrieved from http://www.fema.gov/media-library-data/20130726-1854-25045-2121/
citizen_corps_councils_final_report_9_27_2012.pdf.
    27. FEMA (September 2012). "Citizen Corps Councils Registration and Profile Data."
Retrieved from http://www.fema.gov/media-library-data/20130726-1854-25045-2121/
citizen_corps_councils_final_report_9_27_2012.pdf.

28. FEMA (September 2012). "Citizen Corps Councils Registration and Profile Data." http://www.fema.gov/media-library-data/20130726-1854-25045-2121/citizen_corps_ councils_final_report_9_27_2012.pdf.

29. FEMA. (September 2012). "Citizen Corps Councils Registration and Profile Data." Retrieved from http://www.fema.gov/media-library-data/20130726-1854-25045-2121/ citizen_corps_councils_final_report_9_27_2012.pdf.

30. FEMA (September 2012). "Citizen Corps Councils Registration and Profile Data." Retrieved from http://www.fema.gov/media-library-data/20130726-1854-25045-2121/ citizen_corps_councils_final_report_9_27_2012.pdf.

31. FEMA. (September 2012). "Citizen Corps Councils Registration and Profile Data." Retrieved from http://www.fema.gov/media-library-data/20130726-1854-25045-2121/ citizen_corps_councils_final_report_9_27_2012.pdf.

32. FEMA. (September 2012). "Citizen Corps Councils Registration and Profile Data." Retrieved from http://www.fema.gov/media-library-data/20130726-1854-25045-2121/ citizen_corps_councils_final_report_9_27_2012.pdf; Ready.gov (2013). "Citizen Corps Partner Programs." Retrieved from http://www.ready.gov/citizen-corps-partner-programs.

33. George W. Bush: "Remarks on the Citizens Corps in Knoxville," April 8, 2002. Online by Gerhard Peters and John T. Woolley, *The American Presidency Project.* Retrieved from http://www.presidency.ucsb.edu/ws/?pid=62742.

34. Flint, Courtney G. and Joanne Stevenson. (2010). "Building Community Disaster Preparedness with Volunteers: Community Emergency Response Teams in Illinois." *Natural Hazards Review* p. 118–124.

35. FEMA. (2014). "Community Emergency Response Teams" Retrieved from http:// www.fema.gov/community-emergency-response-teams.

36. FEMA. (September 2012). "Citizen Corps Councils Registration and Profile Data." Retrieved from http://www.fema.gov/media-library-data/20130726-1854-25045-2121/ citizen_corps_councils_final_report_9_27_2012.pdf.

37. Fire Corps, "About Us" Retrieved from http://www.firecorps.org/about-us/overview.

Chapter 8

What Should Be the US Policy Toward the Detainees at Guantanamo Bay?

Introduction

Guantanamo Bay detention camp, also referred to as "Gitmo," is a 45-square-mile military detention facility located on the Guantanamo Bay Naval Base, on the coast of Guantanamo Bay. The camp is located on the southern tip of the island and shares a seventeen-mile border with Cuba. It has a long history as the US's first overseas Naval Base, first established after the Spanish-American War.[1] The facility's remote location allows the Defense Department to limit aircraft flights and control maritime access points, thus providing an additional layer of security for the camp.

According to the Department of Defense, the purpose of military detention such as that at Guantanamo Bay is to remove enemy armed forces from the battlefield. Military detention cannot be equated with criminal incarceration, which serves as a punishment for individuals who have been convicted of violating a criminal law. The Defense Department currently considers most of the individuals held in custody at Guantanamo to be "unprivileged enemy belligerents" under US and international law. Most have been identified as being members of the Taliban or affiliated groups.[2]

Since January 2002, the US has detained a total of 779 individuals at Guantánamo Bay. The last detainee to arrive at that facility was in March 2008. The number of detainees was at its peak in June 2003, when it held about 680 individuals. The US government has transferred over 600 detainees to other countries, either their home country or a third country. As of April 2014, there were 154 detainees still being held in Guantanamo Bay. Three detainees were convicted of crimes by military commissions. Additionally, one detainee was transferred to the US for trial in 2009. He was later convicted in a US civilian court and is currently serving a life sentence in a federal prison in Florence, Colorado. Nine detainees have died while in custody.[3]

Various US laws, including the Detainee Treatment Act and the Military Commissions Act, govern how detainees are treated. However, many human rights and prisoner rights organizations have complained that detainees at Gitmo are not provided with basic human rights as defined by these laws and the Geneva Conventions. They point out that detainees are being held unfairly, without specific charges, with some being subject to torture. Members of these human rights groups have demanded that the facility be closed down.[4] The Supreme Court has made some decisions regarding these allegations and demands, and President Obama has promised to close the facility. Nonetheless, the camp remains open despite significant controversy surrounding the detainees and their treatment. This chapter will provide some history of the facility at Guantanamo Bay and controversies surrounding it.

History

Only three days after the terrorist attacks of 9/11, the US Congress passed the Authorization for Use of Military Force Against Iraq (AUMF) Resolution. This gave the president the right to use all "necessary and appropriate" military force against "those nations, organizations, or persons he determines planned, authorized, committed, or aided the terrorist attacks that occurred on September 11, 2001, or harbored such organizations or persons ..."[5] While the AUMF does not specifically outline the president's authority to detain individuals, President Bush opted to do so based on his interpretation of the AUMF along with his powers as Commander in Chief as described in Article II of the Constitution.[6]

Thus, beginning in fall 2001, hundreds of men, mostly from Afghanistan, were taken into custody and interrogated. On November 13, 2001, President Bush signed a military order entitled the "Detention, Treatment, and Trial of Certain Non-Citizens in the War Against Terrorism." The law provided for the detention, treatment, and trial of noncitizens captured in the War on Terror. He labeled them as "enemy combatants," a term that had not been previously defined by the laws of war or in US law. As described in the order, a suspected terrorist who was not a US citizen would be "detained at an appropriate location designated by the Secretary of Defense." If the individual was charged and faced a trial, they would be tried and sentenced by a military commission as opposed to a criminal court. Further, it would not be a requirement that a commission member be a lawyer, and the rules of military law, or the laws of war, would not apply.[7]

At the time, there was much debate about where the enemy combatants would be housed. There was discussion about keeping the men at Leavenworth (Kansas) or Alcatraz (San Francisco) prisons, but these sites were quickly rejected based on the premise that once a suspected terrorist was held in a facility on American soil, it might mean that they could make appeals to American courts. Guantanamo was chosen as the most appropriate detention site since the base is not part of Cuba, but neither is it part of the US. Thus, the choice was made to detain men who were captured at Guantanamo. It was designated to be the place for long-term military detention operations under the authority of the AUMF and in accordance with international law.[8] The decision was announced to the public on December 27, 2001.

Construction first began on the detention camp early in 2002. At that time, many individuals who had been detained during military operations were transferred to Guantanamo. This included suspected terrorists and suspected members of al-Qaeda or the Taliban who had been captured by US forces in Afghanistan, Iraq, and elsewhere as part of counterterrorism operations. It is estimated that about 40 percent of the detainees at Guantanamo Bay are accused of belonging to a terrorist organization.

The original facilities were referred to as Camp X-Ray, and were only used for ninety-two days in 2002. These buildings were simply chain-link enclosures on concrete slabs. The Defense Department continued to build new wings as the number of detainees grew and as the needs of the facility changed. Many detainees brought to the facility needed to be segregated from others. Thus, other camps were built. These new wings were mostly covered, open-air, single-cell facilities that had steel mesh walls. Some indoor, air-conditioned areas were built later. In total, ten different wings have been built to hold detainees.[9] The Defense Department also operates support services at Guantanamo, such as medical and dental services, as well as behavioral health services.[10]

The camp currently holds detainees in various levels of security, ranging from less secure, communal living areas to maximum security cells in which detainees are in segregated cells from one another and contact is limited.[11] The building referred to as Camp 6 holds the most detainees—about 65 percent of detainees are housed there. It is a medium-security wing much like a county jail found in the US. It consists of eight indoor units of twenty-two individual cells that are air conditioned, plus a single, large common area that is used by detainees to congregate with other detainees. Two of the cells are used as a pantry and a library. Detainees are assigned to units based upon their cultural practices and lifestyles.[12] Inmates assigned to Camp 6 are permitted to have access to one adjacent unit as well as their own unit. The adjacent units are connected by an outdoor recreation area that has exercise equipment and a larger area in which the detainees can play sports such as basketball or soccer. Detainees can move freely for about twenty hours each day in the recreation yard or the nearby housing wing. They must remain in their cells for the remaining four hours each day.[13]

The facility known as Camp 5 is the second-most highly populated unit and holds about one-quarter of the camp's detainees. It is a maximum-security wing of the facility that is comprised of four cell blocks with 100 indoor, climate-controlled cells. Each block has two tiers. There are also twenty-four open-air cells. Most of the cells are segregated housing cells. There are three types of detainees in Camp 5. The first is those being held in segregated cells for a short time as a way to encourage the detainee to comply with the rules. If the inmate complies, they may be transferred to another, less secure, camp. The second type of inmate is those with similar lifestyle habits, who are placed into a shared housing environment. Detainees in this block have access to other inmate's cells and can mingle together. The third type of detainee is those who have been convicted by a military commission and are serving their sentences. These convicted individuals are segregated from other detainees.[14]

Each tier of the facility in Camp 5 also features a media room that has a television which can be used by one resident at a time. There are also three secured outdoor recreation areas that have exercise equipment, but are only large enough for two detainees at a time. All detainees in Camp 5 are allowed to have at least two hours of recreation each day with another detainee. Those who comply with the rules can have up to four hours of recreation each day. All detainees also have access to reading material. Detainees who comply are given other privileges such as the right to move freely within the facility.[15]

There are other facilities at Guantanamo Bay that house small groups of detainees. One is Camp 7 that holds "high value" detainees, such as those accused of planning the September 11 attacks. These inmates are held in air conditioned, segregated housing units where they have only limited contact with other inmates. Those in Camp 7 are given up to four hours of recreation each day. An example of an inmate held here is Pakistani Khalid Sheikh Mohammed, 48, an alleged mastermind of the 9/11 attacks.

Camp Echo holds detainees whose personal security may be at risk if they were housed elsewhere. Camp Echo has ten wooden hut-like structures in which inmates have a sleeping area and a communal area. Detainees in Camp Echo are permitted to recreate together for up to twenty hours each day. Camp Iguana holds detainees who have been cleared for release from Gitmo. Detainees here can move freely within a fenced area at all times.[16] Officials report that all of the facilities were designed based on correctional institutions in the

US, and that they meet the standards set forth by the American Correctional Association.[17]

There are three types of inmates held at Guantanamo Bay. The first are those detainees who have been cleared for release. They are considered to be safe to release to either their home countries or to a third country. If released, the US will continue to monitor these inmates as a way to ensure that they do not take up arms against the US in the future. The second group of inmates are those who are suspected of acts of terrorism, and whom the government is prosecuting, or plans to charge, with specific crimes. The third group is comprised of those detainees who are considered to be too dangerous to release. These inmates may be members of al-Qaeda, may have had explosives training, or in some cases have stated openly that they seek to kill Americans. It may not be possible to put these inmates on trial as much of the evidence against them may have been gathered by means of torture. In some cases, the troops that captured the individual may not have collected enough evidence.[18]

Allegations of Mistreatment

There have been allegations by civil rights groups that the detainees at Guantanamo Bay are not being treated fairly and that the US is violating the rules established by the Geneva Convention, if not basic human rights laws. International human rights groups such as Amnesty International, Human Rights Watch, and the International Committee for the Red Cross, have each condemned the treatment of the detainees at Gitmo. These allegations revolve around detainees being held without charges, a lack of judicial process, and allegations of torture.

Held without Charge

It was alleged that hundreds of detainees were held for years at Gitmo despite not being formally charged with a criminal act. Further, they are not afforded the opportunity to challenge their detentions in a legal environment. In the American justice system, a person cannot be detained for a long period without cause, or a legal reason. Holding an inmate without criminal charges for an extended time violates the Constitution's habeas corpus guarantee, which allows inmates/detainees to request that their incarceration be reviewed to ensure that they are not being held unfairly. Thus, the detainees are in a type of "legal purgatory" in which they are not being charged, yet do not have access to a functioning judicial process that can ensure they are not being held unfairly.

The US Supreme Court reviewed the legality of detaining the legal combatants at Guantanamo. The first case to be heard by the Court was in 2004, in the case of *Hamdi v. Rumsfeld* (542 U.S. 507, 519 (2004)). Yaswer Esam Hamdi, a US citizen fighting with the Taliban, was captured in Afghanistan and subsequently held in military custody in Guantanamo Bay. In 2002, US officials designated him as an "enemy combatant," describing him as "part of or supporting forces hostile to the United States or coalition partners."[19] Further, they claimed that Hamdi had "engaged in an armed conflict against the United States."[20] Hamdi argued that as an American citizen, he had a constitutional right to challenge his designation as an "enemy combatant" and did so.

Supreme Court Justice Sandra Day O'Connor, who wrote the majority decision for the Court, indicated that the Congress authorized Hamdi's detention under the AUMF for those "individuals who fought against the United States in Afghanistan as part of the Taliban, an organization known to have supported the al-Qaeda terrorist network responsible for those attacks." The justices agreed that the AUMF "unmistakably authorized detention" because "detention to prevent a combatant's return to the battlefield is a fundamental incident of waging war."[21] Further, the Court declared that detention for the duration of the conflict was implied within Congress's grant of the use of "necessary and appropriate" force.[22] However, Justice O'Connor also wrote that Hamdi, because he was an American citizen, had a constitutional right to challenge the detention and his status as an enemy combatant before a neutral decisionmaker under the Fifth Amendment of the Constitution.[23] Thus, according to the Supreme Court, certain individuals being held at Gitmo have the right to a habeas corpus review of their status.[24]

Another case that sought to clarify the detainee's rights to appeal their detention was *Rasul v. Bush* (542 U.S. 466 (2004)). In this case, the jurisdiction (or ability) of the federal courts to hear the habeas claims of detainees at Guantanamo Bay was questioned. Under both US law and international human rights law, detainees must be provided a method by which they are able to challenge the legality of their detention. A petition to review the detainment of one detainee, British citizen Shafiq Rasul, was filed in the District Court for the District of Columbia. Officials from the US government argued that US federal courts did not have jurisdiction to review the habeas corpus petitions that were filed on behalf of foreign nationals being held in Guantanamo. The district court agreed, because the detainee in this case was not a US citizen.

The Supreme Court decided the case in 2004 in a 6–3 decision written by John Paul Stevens. The justices reversed the decision of the lower district court, and held that the detainees being held in Gitmo have a legal right to challenge their detention in federal court. Stevens wrote that since the US exercised "complete jurisdiction and control" over the detention facility, the fact that it was in Cuba was irrelevant. Stevens also indicated that the right to habeas corpus is not dependent on citizenship status. The detainees were therefore free to bring suit challenging their detention as unconstitutional.[25] Not long after this decision was made public, Congress responded by passing the Detainee Treatment Act of 2005 to remove the federal courts of the jurisdiction to hear habeas petitions brought on behalf of detainees at Guantanamo.[26]

In recent years, there have been some habeas petitions that have been granted to detainees at Guantanamo and not appealed by the US government. Many of the petitioners were subsequently released after the review process. However, it was unclear if the courts have the power to order the government to release an inmate or simply tell officials to "take all necessary and appropriate diplomatic steps to facilitate the petitioner's release." [27]

This was addressed by the Supreme Court in *Kiyemba v. Obama* (2010). Five detainees who had won their habeas cases but were not released from Guantanamo Bay brought their case to the Supreme Court. The issue was whether a federal judge has the jurisdiction or right to order the release of foreign citizens who had been detained by the US military after being captured abroad and brought onto US soil after a judge ruled that the US did not have the authority to detain them. The court denied certiorari, and the case was sent back to a lower court for reconsideration. This means that the justices believe that the issue has been solved and the current policies are constitutional.[28]

Lack of Trial Proceedings

Another complaint made by human rights organizations regarding those detained at Gitmo has to do with the lack of a "speedy trial," as required by the Constitution. For those few inmates who have been legally charged, there have been no trials to determine if they are indeed guilty and should be detained further or if they should be released.

There is debate over whether the detainees charged with offenses should be tried in a criminal court or in a military court. President Bush created military commissions in 2001 as a way to prosecute the detainees. In these tribunals, military personnel would oversee the process of reviewing a case and determining if a detainee should be released. Bush argued these commissions were necessary because some of the information presented in a hearing could have national security implications. However, because the commissions are not American courtrooms, and are considered to be outside of the US legal process, the legal rights afforded to criminal defendants in the US would not apply.

The legality of the military commissions created by Bush was reviewed by the US Supreme Court in *Hamdan v. Rumsfeld* (548 U.S. 557 (2006)). Hamdan was a bodyguard for Osama bin Laden and thought to be part of the group that planned the 9/11 attacks. He was captured and sent to Guantanamo Bay, then subsequently tried before a military commission for conspiracy to commit terrorism. Hamdan's defense counsel, a Navy JAG officer, filed a habeas corpus petition for him with the Court arguing that the military commissions were illegal. The district court agreed with Hamdan, ruling that the US could not hold a military commission. An appeals court reversed this ruling, deciding that the military commissions were legal.

The case was heard by the Supreme Court, and in June 2006, the Court announced its decision, written by John Paul Stevens. The justices reversed the ruling of the Appeals Court. They held that neither Congress nor the executive branch (the president) had the power to authorize a military commission such as the ones that had been established. Moreover, even if they did have the right to create a military commission, it would have to comply with the laws of the US and the laws of war, including the Geneva Convention and the Uniform Code of Military Justice. Stevens also wrote that the laws could be enforced by the Supreme Court. The decision made it clear that President Bush did not have authority to set up the military commissions, and that they were illegal under both military justice law and the Geneva Conventions.

After the Hamdan decision, Congress passed the Military Commissions Act of 2006, which allowed the military commission trial of "enemy combatants." "Enemy combatants" triable by military commissions were defined as "individual[s] who engaged in hostilities or who purposefully and materially supported hostilities against the US or its co-belligerents."[29] In effect, the legislation restored the legality of the military commissions, despite the Supreme Court ruling. This act denied the right of federal courts to hear habeas corpus petitions filed on behalf of those being detained in Guantanamo Bay.

Another method used by the government to review the status of the detainees at Guantanamo was the Combatant Status Review Tribunals (CSRTs), which were created in 2004. Run by an Administrative Review Board, these tribunals were to review the cases of the detainees being held at Guantanamo Bay to determine if they had been correctly labeled as an enemy combatant. Because they are not trial proceeding, the boards are not forced to follow the legal rules of evidence. The first round of reviews took place from December 14, 2004, until December 23, 2005. On March 6, 2007, the Department of Defense announced the completion of the second round of Administrative Review Boards (ARB). These hearings were conducted from January 30, 2006, to December 6, 2006.

In 2008, the Supreme Court again reviewed the trial status of the detainees at Guantanamo Bay. In *Boumediene v. Bush* (553 US 723 (2008), the justices decided that the Combatant Status Review Tribunals and the limited federal court review process that had been approved by the members of Congress were not adequate and thus did not provide a "meaningful opportunity" for detainees to challenge their detention as provided under the US Constitution.[30] In other words, they decided that the foreign detainees at Gitmo did have a constitutional right to challenge their detention in a federal court. They wrote, "It is immoral, illegal and contrary to the very idea of due process and the rule of law to detain people indefinitely because of possible future crimes, or because we are afraid they will become radicalized, or because we can't figure out where to send them."[31] However, the justices did not provide any description to the lower courts on how the petitions would be implemented. Instead, they allowed the lower courts to define the standards that need to be used.[32]

Torture

Human rights groups have pointed to various forms of torture the detainees must endure during interrogations at Gitmo. They claim that some of the techniques used by guards at the camp to obtain information from the detainees were described by some as torture and abusive treatment, which is a violation of the rights of detainees under the Geneva Conventions. It also violated a treaty that was signed by the US in 1988 and ratified in 1994, called the Convention Against Torture and Other Cruel, Inhuman or Degrading Treatment or Punishment.

A 2006 report by the United Nations' Commission on Human Rights concluded that the US committed acts amounting to torture at Guantanamo Bay. The UN cited methods such as sexual humiliation, a form of mock drowning known as "waterboarding," and the use of dogs to scare detainees.[33] Nonetheless, officials at the Pentagon insist that the detainees are treated humanely and fairly at Guantanamo Bay. They explained that terrorists are often trained to allege that they are being tortured as a way to gain sympathy from the public.

When the first detainees arrived at Gitmo, they were shackled, hooded, and blindfolded. They were held in cages made of chain-link fence and had floodlights pointed at them that were never turned off. An attorney for one of the detainees argued that her client, a high-valued detainee, was subjected to sleep deprivation for over 60 days, prolonged solitary confinement, and military interrogations that resulted in several broken ribs. The detainee claimed to have been questioned by officials while blindfolded, while the sound of a drill was nearby, and the sound of a gun being loaded. He claimed that interrogators showed him a fake letter in which was said that his mother had been arrested. Further, he was told that if he chose not to cooperate, his mother would also be sent to Gitmo where she would be the sole female inmate among all the male detainees. At one point, he was shackled to the floor in a pitch-black room that had strobe-lights flashing. Hardcore rock music was blasted from several speakers in the room.[34]

Officials admitted that they relied on "waterboarding" as a way to interrogate detainees. When a person is waterboarded, he is tied to an inclined bench that is approximately four feet by seven feet. The person's feet are slightly elevated and a cloth is placed over the person's forehead and eyes. Water is poured onto the cloth. As this happens, the cloth is moved so that it covers the person's nose and mouth. The water is continuously poured from about twelve to twenty-four inches above the person. It isn't long before the person feels as if they are drowning. The detainee is allowed a break to take three or four breaths, at which time the procedure is repeated.

Beginning on January 9, 2002, memos were issued by the Office of Legal Counsel in the Bush administration in which they attempted to distinguish acts that were "cruel, inhuman, or degrading" from acts that could be considered to be torture. They also discussed standards of conduct when interrogating detainees. Methods described in the "torture memos" include stripping, exposure to extremes of temperature and light, stress positions, false threats to family members, and the use of dogs to scare detainees into providing intelligence. According to the memo, the practice of using "sleep adjustment," or "adjusting the sleeping times of the detainee" was considered not to be sleep deprivation. These methods were considered to be "enhanced interrogation techniques" used to collect information, as opposed to torture.[35]

Because the detainees were considered to be unlawful combatants who were being detained, the US government argued that it did not have to comply with provisions of the Geneva Convention that outlined treatment of prisoners of war. They argued that these detainees, because they are enemies in the War on Terror, are not like other war prisoners as in the past. They pointed out that al-Qaeda is not a traditional nation—they do not wear a military uniform, do not abide by the laws of war, and are a global network. Thus, it is argued that the US court system and the traditional laws of war are not applicable.[36] Moreover, because of their special status, President Bush argued that the US was not obliged to provide the detainees with any basic constitutional protections, especially since the detention facility was outside of US territory.

Some inmates have protested their unlawful treatment by staging hunger strikes. The first one was in February of 2002 and began after a guard removed a turban from a detainee while he was praying. Soon, the strike turned into a protest over multiple issues: the indefinite detention of the detainees, the living conditions within the camp, and the lack of access to legal proceedings. At the height of the protest, about 194 detainees took part.

There was another hunger strike toward the end of 2002 when detainees protested mistreatment of the Koran by guards. This strike lasted about six weeks. Yet another hunger strike began in June of 2005. The detainees stopped eating to protest the living conditions within the institution and the lack of due process. Specifically, the detainees were demanding the right to send and receive letters from family members, to see the sun, and to have all of the detainees receive equal treatment. Detainees who were housed in all five camps took part, who decided that they would not give up until their demands were met or they died. Officials in Gitmo reported that about 52 detainees took part, but others reported that it was closer to about 200 detainees. The strike ended on July 28, 2005, after officials at Camp Delta agreed to improve conditions of the camp and set up a detainee representative council. A few months later, in August, detainees again staged a hunger strike after officials did not change conditions within the camp as promised. Again, there were conflicting reports about the number of detainees who refused to eat, but it seemed to be somewhere between 100 and 200.

Gitmo and the Obama Administration

During the 2008 presidential campaign, both candidates for the presidency, Democrat Barack Obama and Republican John McCain, made promises to close Guantanamo Bay if elected to the presidency. Two days after his inauguration in January 2009, President Barack Obama attempted to fulfill that campaign pledge when he issued an Executive Order 13492, the Review and Disposition of Individuals Detained at Guantanamo Bay Naval Base and Closure of Detention Facilities. In this, he directed that the Guantanamo Bay detention facility be closed within one year. He indicated that any detainees who remained in Guantanamo Bay when it was closed "shall be returned to their home country, released, transferred to a third country, or transferred to another United States detention facility in a manner consistent with law and the national security and foreign policy interests of the United States."[37] Obama also required that interrogators only use techniques found in the US Army's field manual regarding interrogation, none of which was deemed to be torture.

A month later, in his first State of the Union address, President Obama spoke about the issue. He said, "... [T]here is no force in the world more powerful than the example of America. That is why I have ordered the closing of the detention facility at Guantanamo Bay, and will seek swift and certain justice for captured terrorists."[38] Obama also asked for an immediate case-by-case review of the detainees still being held at the facility. He signed an order that would prohibit the CIA from secretly holding detainees in facilities in other countries.

After Obama issued the executive order, he appointed an interagency working group comprised of officials from the Department of Defense, the Department of Justice, and the Department of Homeland Security to identify existing facilities within the US that could be used to house detainees if the decision was made to transfer detainees for either a trial or further imprisonment. He also sought to move some detainees who had been cleared by the courts to a prison in Illinois. He said closing the prison would return America to the "moral high ground."[39]

There was some precedence for moving detainees into the US prison system from Gitmo. In June 2009, one detainee was formally charged with crimes and transferred to the US. This detainee was transferred into the custody of the Marshals Service which transferred him to the US in order to appear for his trial. In November 2010 he was convicted by a federal court, and was sentenced to life in prison in a federal correctional facility in Colorado.[40]

There is also precedence for holding military members who have been charged and convicted of violations of the Uniform Code of Military Justice (UCMJ) in a facility somewhere in the US that is operated by the Defense Department. In six of these facilities, offenders can be housed for a period of over one year. Five of the facilities hold offenders for less than five years. The sixth facility is the US Disciplinary Barracks at Fort Leavenworth, Kansas, which is operated by the Army. This facility holds inmates with sentences over five years and those inmates sentenced to death. Five of these six corrections facilities are accredited by the American Correctional Association.[41] Under US law, members of the armed forces cannot be held alongside foreign nationals. To comply with this law, the Defense Department may need to relocate some military inmates if detainees from Gitmo were to be moved to existing facilities. Further, the Defense Department regulations prohibit the interaction between unprivileged enemy belligerents with those who have been convicted of criminal offenses. This means that the government would have to ensure that the detainees would be separated from criminal inmates.[42]

In February 2009, after being president for just a few weeks, Obama released the first prisoner from Guantanamo Bay, a first step toward closing the facility. Binyam Mohamed, an Ethiopian citizen, had received asylum in Britain, but it had expired in 2004. Mohamed claims to have been detained in Pakistan and then taken to Morocco where he was tortured. It was after this experience that Mohamed was transferred to Guantanamo Bay. He claimed that the US knew about all of it. Mohamed was transferred to the custody of the UK.[43]

The closure of Guantanamo Bay was halted largely by Republicans in Congress, but some Democrats were also opposed to the move. Those who opposed the idea argued that moving the detainees to US soil would endanger national security efforts. Some claim that the suspects are too dangerous to release and that at least some of them should be permanently imprisoned without charge or trial.[44] In June 2009, the first of many legislative acts that limited or prohibited the use of federal funds to transfer Guantánamo Bay detainees to the US was enacted.

On May 21, 2009, Obama gave a speech at the National Archives entitled, "We Will Not Be Safe If We See National Security As a Wedge That Divides America." In it, he said,

> Now let me be clear: We are indeed at war with al-Qaeda and its affiliates. We do need to update our institutions to deal with this threat. But we must do so with an abiding confidence in the rule of law and due process; in checks and balances and accountability.... First, I banned the use of so-called enhanced interrogation techniques by the United States of America. I know some have argued that brutal methods like waterboarding were necessary to keep us safe. I could not disagree more.... I categorically reject the assertion that these are the most effective means of interrogation. What's more, they undermine the rule of law. They serve as a recruitment tool for terrorists, and increase the will of our enemies to fight us, while decreasing the will of others to work with America.... The second decision that I made was to order the closing of the prison camp at Guantanamo Bay.... So the record is clear: Rather than keeping us safer, the prison at Guantanamo has weakened American national security. It is a rallying cry for our enemies. It sets back the willingness of our allies to work with us in fighting an enemy that operates in scores of countries. By any measure, the costs of keeping it open far exceed the complications involved in closing it. That's why I argued that it should be closed throughout my campaign, and that is why I ordered it closed within one year.[45]

Throughout his term in office, President Obama continued to work toward closing Gitmo. On March 7, 2011, he issued Executive Order 13567, entitled "Periodic Review of Individuals Detained at Guantanamo Bay Naval Station Pursuant to the Authorization for Use of Military Force."[46] In it, the president described a new policy for periodic review for those detainees being held in Guantanamo. Under the new system, the US will continue to hold the detainee only when "it is necessary to protect against a significant threat to the security of the United States." Some have argued that this policy allows for the US to continue to hold a detainee longer than under the AUMF because the standard for continued detention is based on the potential that a person may be harmful to the US without consideration as to whether any armed conflict exists.[47]

In 2011, Congress reacted to the executive order by passing a new policy limiting the power of the Obama Administration to transfer detainees out of Gitmo. Under a provision that is inserted into the Defense Authorization Law each year, detainees cannot be transferred out of Guantanamo Bay without a "certification" from the Secretary of Defense that each individual detainee will not "engage or re-engage in any terrorist activity" and pose a further danger to society.[48] The government must also ensure that the risks of a detainee who is housed elsewhere are low. It also totally banned the policy of bringing prisoners to US soil.[49]

In April of 2013, Obama repeated his belief that holding detainees at Guantanamo is not necessary to keep Americans safe. He told reporters that the policy of indefinite, extralegal detention at the facility is "not sustainable." He said, "It is expensive. It is inefficient. It hurts us in terms of our international standing. It lessens cooperation with our allies on counterterrorism efforts. It is a recruitment tool for extremists. It needs to be closed."[50] Obama followed through with this statement, and on July 24, 2013, a two-page plan was delivered by the White House to Congress in which their plans to close the facility were outlined. The White House later announced the intention to transfer two detainees to Algeria.

The Obama Administration continued to support the closing of Gitmo. On August 1, 2013, in a Joint Statement by President Barack Obama and President Abd Rabuh Mansur Hadi of Yemen, Obama again clearly stated his commitment to closing Guantanamo Bay. In the speech, he described a decision to remove the moratorium on transferring detainees to Yemen. He and the president of Yemen, Hadi, stated that the two governments would cooperate to facilitate the transfer and resettlement of Yemeni detainees who had been approved for such a transfer. Hadi described his plans to create a rehabilitation program for extremists that would focus on the problem of violent extremism within the country of Yemen. This would also facilitate the transfer of Yemeni detainees who were being held at Guantanamo. At the end of the speech, Presidents Obama and Hadi announced their intentions to consult with each other on a continuing basis on this topic.[51]

As of February 2015, Guantanamo Bay remains open.

What Should Be the US Policy toward the Detainees at Guantanamo Bay?

The detention facility at Guantanamo Bay Naval Base is extremely controversial. Many argue that it should be closed and the detainees allowed to return home or sent to a third country. Others believe that Guantanamo Bay is a necessary facility to house those who are identified as enemies of the US and who seek to bring harm to citizens and those who live in America, and therefore should remain open. The debate over what to do with the detainees at Guantanamo remains on-going and the subject of much debate among politicians and non-politicians alike.

To those who believe that Guantanamo should be closed claim that the facility is "an infamous symbol of the US's post-9/11 war on terrorism"[52] and present many reasons to close the facility. One revolves around the belief that the detainees at Guantanamo are being mistreated. Their rights as prisoners and as humans continue to be violated as they are kept out of the American criminal justice system. Many are being held without formal charges, and others are not being tried for crime they allegedly committed. The inmates are unable to have their detention status reviewed by an impartial court, and many face torture and interrogations. Very few of the detainees held at Guantanamo have been convicted of a crime by a military commission, yet are not free to leave. While several hundred detainees have been cleared for released, many remain imprisoned. Many of these policies violate domestic laws of the US and the international Geneva Convention that define the treatment of individuals engaged in war.[53]

Another reason to close Guantanamo Bay is that it is expensive. Each inmate costs $800,000 a year to house, for a total of about $150 million per year.[54] This is a significant amount of money for the US to spend each year on maintaining the facility.

If Guantanamo was closed, the inmates could be released or transferred to prisons within the US. There, the interrogation of the detainees at Guantanamo could continue in facilities that are part of the American justice system. Useful intelligence could be collected in the same way. But in these facilities, the detainees would have fair prosecutions and lawful detention, and be afforded their due process rights.[55]

Some believe that the facility at Guantanamo should be closed because it is harming the reputation and credibility of the US. By housing detainees in possible violation of international conventions, US officials are sending the message that they do not feel the need to obey the treaty signed in years past. Other countries may not trust Americans anymore because of this.

Finally, the argument has been made that Guantanamo should be closed because most of the detainees in the facility were low-level insurgents or innocent bystanders who were "swept up" in the panic in the days after 9/11. Many of the detainees at Guantanamo were "captured" after the US dropped handouts in Pakistan and Northern Alliance villages that offered a $5,000 reward to anyone who turned in members of terrorist groups. Many citizens turned in their neighbors, who were brought into custody. Few of the detainees were actually captured in a battlefield and belong to terrorist organizations. In fact, most of the detainees were captured far from a battlefield and have little knowledge of the groups.[56]

On the other hand, there are reasons to maintain Guantanamo Bay. One reason has to do with the dangerousness of those being detained. It is thought that many of the detainees would, if released, pose a threat to national security and continue to seek ways to bring harm to Americans.[57] Many of the detainees are members of terrorist groups who would certainly return to those organizations and support anti-American violence. There would be a greater potential of further violent attacks on Americans if the detainees were allowed to go free. For those detainees who are deemed to be too dangerous to release, there is currently no plan to detain them elsewhere.

Further, the detainees can provide US officials with key information and intelligence about the activities of these anti-American organizations, the leadership of them, and the training of their members. We have also learned about their future plans. With this intelligence, American officials can prevent future attacks on Americans, both in the US and around the world, and save lives. Even though some of the interrogation tactics used in the past were controversial, the detainees could be questioned in a more humane way in the future.[58]

Those who support further detention at Guantanamo Bay point out that the inmates have been presented with legal counsel and the opportunity to have their cases heard. While they are not being heard in a US courtroom, the military commissions have provided the detainees with a place to have their case heard. And in some cases, once the commissions heard the facts, they have cleared the detainees for release. In fact, many detainees have had their cases reviewed and if it was determined that the individual was not a terrorist, they have been released to their homes.[59] When it comes to the treatment of the individuals being held in Guantanamo, supporters point out that they have been provided with many amenities such as soccer fields, libraries, and television, which are certainly humane conditions.

An additional reason to keep the facilities at Guantanamo open is to house newly captured terrorists, at least until their cases can be heard. If Guantanamo was closed, there is no national plan to handle future offenders. It has been said that what goes on at Guantanamo (specifically the questioning of detainees) will have to occur even if Guantanamo was closed. So chances are, newly captured offenders would just be held and questioned elsewhere. In effect, this makes the closure of Guantanamo Bay a symbolic gesture.[60]

Conclusion

Whatever the future may bring, it is unlikely that the detainees at Guantanamo Bay will go free any time soon. Despite President Obama's promises and actions to close the facility and move the detainees, he has faced great opposition from members of Congress and has been unable to close the facility. The controversy over Guantanamo Bay will continue to exist, probably for many years to come, until the US decides what to do with the detainees at Guantanamo.

Endnotes

1. Schwab, Stephen Irving Max. (2009). *Guantanamo, USA: The Untold History of America's Cuban Outpost* Lawrence, Kansas: University Press of Kansas.

2. U.S Government Accountability Office. (November 2012). "Guantanamo Bay Detainees: Facilities and Factors for Consideration If Detainees were Brought to the United States." Retrieved from http://www.gao.gov/assets/660/650032.pdf.

3. Crowley, Michael. (June 10, 2013). "Why Gitmo Will Never Close." *Time* vol 181, Issue 22, pp. 44; Ackerman, Spencer. (April 19, 2014). "Guantanamo Bay Detainees' Release Upon End of Afghanistan War "unlikely." *The Guardian*. Retrieved from http://www.theguardian.com/world/2014/apr/19/guantanamo-bay-detainees-release-unlikely.

4. Amnesty International. (January 22, 2014). "USA: Close Guantanamo and end Human Rights Hypocrisy." Retrieved from http://amnesty.org/en/news/usa-close-guant-namo-and-end-human-rights-hypocrisy; see also Lepore, Jill. (March 18, 2013). "The Dark Ages". *New Yorker* Vol 89, Issue 5.

5. Authorization for Use of Military Force Against Iraq Resolution, October 2002, 116 Stat. 1498, enacted October 16, 2002, H.J Res 114, Public Law 107–243.

6. Clutter, Mason C. (2011). "Guantanamo Ten Years After 9/11" *Human Rights* Vol 38, Issue 1.

7. Leopore, Jill. (March 18, 2013). "The Dark Ages" *New Yorker* Vol 89 No 5; George W. Bush: "Military Order-Detention, Treatment, and Trial of Certain Non-Citizens in the War Against Terrorism," November 13, 2001. Online by Gerhard Peters and John T. Woolley, *The American Presidency Project*. Retrieved from http://www.presidency.ucsb.edu/ws/?pid=63124.

8. U. S. Government Accountability Office. (November 2012). "Guantanamo Bay Detainees: Facilities and Factors for Consideration If Detainees were Brought to the United States." Retrieved from http://www.gao.gov/assets/660/650032.pdf.

9. U.S. Government Accountability Office. (November 2012). "Guantanamo Bay Detainees: Facilities and Factors for Consideration If Detainees were Brought to the United States." Retrieved from http://www.gao.gov/assets/660/650032.pdf.

10. U.S. Government Accountability Office. (November 2012). "Guantanamo Bay Detainees: Facilities and Factors for Consideration If Detainees were Brought to the United States." Retrieved from http://www.gao.gov/assets/660/650032.pdf.

11. U.S. Government Accountability Office. (November 2012). "Guantanamo Bay Detainees: Facilities and Factors for Consideration If Detainees were Brought to the United States." Retrieved from http://www.gao.gov/assets/660/650032.pdf.

12. U.S. Government Accountability Office. (November 2012). "Guantanamo Bay Detainees: Facilities and Factors for Consideration If Detainees were Brought to the United States." Retrieved from http://www.gao.gov/assets/660/650032.pdf.

13. U.S. Government Accountability Office. (November 2012). "Guantanamo Bay Detainees: Facilities and Factors for Consideration If Detainees were Brought to the United States." Retrieved from http://www.gao.gov/assets/660/650032.pdf.

14. U.S. Government Accountability Office. (November 2012). "Guantanamo Bay Detainees: Facilities and Factors for Consideration If Detainees were Brought to the United States." Retrieved from http://www.gao.gov/assets/660/650032.pdf.

15. U.S. Government Accountability Office. (November 2012). "Guantanamo Bay Detainees: Facilities and Factors for Consideration If Detainees were Brought to the United States." Retrieved from http://www.gao.gov/assets/660/650032.pdf.

16. U.S. Government Accountability Office. (November 2012). "Guantanamo Bay Detainees: Facilities and Factors for Consideration If Detainees were Brought to the United States." Retrieved from http://www.gao.gov/assets/660/650032.pdf.

17. U.S. Government Accountability Office. (November 2012). "Guantanamo Bay Detainees: Facilities and Factors for Consideration If Detainees were Brought to the United States." Retrieved from http://www.gao.gov/assets/660/650032.pdf.

18. Crowley, Michael. (June 10, 2013). "Why Gitmo Will Never Close." *Time* vol 181, Issue 22, pp. 44.

19. "Hamdi, et al. v. Rumsfeld, Secretary of Defense, et al." (2004). FindLaw; Retrieved from http://caselaw.lp.findlaw.com/scripts/getcase.pl?court=us&vol=000&invol=03-6696.

20. "Hamdi, et al. v. Rumsfeld, Secretary of Defense, et al." (2004). FindLaw; Retrieved from http://caselaw.lp.findlaw.com/scripts/getcase.pl?court=us&vol=000&invol=03-6696.

21. "Hamdi, et al. v. Rumsfeld, Secretary of Defense, et al." (2004). FindLaw; Retrieved from http://caselaw.lp.findlaw.com/scripts/getcase.pl?court=us&vol=000&invol=03-6696.

22. Clutter, Mason C. (2011). "Guantanamo Ten Years After 9/11" *Human Rights* Vol 38, Issue 1.

23. Clutter, Mason C. (2011). "Guantanamo Ten Years After 9/11" *Human Rights* Vol 38, Issue 1.

24. "Hamdi v. Rumsfeld."(2004). Oyez; Retrieved from http://www.oyez.org/cases/2000-2009/2003/2003_03_6696/; "Hamdi v. Rumsfeld" (2004). Legal Information Institute. Retrieved from http://www.law.cornell.edu/supct/html/03-6696.ZS.html.

25. Rasul v. Bush. (2004). Oyez. Retrieved from http://www.oyez.org/cases/2000-2009/2003/2003_03_334; Rasul v. Bush. (2004). Legal Information Institute. Retrieved from http://www.law.cornell.edu/supct/html/03-334.ZS.html.

26. Clutter, Mason C. (2011). "Guantanamo Ten Years After 9/11" *Human Rights* Vol 38, Issue 1.

27. Clutter, Mason C. (2011). "Guantanamo Ten Years After 9/11" *Human Rights* Vol 38, Issue 1.

28. Clutter, Mason C. (2011). "Guantanamo Ten Years After 9/11" *Human Rights* Vol 38, Issue 1.

29. Clutter, Mason C. (2011). "Guantanamo Ten Years After 9/11" *Human Rights* Vol 38, Issue 1.

30. Clutter, Mason C. (2011). "Guantanamo Ten Years After 9/11" *Human Rights* Vol 38, Issue 1.

31. Conniff, Ruth. (June 2013). "No Excuse on Guantanamo" *Progressive* VOl 77, Issue 6.

32. Clutter, Mason C. (2011). "Guantanamo Ten Years After 9/11" *Human Rights* Vol 38, Issue 1.

33. United Nations Economic and Social Council, Commission on Human Rights. (February 15, 2006). "Situation of Detainees at Guantanamo Bay" Retrieved from http://www.nytimes.com/packages/pdf/international/20060216gitmo_report.pdf.

34. Hanley, Delinda C. (Mar/Apr 2012). "The Many Reasons Why the Guantanamo Detention Facility Must Close" *Washington Report on Middle East Affairs* Vol 31, Issue 2.

35. Stein, Sam. (June 9, 2009). "Bush Torture Memos Released By Obama: See the Complete Documents" *Huff Post Politics. Retrieved from* http://www.huffingtonpost.com/2009/04/16/bush-torture-memos-releas_n_187867.html.

36. Clutter, Mason C. (2011). "Guantanamo Ten Years After 9/11." *Human Rights* Vol 38, Issue 1.

37. Barack Obama. (February 24, 2009). "Address Before a Joint Session of the Congress," Online by Gerhard Peters and John T. Woolley, *The American Presidency Project.* Retrieved from http://www.presidency.ucsb.edu/ws/?pid=85753.

38. Barack Obama (February 24, 2009). "Address Before a Joint Session of the Congress." Online by Gerhard Peters and John T. Woolley, *The American Presidency Project.* Retrieved from http://www.presidency.ucsb.edu/ws/?pid=85753.

39. Barack Obama (February 1, 2010). "Question-and-Answer Session With YouTube Participants." Online by Gerhard Peters and John T. Woolley, *The American Presidency Project.* Retrieved from http://www.presidency.ucsb.edu/ws/?pid=87467.

40. U.S. Government Accountability Office. (November 2012). "Guantanamo Bay Detainees: Facilities and Factors for Consideration If Detainees were Brought to the United States." Retrieved from http://www.gao.gov/assets/660/650032.pdf.

41. U.S. Government Accountability Office (November 2012). "Guantanamo Bay Detainees: Facilities and Factors for Consideration If Detainees were Brought to the United States." http://www.gao.gov/assets/660/650032.pdf.

42. U.S. Government Accountability Office, November 2012. "Guantanamo Bay Detainees: Facilities and Factors for Consideration If Detainees were Brought to the United States." Retrieved from http://www.gao.gov/assets/660/650032.pdf.

43. Greenberg, Karen J. (2009). "Detention Nation" *National Interest* Issue 101.

44. Hanley, Delinda C. (March/April 2012). "The Many Reasons Why the Guantanamo Detention Facility Must Close" *Washington Report on Middle East Affairs* Vol 31, Issue 2.

45. Barack Obama, (May 21, 2009). "Remarks at the National Archives and Records Administration." Online by Gerhard Peters and John T. Woolley, *The American Presidency Project.* Retrieved from http://www.presidency.ucsb.edu/ws/?pid=86166.

46. Obama, Barack. (March 7, 2011). "Executive Order 13567—Periodic Review of Individuals Detained at Guantanamo Bay Naval Station Pursuant to the Authorization for

Use of Military Force" *Daily Compilation of Presidential Documents* DCPD number DCPD 201100151.

47. Clutter, Mason C. (2011). "Guantanamo Ten Years After 9/11" *Human Rights* Vol 38, Issue 1.

48. Conniff, Ruth. (June 2013). "No Excuse on Guantanamo" *Progressive* Vol 77, Issue 6.

49. Hanley, Delinda C. (March/April 2012). "The Many Reasons Why the Guantanamo Detention Facility Must Close" *Washington Report on Middle East Affairs* Vol 31, Issue 2.

50. Barack Obama. (April 30, 2013). "The President's News Conference." Online by Gerhard Peters and John T. Woolley, *The American Presidency Project*. Retrieved from http://www.presidency.ucsb.edu/ws/?pid=103552.

51. Obama, Barack and Abd Rabuh Mansur Hadi. (August 1, 2013). "Joint Statement by President Barack Obama and President Abd Rabuh Mansur Hadi of Yemen." Daily Compilation of Presidential Documents, Superintendent of Documents; DCPD number: DCPD201300545.

52. Crowley, Michael. (June 10, 2013). "Why Gitmo Will Never Close." *Time* vol 181, Issue 22, pp. 44.

53. Clutter, Mason C. (2011). "Guantanamo Ten Years After 9/11" *Human Rights* Vol 38, Issue 1.

54. Crowley, Michael. (June 10, 2013). "Why Gitmo Will Never Close." *Time* vol 181, Issue 22, pp. 44.

55. Clutter, Mason C. (2011). "Guantanamo Ten Years After 9/11" *Human Rights* Vol 38, Issue 1.

56. Hanley, Delinda C. (March/April 2012). "The Many Reasons Why the Guantanamo Detention Facility Must Close" *Washington Report on Middle East Affairs* Vol 31, Issue 2.

57. McKeon, Buck. (May 2, 2013). "Keep Guantanamo Open: Opposing View." *USA Today*. Retrieved from http://www.usatoday.com/story/opinion/2013/05/02/guantanamo-bay-buck-mckeon-editorials-debates/2131137/; Daskal, Jennifer. (January 10, 2013). "Don't Close Guantanamo." *New York Times* Retrieved online at http://www.nytimes.com/2013/01/11/opinion/don't-close-guantanamo.html.

58. McKeon, Buck. (May 2, 2013). "Keep Guantanamo Open: Opposing View." *USA Today*. Retrieved from http://www.usatoday.com/story/opinion/2013/05/02/guantanamo-bay-buck-mckeon-editorials-debates/2131137/.

59. Rogan, Tom. (September 24, 2012). "Why Guantanamo Bay Should Remain Open." *The Daily Caller* Retrieved from http://dailycaller.com/2012/09/24/why-guantanamo-bay-should-remain-open/#!.

60. "Why Guantanamo Should Stay Open." (June 10, 2005). *National Public Radio* Retrieved from http://www.npr.org/templates/story/story.php?storyId=4697513.

Chapter 9

Should the USA PATRIOT Act Be Eliminated?

Introduction

After the terrorist attacks of September 11, 2001, the US Attorney General drafted new legislation that was designed to prevent and combat future acts of terrorism in the US and around the world. The law, formally entitled "Uniting and Strengthening America by Providing Appropriate Tools Required to Intercept and Obstruct Terrorism Act of 2001," (USA PATRIOT Act) became more widely known as the Patriot Act. The bill was signed into law on October 26, 2001 (PL 107-56) by President George W. Bush. As he signed the new law, he said: "The law allows our intelligence and law enforcement officials to continue to share information. It allows them to continue to use tools against terrorists that they used against—that they use against drug dealers and other criminals. It will improve our nation's security while we safeguard the civil liberties of our people. The legislation strengthens the Justice Department so it can better detect and disrupt terrorist threats. And the bill gives law enforcement new tools to combat threats to our citizens from international terrorists to local drug dealers."[1]

The Patriot Act revised existing counter-terrorism laws to enhance the investigatory authority of US law enforcement agencies. Law enforcement agencies were given increased surveillance power so that they could perform searches for information and intelligence more easily, often without a court order. The new law allowed law enforcement to intercept communications and collect relevant intelligence. Law enforcement can also delay notifying a suspect that a search was carried out as a way to prevent a suspect from destroying possible evidence or fleeing the area. This was all done based on the argument that it will prevent further terrorist attacks on Americans.

Some argue that the searches infringe on the constitutional rights of American citizens and foreigners who are living in the US. The rights of citizens against unreasonable searches and seizures are protected in the Fourth Amendment of the US Constitution. However, critics argue, these rights were eroded when the Patriot Act was passed. Not only did the Patriot Act increase the powers of law enforcement to search homes without notice, it also effectively eliminated judicial oversight that may prevent abuse by law enforcement. The law also tightened the borders to foreign terrorists and allows the government to detain and remove threats from within the borders of the US.[2]

This chapter poses the question, should citizens allow their civil liberties to be eroded in order to prevent another major terrorist attack? Should the government be permitted to search the personal property and read the e-mail communications of its citizens as well as those visiting the country? Should companies based in the US also be monitored, regardless if they are headquartered in America or a subsidiary of a larger, non-US-based company? Should the US limit ease of travel at the border, and if so, to what extent? Should the Congress eliminate the USA Patriot Act?

Expanded Powers

The Patriot Act gave law enforcement expanded powers to track the communications and activities of those who are suspected of plotting terrorist activity. This was done by amending and strengthening some existing laws, including the Foreign Intelligence Services Act (FISA) and the Electronic Communications Privacy Act (ECPA). By changing these laws, it is hoped that agencies such as the CIA and FBI will be able to identify terrorist networks that are operating both within and outside the US, then disband them before they are able to carry out any violent acts. Federal prosecutors can then use any evidence collected during the search to punish those who planned or carried out these acts.

The Patriot Act increased law enforcement's surveillance powers in multiple ways. One is by expanding the government's ability to carry out searches of a person's records or behaviors that are held by a third party regarding suspicious activity (in Section 215 of the law). Law enforcement can require that businesses or organizations such as libraries, video stores, doctors, libraries, bookstores, banks, schools, universities, and internet service providers make records related to the behaviors or activities of their clients or customers available for review. Officials can gather "any tangible thing" (i.e., records, books, papers, documents) that may be related to an investigation. These "things" can be collected even if there is no proof that the item is related to a suspected terrorist or their activities. Instead, the records can be collected if they are sought in connection with a possible terror investigation.

Another section of the Patriot Act (Section 505) includes provisions that permit a law enforcement agency to use an alternative type of subpoena, called a National Security Letter, as a way to carry out a search. The letter, issued independently by FBI field offices, simply states that the desired information is relevant to a national security investigation. The letter is not subject to judicial approval or review unless a case comes to court. By simply filing a letter, the FBI and other government agencies can force businesses and organizations turn over a person's personal documents and records (i.e., financial records, communications information) to law enforcement. Since the law was passed, the FBI has issued hundreds of these letters.[3]

A second expanded power under the Patriot Act pertains to searches of private property. With the new law, law enforcement is permitted to carry out searches of private property without notifying the owner of that property (section 213). Prior to the Patriot Act, law enforcement generally could not go onto a person's private property without their consent or prior notification of a search. Now, the government is allowed to carry out a search without notifying the owner for permission, or even notifying them after the search has been conducted.[4] In other words, police can now enter a person's home or office when the occupant or owner is not there, search the property (take pictures or even seize property), and not inform the owner or residents, or delay notifying the owner/resident of the search or that they are being investigated. The search can be carried out in connection to any federal crime, including misdemeanors, and for criminal investigations as well as investigations related to possible terrorism. This has been called "sneak and peak" powers.[5]

Law enforcement officials, particularly from the Justice Department, report that the "sneak and peak" provision has allowed them to search the homes of dangerous drug dealers and other criminals without providing notice that might have jeopardized an investigation. Had they been forced to inform these criminals that they were under investigation and their properties were being searched, the individuals would have fled the area and any possible co-conspirators would have been tipped off.

A third expanded power found in the Patriot Act has to do with intelligence searches and wiretaps. The Patriot Act amends the Foreign Intelligence Surveillance Act (FISA), passed in 1978, that created an exception to the Fourth Amendment's requirement that law enforcement show probable cause when the wiretap or search is intended to collect foreign intelligence (i.e., for spying). Thus, if a case involved foreign intelligence, the investigators could use a wiretap to gather evidence without proving probable cause to a judge prior to installing the tap. Otherwise, wiretaps could only be issued to investigate only crimes that were specifically listed in the Federal Criminal Code. The Patriot Act adds to the list of crimes for which wiretaps can be used. Moreover, wiretaps and searches can now be used in order to collect evidence for domestic criminal cases, not just foreign offenses.[6]

A fourth expanded power given to law enforcement in the Patriot Act has to do with "Trap and Trace" searches (Section 214). In another Fourth Amendment exception for evidence collection, law enforcement can now collect "addressing" information about the origin and destination of communications (as opposed to the content). Wiretaps that only collect information on the addressing information are called "Pen register/trap and trace" searches. Similarly, pen registers trace all numbers that are called from a phone. The Patriot Act allows law enforcement to use trap and trace devices and pen registers for electronic communications such as e-mail in more situations than in the past.[7]

Under the Patriot Act, there are few requirements for getting a pen register/ trap and trace warrant. Law enforcement is not required to show probable cause or reasonable suspicion of criminal activity before using the warrant. It must only certify, but not prove, to a judge that such a search would be "relevant" to an ongoing criminal investigation. The judge does not have the authority to reject the application. Further, pen register/ trap and trace requests that are approved by a judge can be used anywhere—not only in that single jurisdiction. This also means that the judge who approves the device may not be able to monitor its use.

Now, law enforcement agents can use the "header" of an e-mail message as information that is accessible with a pen register/ trap and trace warrant. They have also examined all of the URLs or website addresses that a person visits with these warrants. This means that law enforcement has the ability to track the websites an individual visited and when. They can also know how long a person was on a website and if any products were purchased or a donation made. If that happened, law enforcement would also know the credit card or bank account numbers of the user. This means that law enforcement agents are able to monitor the online activities of all Americans as well as track the websites people visit by simply telling a judge anywhere in the US that the investigation could lead to information that is "relevant" to an ongoing criminal investigation. Further, the person who is being investigated does not have to be the primary target of the investigation. Moreover, the government is not obligated to inform person being watched that the investigation occurred, or even tell the court of any findings.[8]

In Section 206 of the Patriot Act, referred to as the "roving John Doe wiretap" provision, law enforcement was given the power to obtain surveillance orders that identify neither the exact person nor the precise facility to be tapped. Before this, law enforcement officers had to obtain a separate court order for every device that was used by a suspect. That means that an officer would have to get separate warrants from a judge to tap a suspect's computer, laptop, cell phone, or any other communications device. Under the Patriot Act, "roving wiretaps," which are not attached to one specific device, can be used. These wiretaps can be moved from one phone to another phone, or from one computer to another computer. Thus, officials can watch a suspect even if he or she uses multiple methods of communication.[9]

A related provision of the Patriot Act is Section 6001 that describes the "Lone Wolf" provision. This provision broadens the definition of "agent of a foreign power" under the FISA Act to include a non-US citizen who is not affiliated with a foreign organization but who is thought to have engaged in acts of terrorism. In the past, that person had to be affiliated with a foreign power to be the subject of a search. Once identified as a "Lone Wolf," (a designation granted only in secret courts), law enforcement can carry out investigations as described above.[10]

The fifth way that law enforcement surveillance powers are expanded by the Patriot Act is by encouraging cooperation between US law enforcement and foreign intelligence officers. Under the Patriot Act, some of the laws that limit foreign intelligence gathering within the US were loosened, and in Sections 203(b) and 203(d) of the law, increased information sharing is encouraged. This is relevant because both the CIA and FBI had pieces of information regarding September 11 hijackers but they did not share it with other agencies, so the pieces were not put together and the suspects were not detained. Officials claim that procedures at the time made law enforcement hesitant to share information between the intelligence side and criminal aspects of the investigation. It is thought that the new provisions of the Patriot Act will permit more information sharing within the FBI, and with other intelligence agencies.

Thus, there is an increased amount of information sharing between domestic law enforcement and intelligence agencies under the Patriot Act. Now, any information collected from a wiretap, grand jury proceeding or any other evidence that has been collected in a criminal case can be provided to government intelligence agencies if it is thought that the information is related to foreign intelligence. It is typical in a criminal grand jury investigation that business and personal records will be subpoenaed from companies such as banks (for financial records), schools, and retailers (e.g., bookstores and video stores). The Patriot Act allows intelligence agents to retrieve these same documents.[11]

When it comes to investigating outside of the US, the Patriot Act allows US law enforcement and intelligence agencies to access European data that is stored in the "cloud," despite strong laws in Europe regarding data protection and the privacy of its citizens. These provisions could be used by US law enforcement to gather information on individuals and businesses thought to be committing illegal acts. While most cloud providers are maintained within the jurisdiction of the US (since most are US companies or conduct business in the

US), some businesses and schools are located outside the US could be forced by US agents to provide data to law enforcement.[12]

Other powers were given to law enforcement in the Patriot Act. For example, there are new provisions to detect and punish money laundering. New crimes regarding money laundering were established and penalties for existing crimes were increased. Under the new law, government officials can also confiscate the property of any person who either plans or participates in an act of domestic or international terrorism. They can also confiscate any property that was derived from or used to facilitate domestic or international terrorism.

Other new laws were defined in the Patriot Act. For example, it is now illegal to plan or carry out a terrorist attack on a mass transportation facility. It is also now illegal to harbor terrorists, or to provide material support to terrorists. The new law increased penalties for conspiracy to commit certain terrorist offenses, and increases the penalties for counterfeiting, cybercrime, and charity fraud. Under the Patriot Act, the attorney general is permitted to gather DNA samples from prisoners who were convicted of any federal crime of violence or terrorism. The Patriot Act also increased the penalties for those who were found to have committed crimes of terrorism, and eliminated the statutes of limitations for certain terrorism crimes.[13]

Sunset Provisions

Many provisions in the Patriot Act had a sunset provision of December 31, 2005, meaning that they would expire if not renewed by the US Congress and the president. The sunset provisions were intentionally included in the original legislation as a way to provide Congress with the opportunity to review the law at a later date to determine if changes were needed. This way, Congress could evaluate the original law that granted increased surveillance powers to the government to determine if they were being used fairly and responsibly by law enforcement.

There were multiple sections of the Patriot Act that needed to be renewed by Congress. They included provisions allowing for wiretapping in cases of terrorism, or for cases of computer fraud and sharing of wiretapping information. The sections that modified pen register/trap and trace wiretaps, lone wolf, and roving wiretaps also needed to be renewed by Congress.

The Patriot Act renewal was very controversial. Those opposed to renewing the law argued that there needed to be more protections in the law to protect innocent people from government surveillance. They believed that the law gave the government too much power and did not protect the rights of citizens.

Those who supported the bill argued that the surveillance powers were needed to protect Americans and the nation's security.

Despite the controversy, Congress passed the USA Patriot and Terrorism Prevention Reauthorization Act of 2005 in July 2005. In addition to reauthorizing provisions of the original bill, the new law had sections to increase security at seaports, gave the Secret Service additional powers, and new provisions related to the death penalty. Another reauthorizing act was passed in February 2006, and was called the USA Patriot Act Additional Reauthorizing Amendments Act.

In 2010, the Patriot Act again faced sunset provisions that were to take effect on some parts of the law if not renewed. On February 27, 2010, however, President Obama signed a temporary extension of the Patriot Act for one year. In this legislation, the Patriot Act was set to expire on February 28, 2011, if not granted a renewal. Just before the provisions were set to expire, the Congress passed additional legislation to extend the sunset deadline. The reauthorizing legislation was passed in February 2011, and again signed by President Obama. This was called the PATRIOT Sunsets Extension Act of 2011. This law extended provisions of the original Patriot Act for four years, but it also set new limits on the use of surveillance devices and the ability of law enforcement to conduct searches.

Travel

In addition to increasing law enforcement powers to gather intelligence against potential terrorists, the Patriot Act also created new policies regarding travel into and out of the US as a way to increase the nation's security levels. Title IV of the Patriot Act has to do with protecting the border. Subtitle A of this title defines new rules for protecting the northern border with Canada. The law increases the number of personnel who monitor travel at the border by tripling the number of US Customs and Border Protection personnel and immigration inspectors along the northern border. It also provides for an additional $50 million for US Citizenship and Immigration Services (USCIS) to improve monitoring technology. The law provided for extra funds for the extra pay and overtime as well as for more funds to upgrade border security.

Another way the Patriot Act increases security at the border is to require that all travelers verify their identity. Section 403 of the Patriot Act gives USCIS and State Department personnel access to the FBI's Most Wanted Persons File as a way to check the criminal history of every visa applicant. This section also instructs the attorney general and the secretary of state to develop new technology that can be used to verify the identity of those who apply for visas. The new technology will also be used as the basis of a new system that will be able to verify every visitor's identity at all ports of entry, and then share that information with other law enforcement agencies. Other provisions regarding travel found in the Patriot Act are described in Table 9.1.

Table 9.1. Travel Restriction from USA Patriot Act

- Section 413: authorizes the secretary of state to share information that is being held in their visa database and information on individual aliens with foreign governments.
- Section 405: requires the US attorney general to report to Congress on the feasibility of expanding the FBI's Integrated Automated Fingerprint Identification System (IAFIS) to include visa applicants and visa holders who may be wanted in connection with a criminal investigation. This information can be used to deny a visa to an unwanted individual, or to identify them upon entry into or exit from the US.
- Section 411: increases the reasons for excluding people identified as possible terrorists or aliens with ties to terrorist groups from entering the US. The law also authorizes the exclusion of the spouses and children of these individuals.
- Section 412: permits the US attorney general to detain a person at the border if it can be shown that they have engaged in terrorist activities or is affiliated with an identified terrorist organization. If this occurs, the attorney general must, within seven days, begin removal proceedings against the individual, charge them with a criminal offense, or release them.
- Section 414: requests that the US attorney general implement computer data base for those seeking to enter or exit the US. The system would be used at airports, seaports, and land border ports and would include biometric technology as well as machine-readable documents and would be connected to law enforcement databases.
- Section 416: requests that the US attorney general implement a system to track foreign students attending schools in the US. The data would include the date they arrived, the port of entry that was used, the school the student is attending and degree sought, among other information.

Effects on Travel and Relations with Canada

For years, Canada and the US have cooperated to maintain the easy movement of goods, services, and travelers across the border. Because of these agreements, travel between the two countries has grown each year.[14] However, the comfortable relationship between the two countries changed dramatically after the terrorist attacks of September 11, 2001. In the days immediately following the attacks, the US shut down the border and increased security measures. This had an immediate impact on travel between the countries. With more security restrictions on the border, travel was more difficult. This has been referred to as the "thickening of the border" and was a real concern to Canadians.

More "border thickening" occurred when Congress passed the Western Hemisphere Travel Initiative (WHTI) that included a requirement that all travelers entering into the US, whether they are US citizens or from other countries, must present a valid passport to enter the country. In other words, it would be necessary for all travelers (even US citizens) entering the country by land, air, or sea, to present a passport and proof of citizenship. This new law offended many Canadians who, for many years, had easy access to the US.[15] After a great public outcry from both Canadians and Americans, Congress delayed the implementation of WHTI until June 2009.[16] In the first month of the new policy, the eleven busiest US–Canada bridges had approximately 2.6 million vehicles—a drop of nearly 23 percent from the same time in the previous year.[17]

Nonetheless, security at the border has become a priority for the US. Canada responded in kind and change their security measures as well. Canada agreed to hire additional officers and staff at the ports, increase the number of CBSA personnel, and Border Patrol officers.[18] The Canadian government agreed to spend $7.7 billion (CAN) over a five-year period to improve border infrastructure and enforcement. They also allocated $1.2 billion to boost the country's military.[19] Canada also reorganized its border law enforcement by merging Canada Customs, Citizenship and Immigration Canada, and the Canadian Food Inspection Agency to form the Department of Public Safety and Emergency Preparedness Canada.[20] The new agency focuses on managing the border. They also restructured the Canadian military command system and tightened immigration and refugee policies to allay US fears that terrorists could enter the US illegally from Canada.

Not all Canadians support the increased security measures in the Patriot Act. One very controversial component of the increased security policies revolves around the privacy of citizens. Canadians have very different standards regarding privacy than Americans. Canada has very strict privacy laws, with "data protection authorities" and "privacy officers" which do not exist in the US. On the whole, Canada expects far more in terms of privacy laws than do citizens in the US, and they have different perspectives of what the government should and can do.[21] Canadians are opposed to sharing personal information with many groups as encouraged by the Patriot Act. Many Canadians say that privacy issues are being violated as a result of the post 9/11 changes.

Many Canadians also believe that Canadian officials made concessions on the sharing of personal information as required in the Patriot Act. In particular, the US required Canadian-based airlines to send information to the US that many Canadians feel they have no right to collect. Under the Patriot Act, information on travelers travelling to or passing through Canada is collected by the US. To many Canadians, that information is not protected. Once the US collects the information, it can give it to a third country without the approval of the Canadian government.[22] Furthermore, there is nothing that Canadians can do to protect their personal data. In the end, Canada is losing control of their information. This angers many Canadians.

Canada and the US also differ concerning immigration. The countries have different policies and rules for immigration. The US depends on Canada from becoming a transit point for terrorists who seek to attack the US.[23] Canada would let people into their country that American would turn away, and vice-versa. Some American officials say that the Canadians have a generous asylum policy that is much more generous than that in America, and some seek to abuse this. The Patriot Act includes many provisions that are intended to prevent foreign terrorists from entering the US, particularly through Canada. Authorities can detain and deport any alien terrorists and those who support them.

Should the Patriot Act Be Eliminated?

There are many critics of the Patriot Act who say that the law should be eliminated. They argue that the act erodes the personal liberties and privacy rights guaranteed to citizens in the Constitution. They point out that many of the provisions in the Patriot Act violate the Fourth Amendment of the Constitution regarding search and seizure. Generally, US laws regarding searches and seizures require that law enforcement officers prove to a judge that there is a reasonable suspicion of criminal activity or probable cause of illegal behavior prior to undertaking an investigation that infringes upon a person's privacy. However, under the Patriot Act, law enforcement officers are permitted to review a person's private records without proving that the person being investigated is an "agent of a foreign power," or that the records are somehow related to possible terrorist criminal activity. Instead, they are only required to indicate that the search is related to an ongoing investigation into possible terrorism or foreign intelligence. The agents are not required to show evidence or proof of wrongdoing on the part of the suspect, and in many cases the presiding judge does not have the power to reject the application. Thus, under the Patriot Act, law enforcement can search (and seize) personal records or other evidence without first proving probable cause to a judge.

Further, many of these searches do not require that the suspect be informed that law enforcement performed the investigation. This removes a critical check on the government's power and potential for abuse. Those who are the target of a search lose the ability to question the need for the search or that proper procedures were followed by police. They also point out that the Patriot Act authorizes the use of this technique for any crime, no matter how minor, and not just those related to terrorism.

When it comes to the use of roving wiretaps and lone wolf wiretaps, it is argued that these also violate the Fourth Amendment, which states that a warrant must show the "place to be searched, and the persons or things to be seized." Now, agents do not need to demonstrate to a judge that the phones or computers are being used by a particular suspect under investigation, or even identify the person who is the subject of the investigation. They also do not need to identify the information they seek to collect from that device. Opponents argue that this provision of the Patriot Act is unconstitutional and that these taps could result in privacy violations of anyone who comes into casual contact with the person under investigation.

Civil libertarians point out that the expanded investigative powers given to law enforcement in the Patriot Act means that police can search an individual's personal financial records, medical histories, Internet searches, books purchased at a bookstore, material borrowed from a library, travel patterns, or any other activity for which there is a record. Moreover, an agency is required to provide that information to law enforcement without disclosing to the individual that their records have been requested (the gag order). It has been pointed out that these gag orders are a violation of a person's First Amendment rights of freedom of speech because they prohibit a person or agency (e.g., a video store owner, a librarian) from telling someone about the searches performed.

Other criticisms revolve around the changes in the border policies with Canada. Because of the Patriot Act, travel and trade with that country have become much more difficult. There are longer lines and longer waiting periods to enter the US, resulting in less travel and tourism. The demands made by the US for increased information sharing have angered many Canadian citizens who feel that the US is "bullying" them into providing unnecessary personal information that could be used inappropriately. Many Canadians also feel that the US is making demands that Canada increase their border security, a policy to which many Canadians do not agree.

While many criticize the Patriot Act, there are many supporters of the law who deem it necessary in the post-9/11 era to keep Americans safe from terrorists, both international and domestic, who carefully plan acts of violence and who have been trained to evade detection. They point out that the new investigative powers are needed to give law enforcement the ability to use surveillance against those who are suspected of committing acts of terrorism. Now, law enforcement can review a person's records and communications more easily to determine if plans are being made to commit violence. The investigations can be done covertly, without tipping off the suspect. In the end, the goal is to make it easier for law enforcement to detect possible acts of terrorism before they occur. It is essential that law enforcement have the ability to investigate in more advanced ways than in the past, and the Patriot Act provides for this. It is also said that the terrorists are using non-traditional criminal techniques to carry out their crimes, so law enforcement must have advanced investigative techniques as well.

The law also encourages increased communication and cooperation between law enforcement agencies. This is obviously critical as separate agencies may collect intelligence information they believe is isolated, when in fact it is not. Increased information sharing between agencies, both domestic and international, will allow for better and quicker detection of possible terrorist activities.

Those who support the law argue that no law abiding citizen has anything to fear from the Patriot Act. Chances are, investigators will not be interested in the routine activities of the average citizen. Additionally, legal protections against law enforcement abuses still exist so if a person believes their rights have been ignored, a court will review the facts. As another check, there will be a constant review of the controversial aspects of the law. Many of the provisions in the act must be renewed after a few years by the members of Congress. That means if there are indications that law enforcement is abusing their powers, the law can be revised, amended, or allowed to expire.

Another motivation for maintaining the Patriot Act is that it increases security at the border so that individuals intending to carry out acts of terror will be caught before entering the country. The long waiting times that occurred in the aftermath of new policies will eventually be reduced as more personnel are hired and advanced technology is implemented. That has already begun in some border crossing stations. The law does not preclude approved travelers from entering the US, or legal immigrants from becoming citizens.

Conclusion

It is a foregone conclusion that the world is a more dangerous place than it once was. Advancements in technology, communications, and travel, although beneficial in many ways, have also made it easier for terrorists to carry out acts of violence against Americans. The Patriot Act was intended to enhance the nation's security by giving law enforcement investigative powers. At the same time, these expanded powers have angered many civil libertarians who believe that the provisions of the new law erode American's freedoms and violate citizen's constitutional rights. The Patriot Act has also made significant changes in the border policies with Canada, angering many Canadian residents as well. Calls for revising or eliminating the Patriot Act have come from many diverse groups, but what should be done remains unclear.

To what extent will Americans give up their privacy in order to protect their safety? It is, to some extent, a personal issue. Some are more willing to allow the government to read their e-mails than others. There is no doubt that the nation will continue to struggle with this question in the years to come as terrorists devise new methods to attack the US and seek to cause harm to Americans and those who visit there.

Endnotes

1. George W. Bush. (October 26, 2001). "Remarks on Signing the USA PATRIOT ACT of 2001." Online by Gerhard Peters and John T. Woolley, *The American Presidency Project*. Retrieved from http://www.presidency.ucsb.edu/ws/?pid=63850.

2. Doyle, Charles. (April 18, 2002). "The USA PATRIOT ACT: A Sketch." Congressional Research Service, Library of Congress.

3. "National Security Letters." (January 10, 2011). American Civil Liberties Union, Retrieved from https://www.aclu.org/national-security-technology-and-liberty/national-security-letters; Mueller, Robert S., III, (March 27, 2007). "Statement Before the Senate Committee on the Judiciary. Retrieved from http://www.fbi.gov/news/testimony/the-fbis-use-of-national-security-letters-2.

4. "Surveillance Under the USA PATRIOT Act" (December 10, 2010). American Civil Liberties Union. Retrieved from https://www.aclu.org/print/national-security/surveillance-under-usa-patriot-act.

5. "How PATRIOT Threatens Online Civil Liberties" Electronic Frontier Foundation. Retrieved from http://w2.eff.org/patriot/why.php; "How the USA-Patriot Act Expands Law Enforcement "Sneak and Peek" Warrants" (March 7, 2002). American Civil Liberties Union. Retrieved from https://www.aclu.org/print/technology-and-liberty/how-usa-patriot-act-expands.

6. DeRosa, Mary. (2005). "Section 215: Access to Business Records under FISA and Section 214: Pen Register and Trap and Trace Authority under FISA: A Summary." Patriot Debates, American Bar Association. Retrieved from http://apps.americanbar.org/natsecurity/

patriotdebates/sections-214-and-215; "Section 214" Patriot Debates, American Bar Association. Retrieved from http://apps.americanbar.org/natsecurity/patriotdebates/act-section-214; Abramson, Larry And Maria Godoy. (December 16, 2005). "The Patriot Act: Key Controversies" National Public Radio. Retrieved from http://www.npr.org/news/specials/patriotact/patriotactdeal.html.

7. "Analysis of the USA Patriot Act related to Libraries" American Library Association. Retrieved from http://www.ala.org/offices/oif/ifissues/issuesrelatedlinks/usapatriotactanalysis; DeRosa, Mary. (2005). "Section 215: Access to Business Records under FISA and Section 214: Pen Register and Trap and Trace Authority under FISA: A Summary" Patriot Debates, American Bar Association. Retrieved from http://apps.americanbar.org/natsecurity/patriotdebates/sections-214-and-215; "Section 214" Patriot Debates, American Bar Association. Retrieved from http://apps.americanbar.org/natsecurity/patriotdebates/act-section-214.

8. "EFF Analysis of the Provisions of the USA Patriot Act." (October 27, 2003). Electronic Frontier Foundation; Retrieved from http://w2.eff.org/Privacy/Surveillance/Terrorism/20011031_eff_usa_patriot; "News" Electronic Privacy Information Center. Retrieved from http://epic.org/privacy/terrorism/usapatriot/; Abramson, Larry and Maria Godoy. (December 16, 2005). "The Patriot Act: Key Controversies" National Public Radio. Retrieved from http://www.npr.org/news/specials/patriotact/patriotactdeal.html.

9. "EFF Analysis of the Provisions of the USA Patriot Act." (October 27, 2003). Electronic Frontier Foundation. Retrieved from http://w2.eff.org/Privacy/Surveillance/Terrorism/20011031_eff_usa_patriot; "News" Electronic Privacy Information Center. Retrieved from http://epic.org/privacy/terrorism/usapatriot/; Abramson, Larry and Maria Godoy. (December 16, 2005). "The Patriot Act: Key Controversies" National Public Radio. Retrieved from http://www.npr.org/news/specials/patriotact/patriotactdeal.html.

10. "EFF Analysis of the Provisions of the USA Patriot Act." (October 27, 2003). Electronic Frontier Foundation. Retrieved from http://w2.eff.org/Privacy/Surveillance/Terrorism/20011031_eff_usa_patriot; "News" Electronic Privacy Information Center. Retrieved from http://epic.org/privacy/terrorism/usapatriot/; Abramson, Larry and Maria Godoy. (December 16, 2005). "The Patriot Act: Key Controversies" National Public Radio. Retrieved from http://www.npr.org/news/specials/patriotact/patriotactdeal.html.

11. Sales, Nathan A. (September 8, 2011). "A Vital Weapon" *New York Times*. Retrieved from http://www.nytimes.com/roomfordebate/2011/09/07/do-we-still-need-the-patriot-act.

12. Whittaker, Zack. (December 4, 2012). "Patriot Act can 'obtain' Data in Europe, Researchers Say." CBS News. Retrieved from http://www.cbsnews.com/news/patriot_act_can_obtain-Data-in-europe-researchers-say/.

13. U.S. Department of Justice, "The USA Patriot Act: Preserving Life and Liberty" Retrieved from http://www.justice.gov/archive/ll/what_is_the_patriot_act.pdf.

14. Bradbury, Susan L. and Daniel E. Turbeville III. (2009). "Are Enhanced Trade and Enhanced Security Mutually Exclusive? The Western Canada-US Borderland in a Post-9/11 World." *American Review of Canadian Studies*, 39: 3, 317-340: 320-321.

15. Sands, Christopher (2009). "Toward a New Frontier: Improving the U.S. Canadian Border." Washington, D.C.: The Brookings Institution.

16. Jason Ackleson (2009). "From 'Thin' to 'Thick' (and Back Again?): The Politics and Policies of the Contemporary US-Canada Border." *American Review of Canadian Studies"* Vol 39, No. 4, pp. 336-351.

17. Herring, Chris. (August 14, 2009). "At Canada Border, Businesses Take a Hit." *The Wall Street Journal*; Retrieved from http://online.wsj.com/article/SB125020948175430687.html.

18. Bradbury, Susan L. and Daniel E. Turbeville III. (2009). "Are Enhanced Trade and Enhanced Security Mutually Exclusive? The Western Canada-US Borderland in a Post-9/11 World." *American Review of Canadian Studies*, 39: 3, 317-340: 323.

19. Berry, Donald. (2003). "Managing Canada-US Relations in the Post-9/11 Era: Do We Need a Big Idea?" Center for Strategic and International Studies, Policy Paper on the Americas, Volume XIV, Study 11: 11; Pardy, Guy. (September 2011). "Shared Vision or Myopia: The Politics of Perimeter Security and Economic Competitiveness." Rideau Institute. Retrieved from www.rideauinstitute.ca; Bradbury, Susan L. and Daniel E. Turbeville III, (2009). "Are Enhanced Trade and Enhanced Security Mutually Exclusive? The Western Canada-US Borderland in a Post-9/11 World." *American Review of Canadian Studies*, 39: 3, 317-340:322.

20. Susan L. Bradbury and Daniel E. Turbeville III. (2009). "Are Enhanced Trade and Enhanced Security Mutually Exclusive? The Western Canada-U.S. Borderland in a Post-9/11 World" *American Review of Canadian Studies* 38:3, 317-340: 321.

21. Denholm Crosby, Ann. (2010). "Canada-US Defence Relations: Weapons of Mass Control and a Praxis of Mass Resistance" in J. Marshall Beier and Lana Wylie, eds. *Canadian Foreign Policy in Critical Perspective*. (Ontario: Oxford University Press), pp. 29-43: 30.

22. Hale, Geoffrey (2012). *So Near Yet So Far: The Public and Hidden Worlds of Canada-US Relations*. Vancouver, BC: UBC Press: 39.

23. Jockel, Joseph T., "North American Defense Relations: Some Preliminary Thoughts," in Donald Barry, ed., Toward a North American Community? Canada, the United States, and Mexico. (Boulder: Westview Press, 1995), 212; cited in Donald Barry and Duane Bratt (2008). "Defense Against Help: Explaining Canada-US Security Relations." *American Review of Canadian Studies*, 38: 1, 63-89: 67.

Chapter 10

Cybersecurity: How Protected Is America's Critical Infrastructure?

Introduction

In April 2007, the tiny country of Estonia announced to the world that their country was "under a cyberattack" by the Russian government. In a series of massive coordinated denial-of-service (DoS) attacks, the Estonian public and private sectors were crippled. Primary targets were the Estonian presidency and its Parliament, almost all of the country's government ministries, two of the biggest banks, and three of the country's largest news organizations.[1] These cyberattacks were launched in protest after the Estonian government removed the Bronze Soldier statue in Tallinn, a controversial Soviet war monument erected in 1947.[2] Considered to be the most "wired" and advanced country in all of Europe, Estonia suffered greatly in this intent to shut down their information infrastructure. The attacks used Botnets (swarms of computers hijacked by malicious code) to overload sites and networks by saturating them with phony requests for information.[3] Routers were damaged, routing tables were changed, and DNS servers were overloaded. In total, these attacks lasted about three weeks and involved an estimated 1 million computers.[4] Citizens were unable to execute financial transactions, including the use of ATM machines. At the peak of the attack, those who wanted to use payment cards for groceries or gas had to wait because the traffic overload stalled the banks' ability to verify funds.[5]

Some have claimed that Estonia was the first real "cyberwar"; others maintain it was the first time a country claimed publically it was under attack.[6] Regardless, the lessons from Estonia are clear: cyberattacks and cyberwarfare are a real threat. We live in a digital world. We rely on portable devices and the information they store for banking, commerce, infrastructure, communications, transportation, entertainment, and virtually every other aspect of our lives.

As the world becomes more intertwined with digital technologies and the internet, we face newer and unpredictable cyber threats. In some cases, the world is applying these technologies faster than our ability to understand the security implications and mitigate potential risks.[7]

In recent years cyber intrusions and attacks have increased dramatically, exposing sensitive personal and business information, disrupting critical operations, and imposing high costs on the economy. Testifying before the Senate Homeland Security Committee in 2013, FBI Director James B. Comey warned that cyberattacks are increasingly becoming the primary threat against the US.[8] In 2014 James Clapper, the Director of National Intelligence testified that the cyber risk is so dire, it tops the list of global threats for the second consecutive year, surpassing terrorism, espionage, and dangers posed by weapons of mass destruction.[9]

What are the risks of cyberattacks on our US critical infrastructure? How well-protected is the US power grid? How vulnerable are our nuclear power plants and other critical infrastructures? What efforts are in place to thwart would be "hackers" and why is cybersecurity considered one of the most pressing threats of our time? This chapter explores the serious issue of cybersecurity and the potential risks of attacks on US soil.

What Is Cybersecurity?

Defined as "measures taken to protect a computer or computer system (as on the internet) against unauthorized access or attack," cybersecurity has become one of the most pressing concerns of our time. Each day the US faces a myriad of threats in cyberspace, from the theft of US intellectual property through cyber intrusions to denial-of-service attacks against public facing websites and attempted intrusions of US critical infrastructures.[10] In the private sector, big-box retailers like Target and Home Depot have been attacked by hackers breaking into their computer systems and stealing millions of customer credit card and debit card numbers. Even the newest of technologies, the iCloud, was compromised when several celebrities' nude photos were hacked from their iCloud accounts and posted on the web.

In May 2009, President Barack Obama declared the safety of our digital infrastructure to be a national security priority. Since then, efforts have been underway to strengthen our national policy on critical infrastructure security and resilience. The Department of Homeland Security (DHS) is the lead agency which manages the nation's cyber threats through its risk management division, the Directorate for National Protection and Programs.[11] In 2014 DHS published the second edition of the *Quadrennial Homeland Security Review* and in it renewed the nation's commitment to safeguarding and securing cyberspace. In it, DHS personnel reports that "We must, over the next four years, continue efforts to address the growing cyber threat, illustrated by the real, pervasive, and ongoing series of attacks on our public and private infrastructure."[12] DHS identifies these strategic priorities as:

- Strengthen the security and resilience of critical infrastructure
- Secure the federal civilian government information technology enterprise
- Advance law enforcement, incident response, and reporting capabilities
- Strengthen the ecosystem.[13]

Critical Infrastructure Protection

One of the cornerstones of homeland security is critical infrastructure protection. The Department of Homeland Security (DHS) defines critical infrastructure as "assets, systems and networks, whether physical or virtual, so vital to the US that their incapacitation or destruction would have a debilitating effect on security, national economic security, public health or safety, or any combination thereof."[14] Cybersecurity or protection of the information technology sector—is part of the critical infrastructure matrix.[15]

Brief History

National policies for the protection of critical infrastructures have evolved over the past 50 years as our government has increasingly recognized the importance of protecting essential infrastructures. One of the earliest attempts at a national strategy can be traced to the Kennedy administration and the establishment of the National Communications System (NCS) in 1963.[16] This move was in response to the 1962 Cuban Missile Crisis and the difficulties President Kennedy and Premier Khruschev had communicating during it. The NCS was established to ensure the federal government's ability to communicate in emergency situations including a nuclear attack. It is interesting to note that the telecommunications industry was the first infrastructure sector to be considered "critical."

In March 1979, FEMA was officially established with President Jimmy Carter's signing of Executive Order 12127. Along with this new entity came the responsibilities for civil defense and hurricane and earthquake risk reduction. In the 1980s our current understanding of critical infrastructure began to evolve when President Reagan, in another executive order, charged the head of each federal department and agency the responsibility of protecting essential resources and facilities within their organizations.

Probably the most significant presidential action on critical infrastructure protection occurred in 1996 when President Clinton established the Presidential Commission on Critical Infrastructure Protection. As a result, Clinton issued Presidential Decision Directive/NSC-63 in May of 1998. PDD-63 established eight critical infrastructure sectors and the foundation of an emerging national strategy. The Marsh Report of 1997 was instrumental in getting these first sectors identified and established the first working definition of infrastructure as "a network of independent, mostly privately-owned, man-made systems that function collaboratively and synergistically to produce and distribute continuous flow of essential goods and services."[17]

A rapid expansion of critical infrastructure protection and risk assessment efforts came in the aftermath of September 11, 2001. Most notably two key documents—the Homeland Security Act of 2002 and the Homeland Security Presidential Directive 7 (HSPD-7)—provided the necessary power for the federal government to develop critical infrastructure protections. HSPD-7 replaced PDD-63 and expanded critical infrastructure to thirteen sectors and added five key resources. Also related to these efforts was the issuing of the Homeland Security Presidential Policy Directive 8 (HSPD-8), the National Preparedness Directive. This required the establishment of a national domestic all-hazards preparedness goal. In all, these documents led to the publication of the first National Infrastructure Protection Plan (NIPP) in 2006 with scheduled revisions every three years. It was revised in 2009 and more recently in 2013.

The NIPP provides the structure for coordination and integration of the wide range of efforts to enhance protection and resiliency of the nation's critical infrastructures and key resources (CIKR) into a single national program. The goal of NIPP is to "build a safer, more secure and resilient America by preventing, deterring, neutralizing, or mitigating the effects of deliberate efforts to destroy, incapacitate, or exploit elements of our nation's CIKR and to strengthen national preparedness, timely response, and rapid recovery of CIKR in the event of an attack, natural disaster, or other emergency."[18] In February 2013, this structure was expanded to include a cybersecurity and resiliency framework issued by President Obama in Presidential Policy Directive—21 (PPD-21) Critical Infrastructure Security and Resilience. This was developed through a collaborative process involving stakeholders from all 16 critical infrastructure sectors, all 50 states, and from all levels of government and industry. The National Infrastructure Protection Plan (NIPP) 2013 was then issued in response to PPD-21. Key concepts addressed in this latest version include a greater focus on integration of cyber and physical security efforts, increased focus on cross sector and cross jurisdictional coordination, and an integration of information-sharing as an essential component of the risk management framework.[19] The current list

**Table 10.1. Critical Infrastructure Sectors As Established by
Presidential Policy Directive 21 (PPD-21)**

Chemical Sector	Defense Industrial Base Sector
Communications Sector	Energy Sector
Dams Sector	Food and Agriculture Sector
Emergency Services Sector	Healthcare and Public Health Sector
Financial Services Sector	Information Technology Sector
Government Facilities Sector	Transportation Systems Sector
Commercial Facilities Sector	Nuclear Reactors, Materials, and Waste Sector
Critical Manufacturing Sector	Water and Wastewater Systems Sector

Source: The Department of Homeland Security Critical Infrastructure Sectors. www.dhs.gov.

of critical infrastructure sectors identified in PPD-21 supersedes those which were previously established by HSPD-7 (see Table 10.1).

Each of these sectors contains physical, human, and cyber elements. The proportion of these elements and the associated vulnerabilities vary between sectors. Some sectors such as Water and Wastewater Systems, Energy, and Government Facilities rely heavily on physical elements while others—like the Financial Services sector—have mostly cyber elements.

Recent government action taken to address cybersecurity risks can be found in the *Framework for Improving Critical Infrastructure Cybersecurity*. Under Executive Order 13636, Improving Critical Infrastructure Cybersecurity, The National Institute of Standards and Technology (NIST) are responsible for leading the development of a voluntary framework for reducing cybersecurity risk to critical infrastructure.[20] Touted as a "living document," it's a collaborative effort between industry and government to detail cybersecurity best practices and standards. The framework is a risk-based approach to managing cybersecurity risk and is composed of three parts:

- **Framework Core**—a template of activities and outcomes that organizations can use with their best practices.

- **Framework Implementation Tiers**—assist organizations rate their cybersecurity readiness based on four levels of maturity.
- **Framework Profile**—helps organizations align their cybersecurity activities with their business requirements, risk tolerances, and resources.[21]

Adoption of the framework is voluntary. But because the framework represents the recommendations of hundreds public and private sector organizations and companies, rather than just government, industry experts are optimistic that businesses will take them seriously.[22]

As with any new effort, the cybersecurity framework is not without its critics. One of the criticisms of the framework is the voluntary nature. Although it is in the interests of critical infrastructure operators to follow the framework, some argue it will still take incentives from Congress and prodding from regulators to ensure widespread adoption. Even if the operators follow the NIST guidelines to the letter, it still may only deter, not thwart, an attack. Furthermore, it does not tell critical infrastructure operators what to do or which tools to use. It is technology-neutral.[23] More government regulation is another criticism leveled against the new framework. Some have called it a "semi-coercive" effort and a back-door attempt at regulating the industry. Those who do not adopt it may also be subject to liability and lawsuits.[24] On the other hand, the strength of the framework is that is allows industry and government to establish standards and best practices for identifying, detecting, protecting against, and responding to, threats and attacks. The need to improve cybersecurity is a goal most everyone can agree on. The framework in this sense is a step in the right direction.

How Protected Is America's Critical Infrastructure?

US Power Grid

The US power grid is a complex network of transmissions and power lines that carry power from plants to consumers. The power grid consists of large, high-voltage power lines and the hardware that links them together. The basic process is simple: electric power is generated at power plants and then moved by transmission lines to substations. A local distribution system, of smaller, lower-voltage transmission lines then moves power from substations to customers. Thomas Edison launched the first commercial power grid, The Pearl Street Station, in lower Manhattan, in 1832. It initially served eighty-five customers and provided electricity to 400 lamps. Today the US has over 160,000 miles of transmission lines that moves power from plants to cities and towns and from one part of the system to another. The grid is designed to handle natural and manmade disasters as well as fluctuations in demand. For example, if demand goes up in one location or a major power line or transmission goes down due to weather, a technical malfunction, or even a terrorist attack, power can be rerouted to prevent blackouts. The grid, however, is not always effective, as the big 2003 blackout in the Eastern connection demonstrated. Lasting two days, the infamous blackout cut off power to over 50 million people in eight states and millions of Canadians in one province. Terrorism was quickly ruled out as a cause. Rather, the blackout was the result of a software bug in the alarm system at a control room at First Energy Corporation in Akron, Ohio. At fault: a section of overgrown trees which were hit by overloaded transmission lines. What should have been a manageable blackout turned into a widespread distress on the electric grid because operators were unaware of the need to re-distribute power. In the final report on the causes of the blackout, the US-Canada Power System Outage Task Force identified poor vegetation management, computer failures, inadequate training, and lack of real-time situational awareness of grid conditions as the main factors behind the disaster.[25]

The US grid is actually three separate grids known as the Western, the Texas, and the Eastern interconnections. An interconnection, also known as a wide area synchronous grid, is a region of interconnected AC power systems operating at the same frequency and phase with one another. This allows all of the independent electrical networks in a particular area to be connected by synchronizing the electrical frequency between them. Each interconnection in turn consists of from one to several regional Reliability Councils overseeing at least part of the total interconnection. These Reliability Councils are comprised of individual utility companies, power producers, and distributors, as well as larger groups/networks of such entities.

While the US power grid is susceptible to natural disasters and manmade errors, as we saw in the 2003 blackout, is it safe from a large-scale attack? Some experts believe it's virtually impossible for an online-only attack to cause a widespread or prolonged outage of the North American power grid.[26] Hackers could penetrate the networks of bulk power providers, but there is a huge gap between that and causing a civilization-ending sustained outage of the grid.[27] Experts knowledgeable about the bulk power system—power generators and high voltage transmission entities—argue that electrical-grid hacking scenarios mostly overlook the engineering expertise necessary to intentionally cause harm to the grid. Because the grid is designed to lose utilities all the time, the ability to cause a nationwide cascading failure for any extended period of time is highly unlikely.[28]

Despite these expert claims, recent events have demonstrated vulnerabilities do exist in the electric grid system. In San Jose, California, for example, just after midnight on April 16, 2013, someone slipped into underground tunnels and cut the phone lines running into the PG&E Metcalf power substation. Then two snipers proceeded to fire over 100 rounds into the substation in a matter of nineteen minutes, knocking out seventeen transformers. While the electric company was able to prevent a widespread blackout, security officials feared the attack could be a dry run for a larger-scale terrorist attack.[29] In October 2013, the US Justice Department charged an individual with attacks on the transmission grid in Arkansas, including a deliberate fire set at a substation in Lonoke County. Although the fire destroyed the substation, electrical service was not interrupted.[30] At a Progress Energy Substation in Florida, a rile attack ruptured a transformer oil tank, resulting in an explosion and local blackout.[31]

The US power grid is arguably the most important sector of the critical infrastructure, since none of the other sectors could function without it. Substations, generation facilities, and control centers are just a portion of the vulnerabilities in the overall electric grid. Weaknesses within the software, supply chain, operational technologies, and personnel all pose cyber threats.[32] So what efforts are being put forth to protect the grid?

The main risk from a physical attack against the electric power grid—primarily towers and transformers—is a widespread power outage lasting for days or longer. As discussed above, utilities regularly experience damage to transmission towers due to both weather and malicious activities and are able to recover from this damage fairly rapidly. Therefore, physical attacks on towers generally have not resulted in widespread or long-lasting outages.[33] Similarly, the power industry has experienced mechanical failure of individual HV transformers, however no region in the US has experienced simultaneous failures of multiple HV transformers. Experts have predicted that a coordinated and simultaneous attack on multiple HV transformers could have severe implications over a widespread area. Such an event would result not only in massive blackouts, but also have serious economic and social consequences.[34] Furthermore, it is very difficult to restore a damaged HV transformer substation. Most HV transformers currently in use are custom designed and, therefore, cannot be generally interchanged.[35] Transformer substations cost $3–5 million dollars for each unit, which in turn makes keeping an inventory of spare HV transformers solely as an emergency replacement expensive.[36]

A recent Congressional Research Service report on the physical security of the power grid identified a number of measures to help prevent an intentional attack against a transformer substation.[37] Although these will vary depending upon the substation's particular configuration and operating profile, a general set of categories are as follows:

- **Protecting information**—about critical HV substations; for example, engineering drawings, power flow modeling runs, and site security information which could be useful to a potential attacker.
- **Surveillance and monitoring**—through the use of video cameras, motion detectors, imaging, acoustical monitors, aerial drones, and periodic inspection by security employees.
- **Restricting physical access**—limiting entry to necessary employees, installing electronic locks and other access controls, and erecting physical barriers and controls for vehicle entry. Another option is to post full-time guards.
- **Shielding assets**—from offsite attacks using visual barriers such as opaque or hardened fencing, erecting taller fences, or erecting protective walls.
- **Modifying substation designs**—to make them more resistant to physical damage.[38]

In addition to these measures, the electric utility industry and government agencies have engaged in a number of initiatives to secure HV transformers from attacks and to improve resilience. These initiatives include coordination and information sharing, spare equipment programs, security standards, and grid security exercises.[39]

While there is widespread agreement among government, utilities, and manufacturers that HV transformers in the US are vulnerable to a terrorist attack, the most serious of such attacks would require operational information and a certain level of sophistication on the part of the potential attackers.[40] However, the Metcalf incident and others exposed the weaknesses in the US critical infrastructure. Furthermore, there continues to be uncertainty about the risk of terror attacks on the power grid, and what measures are economically justified in addressing them.[41]

Nuclear Power Plants

In the aftermath of September 11, 2001, the physical security of nuclear power plants and their vulnerability to the deliberate acts of terrorism was elevated to a national security issue. Congress enacted new security requirements and has repeatedly focused attention on regulation and enforcement by the Nuclear Regulatory Commission (NRC).[42] The US nuclear energy industry is one of the few industries where security is regulated by the federal government. The Energy Policy Act of 2005 (EPACT05, P.L. 109-58) imposed specific criteria for NRC to consider in revisiting the "Design Basis Threat (DBT)," which specifies the maximum severity of potential attacks that a nuclear plant's security force must be capable of repelling.[43] There are currently 62 commercially operated nuclear power plants with 100 nuclear reactors operating in 31 states in the US. Thirty-five of these plants have two or more reactors.[44] Many of these were designed in the 1960s and 70s, and are controlled primarily by analog systems that are resistant to cyberattacks. However as these plants age, obsolete technology is being replaced with digital technologies and modern networking and communications equipment, resulting in potential cyber vulnerabilities.[45]

A classic debate over critical infrastructures and their vulnerability to a cyberattack centers on the argument that the process control systems use specialized hardware and propriety protocols. Therefore they are immune to internet hackers. However, since the 1990s, many of these control systems have been integrated with computer networks build from commercial off-the-shelf operating systems such as Windows and Unix.[46] Although this has simplified the task of managing facilities remotely, it has made the process control systems (PCS) vulnerable to attacks over the internet. On the one side, alarmists point to these connections as vulnerabilities that pose a huge threat. Others dismiss these fears claiming that the necessary measures to prevent a cyberattack have already been implemented with layers of security and federal regulations.[47] In truth, vulnerability of the process control systems that support our nuclear power plants lie somewhere in between this debate. For many years, operators of process control systems believed that they were invulnerable to cyberattacks for two reasons: (1) they are isolated from the internet, and (2) PCS generally use proprietary protocols and specialized hardware not compatible with ordinary computers and common networks. However, there has been a steady move towards the use of open protocols and off-the-shelf hardware to manage process control systems, even connecting them to the internet— sometimes inadvertently.[48] Some argue this increases the risk for replicating a nuclear reactor shutdown through a cyberattack.

How protected are our nuclear facilities? What would a cyberattack entail? A look at the history of cyber incidents offers a glimpse into the potential risks.

Davis-Besse Worm Infection

In January 2003, a "Slammer" worm exploited a vulnerability in Microsoft SQL Server, infecting 75,000 servers worldwide. Among the victims was the Davis-Besse nuclear power plant near Oak Harbor, Ohio. The worm traveled from a consultant's network, to the corporate network of First Energy Nuclear, the licensee for Davis-Besse, then to the process control network for the plant. Corporate and control networks were clogged for well over four hours. As a result, the plant personnel could not access the Safety Parameter Display System (SPDS), which shows sensitive data about the reactor core—and would indicate meltdown conditions. This incident highlighted the fact that most nuclear power plants, by retrofitting their SCADA systems for remote monitoring from their corporate network, had unknowingly connected their control networks to the internet. At the time, the NRC did not permit remote operation of plant functions, however that policy has changed.[49]

Browns Ferry Shutdown

In August 2006, Unit 3 of the Browns Ferry nuclear power plant in Alabama was manually shut down after the failure of both reactor and recirculation pumps and the condensate demineralizer controller.[50] This was necessary because without the recirculation pumps, the power plant could not cool the reactor, making a shutdown necessary to avoid melting the reactor core. Both the recirculation pumps and demineralizer controller have embedded microprocessors that can communicate data over the ethernet. Both devices however, are also prone to failure in high-traffic environments. The Browns Ferry network produced more traffic than its controllers could handle. While the failure was not the result of a cyberattack, the incident demonstrates the effect one component can have upon the entire PC network. Combined with the Davis-Besse worm infection, the Browns Ferry shutdown presents a possible attack scenario.[51]

Hatch Automatic Shutdown

In March 2008, Unit 2 of the Hatch nuclear power plant near Baxley, Georgia, automatically shut down after an engineer applied a software update to a single computer on the plant's business network. Used to collect diagnostic data from the process control network, the computer was updated and designed to synchronize data on both networks. When the engineer rebooted the computer, the synchronization program reset the data on the control network. The control systems interpreted the reset as a sudden drop in the reactor's water reservoir and initiated an automatic shutdown.[52] While not a critical incident, the mistake here shows how malicious hackers could make simple changes to a business network that end up affecting a nuclear reactor.[53]

Stuxnet

Stuxnet is a computer worm with cyber-weaponry characteristics. It is purpose-built, technologically sophisticated, precisely engineered, and complex.[54] It is designed to attack industrial control systems that are used to monitor and control large scale industrial facilities like power plants, dams, waste processing systems, and other similar operations. It allows the attackers to take control of these operations without the operators knowing. In 2010, the Stuxnet worm infiltrated Iran's secret Natanz nuclear fuel enrichment facility and is believed to have destroyed 984 centrifuges. An analysis of the event found that Stuxnet may have been created for that purpose. However it also demonstrates the limitations that even a sophisticated adversary would face in launching an attack against process control systems. Findings from the incident further revealed that the Stuxnet attack, though it successfully disrupted the Iranian centrifuge program, did not slow down Iran's accumulation of low-enriched uranium. While the attack is noted for its sophistication, it did not pose an epic threat to Iran.[55] Rather, the Stuxnet attack against the Iranian nuclear program demonstrates the impact that a sophisticated adversary with a detailed knowledge of process control systems can have on critical infrastructures.[56]

Following the 9/11 attacks greater attention was drawn to the potential severity of credible terrorist threats. The Nuclear Regulatory Commission (NRC) evaluated the extent to which nuclear plant security forces should be able to defend against such threats and ordered a strengthening of the Design Basis Threat (DBT), along with other security measures.[57] For example, plant data networks (PDN) have advanced to improve the efficiency and reliability of the protection, control, and monitoring of systems. Policies have been developed which create better plans to secure network access and its operation. In addition, monitoring the network and using newer techniques such as the application of digital signatures to ensure that the loaded code originated from a legitimate engineering station have been implemented. [58] However despite these increased efforts, some argue the potential of cyberattacks has escalated into a serious threat for nuclear power plants.

In a report prepared by the Nuclear Proliferation Prevention Project (NPPP), "Protecting US Nuclear Facilities from Terrorist Attacks: Re-assessing the Current Design Basis Threat," it was concluded that US commercial and research nuclear facilities remain inadequately protected against two credible threats. These are the theft of bomb-grade material to make a nuclear weapon, and sabotage attacks intended to cause a reactor meltdown.[59] The report also found that none of the 104 commercial nuclear power reactors in the US is protected against a maximum credible terrorist attack, similar to one pulled off on 9/11.[60] Additionally, the report found:

- Those nuclear power plants that are vulnerable to terrorist attacks from the sea are not required to protect against such ship-borne attacks. Examples include Diablo Canyon in California, St. Lucie in Florida, Brunswick in North Carolina, Surry in Virginia, Indian Point in New York, Millstone in Connecticut, Pilgrim in Massachusetts, and the South Texas Project.[61]

- Three civilian research reactors fueled with bomb-grade uranium are vulnerable to theft to make nuclear weapons. The University of Missouri in Columbia, the Massachusetts Institute of Technology in Cambridge, and the National Institute of Standards and Technology (located just 2 dozen miles from the White House in D.C.) are the three reactors. These facilities are not defended against a posited terrorist threat, unlike military facilities that hold the same material.[62]

Although some US government nuclear facilities are protected by or against all of the above threats, others remain unprotected and are deemed to have less credible threats. Furthermore, security officials claim that terrorists do not value some of the sites or that the consequences would not be catastrophic.[63] The threat to digital systems at US nuclear power plants is considerable, but the sector is actually better prepared to defend itself against potentially devastating cyberattacks than most other utilities. While some cybersecurity incidents have occurred at nuclear power plants, so far the potential for damaging a nuclear reactor appears theoretical.[64] Nuclear power plants must comply with stronger safety regulations and inspections and many believe this prevents potential hackers from triggering a meltdown. Thus far, no catastrophic damage has resulted from a cyberattack against a nuclear facility.

Conversely, with the increasing digitalization of instrumentation and control systems and the adoption of the open-system architecture based on the information technology (IT), the potential of cyberattacks on nuclear power plants has escalated. Even in the most strictly controlled access environments and "air-gap" type network structures (meaning the network is physically isolated from the public internet), cyber threats to nuclear power plants have become real.[65] Furthermore, new cyberattacks on malicious software programs spawned by Stuxnet have the potential to be smarter, stronger, and more resilient. The nuclear industry needs to consider all cybersecurity issues and potential scenarios.

Other Critical Infrastructures

All 16 critical infrastructure sectors must be secured from cybersecurity threats. Pipelines, water and waste water systems, and the financial services sector are just a few examples. Each sector increasingly relies on digital technology and potential access through the internet leaves these vulnerable to attacks.

Pipelines

There are approximately half a million miles of high-volume pipeline transporting natural gas, oil, and other hazardous liquids across the US. Integral to

US energy supply, these pipelines also have links to other critical infrastructures. While pipelines are vulnerable to accidents, they may also be intentionally damaged by vandals and terrorists. The supervisory control and data acquisition (SCADA) systems may also be susceptible to cyberattacks. In June 2007, the US Department of Justice arrested members of a terrorist group planning to attack jet fuel pipelines and storage tanks at the JFK Airport in New York.[66]

Water and Waste Water Systems

There are approximately 160,000 public drinking water systems and more than 16,000 publically owned wastewater treatment systems in the US. The water and waste water system is vulnerable to a variety of attacks including contamination with deadly agents, physical attacks, and cyberattacks. Cyber espionage and denial-of-service attacks against industrial control systems are a major concern. Reports have indicated that cyber incidents at water and waste water plants have gone up by as much as 60 percent in recent years.[67]

Financial Services Sector

Represents a vital component of our critical infrastructure. Financial institutions provide a broad array of products allowing customers to deposit funds and make payments to other parties; provide credit and liquidity to customers; invest funds; and transfer financial risks between customers.[68] The sector includes more than 18,800 federally insured depository institutions. Cyberattacks against financial institutions have become more frequent, more sophisticated, and more widespread. J.P. Morgan, Goldman Sachs, Bank of America, and Wells Fargo are some of the larger financial institutions which have recently been targeted by cyber criminals.

National Cybersecurity and Critical Infrastructure Protection Act 2014

H.R. 3696 The National Cybersecurity and Critical Infrastructure Protection Act amends the Homeland Security Act of 2002 to improve cybersecurity and critical infrastructure protection. Introduced on December 11, 2013, by Rep. Michael McCaul (R-TX), the bill would direct DHS to leverage industry-led organizations to facilitate critical infrastructure protection and incident response. One of the key provisions is the Homeland Security Cybersecurity Boots-on-the-Ground Act, which would upon passage require the Secretary of Homeland Security to establish cybersecurity occupation classifications, assess the cybersecurity workforce, and develop a strategy to identify gaps in the cybersecurity workforce, among other purposes.[69] The bill passed in the House on July 24, 2014, and goes to Senate for the next consideration.

Conclusion

Cyberattacks present significant threats to the US economy and to national security. Protecting our critical infrastructure has become increasingly important as technology advances and many of our systems rely entirely on digital technologies. The lessons from Estonia are clear: cyberattacks and cyberwarfare are real threats and nations need to be better prepared. Combating cyber threats is a shared responsibility. By building stronger partnerships with public, private, and non-profit sectors, the US can more fully secure the nation's cyber networks.

While many experts agree that critical infrastructure is increasingly vulnerable to cyberattacks, there is debate over which sectors are more at risk. Some argue that the electric power grid is too sophisticated for hackers to successfully attack the entire system. Others maintain that increased digitalization and heavy reliance on the internet leave potential gaps for hackers to insert viruses, malicious codes, and worms. Similarly, nuclear power plants are believed to be at risk due to the process control system (PCS) that are increasingly being updated with open protocols and off-the-shelf hardware. But some argue the layers of security and federal regulations make it simply impossible to shut down reactors through cyber intrusions. Officials and experts do agree, however, that the country has begun to pay more attention to cybersecurity over the last several years. Still, more needs to be done to counter the ever-evolving threat to our nation's critical infrastructure. The Cybersecurity Framework 1.0 and the pending National Cybersecurity and Critical Infrastructure Protection Act of 2014, along with the Homeland Security Cybersecurity Boots-on-the-Ground Act, are steps in the right direction. Only time will tell if these efforts are successful enough to secure the entire US cyber system.

Endnotes

1. Traynor, I. (2007) "Russia accused of unleashing cyberwar to disable Estonia." *The Guardian*. Retrieved online at www.theguardian.com.

2. Richards, J. (2009) "Denial-of-Service: The Estonian Cyber-Warfare and Its Implications for U.S. National Security." *International Affairs Review*. Vol XVIII, No. 1: April 4, 2009.

3. Coleman, K. (2007) "World War III: A cyber war has begun." A White Paper. *The Technolytics Institute*.

4. Coleman, K. (2007) "World War III: A cyber war has begun." A White Paper. *The Technolytics Institute.*

5. Coleman, K. (2007) "World War III: A cyber war has begun." A White Paper. *The Technolytics Institute.*

6. Rheman, S. (2013, January 14). "Estonia's Lessons in Cyberwarfare." *U.S. News World Report.* Retrieved online at www.usnews.com.

7. Clapper, J.R. Statement of Record, Senate Select Committee on Intelligence. *U.S. Intelligence Community WorldWide Threat Assessment,* Hearing, March 12, 2013.

8. Miller, G. (2013, November 13) "FBI director warns of cyberattacks; other security chiefs say terrorism threat altered." *The Washington Post.*

9. Clapper, J.R. Statement of Record, Senate Select Committee on Intelligence. *U.S. Intelligence Community WorldWide Threat Assessment,* Hearing, March 12, 2013.

10. Department Homeland Security 2014 *Quadrenniel Homeland Security Review Report*

11. Bullock. J.A., Haddow, G.D., & Coppola, D.P. (2013) *Introduction to Homeland Security.* 4th edition.

12. Department Homeland Security 2014 *Quadrenniel Homeland Security Review Report*

13. Department Homeland Security 2014 *Quadrenniel Homeland Security Review Report* Fact Sheet.

14. Department of Homeland Security. (2013, November 1). *What is critical infrastructure.* Retrieved from http://www.dhs.gov/what-critical-infrastructure.

15. Bullock. J.A., Haddow, G.D., & Coppola, D.P. (2013) *Introduction to Homeland Security.* 4th edition.

16. Lewis, T.G. (2006). *Critical Infrastructure Protection in Homeland Security.* Wiley Publishing.

17. Lewis, T.G. (2006). *Critical Infrastructure Protection in Homeland Security.* Wiley Publishing.

18. Department of Homeland Security. National Infrastructure Protection Plan (2009).

19. Department of Homeland Security. National Infrastructure Protection Plan (2013).

20. National Institute of Standards and Technology (February 12, 2014) *Framework for Improving Critical Infrastructure Cybersecurity* 1.0.

21. National Institute of Standards and Technology (February 12, 2014) *Framework for Improving Critical Infrastructure Cybersecurity* 1.0.

22. Jackson W. (2014, April 21) "Protecting Critical Infrastructure: A new Approach" *Information Week.* Retrieved online at www.informationweek.com.

23. Jackson W. (2014, April 21) "Protecting Critical Infrastructure: A new Approach" *Information Week.* Retrieved online at www.informationweek.com.

24. Jackson W. (2014, April 21) "Protecting Critical Infrastructure: A new Approach" *Information Week.* Retrieved online at www.informationweek.com.

25. U.S.-Canada Power System Outage Task Force (August, 2004) *Final Report on the August 14, 2003 Blackout in the United States and Canada: Causes and Recommendations.*

26. Perera, D. (2014, September 10) "U.S. grid safe from large-scale attack, experts say." *Politico.* Retrieved online at www.politico.com.

27. Perera, D. (2014, September 10) "U.S. grid safe from large-scale attack, experts say." *Politico.* Retrieved online at www.politico.com.

28. Perera, D. (2014, September 10) "U.S. grid safe from large-scale attack, experts say." *Politico.* Retrieved online at: http://www.politico.com"www.politico.com.

29. Ferris, J. (2014, February 19). "Terrorist Attack Shows Vulnerability in Critical Infrastructure." *Heritage Foundation.*

30. Carter, C.J. (2013, October 12) "Arkansas Man Charged in Connection with Power Grid Sabotage," CNN.

31. Parfomak, P.W. (2014, June 17) "Physical Security of the U.S. Power Grid: High-Voltage Transformer Substations." CRS Report R43604. Retrieved online at www.crs.gov.

32. Ferris, J. (2014, February 19). "Terrorist Attack Shows Vulnerability in Critical Infrastructure." *Heritage Foundation.*

33. Parfomak, P.W. (2014, June 17) "Physical Security of the U.S. Power Grid: High-Voltage Transformer Substations." CRS Report R43604. Retrieved online at www.crs.gov.

34. Parfomak, P.W. (2014, June 17) "Physical Security of the U.S. Power Grid: High-Voltage Transformer Substations." CRS Report R43604. Retrieved online at www.crs.gov.

35. Parfomak, P.W. (2014, June 17) "Physical Security of the U.S. Power Grid: High-Voltage Transformer Substations." CRS Report R43604, p. 7. Retrieved online at www.crs.gov.

36. Parfomak, P.W. (2014, June 17) "Physical Security of the U.S. Power Grid: High-Voltage Transformer Substations." CRS Report R43604, p. 7. Retrieved online at www.crs.gov.

37. Parfomak, P.W. (2014, June 17) "Physical Security of the U.S. Power Grid: High-Voltage Transformer Substations." CRS Report R43604, Retrieved online at www.crs.gov.

38. Parfomak, P.W. (2014, June 17) "Physical Security of the U.S. Power Grid: High-Voltage Transformer Substations." CRS Report R43604, p. 9. Retrieved online at www.crs.gov.

39. Parfomak, P.W. (2014, June 17) "Physical Security of the U.S. Power Grid: High-Voltage Transformer Substations." CRS Report R43604. Retrieved online at www.crs.gov.

40. Parfomak, P.W. (2014, June 17) "Physical Security of the U.S. Power Grid: High-Voltage Transformer Substations." CRS Report R43604, p. 26 Retrieved online at www.crs.gov.

41. Parfomak, P.W. (2014, June 17) "Physical Security of the U.S. Power Grid: High-Voltage Transformer Substations." CRS Report R43604, p. 7. Retrieved online at www.crs.gov.

42. Holt, M. & Andrews A. (2014, January 3). "Nuclear Power Plant Security and Vulnerabilities." Congressional Research Service Report (CRS) RL34331. Retrieved online at www.crs.gov.

43. Holt, M. & Andrews A. (2014, January 3). "Nuclear Power Plant Security and Vulnerabilities." Congressional Research Service Report (CRS) RL34331, p. 7 Retrieved online at www.crs.gov.

44. U.S. Energy Information Administration. Independent Statistics & Analysis.

45. Weiss, J. (2007). Cyber Security in the Control Room. *Power Engineering, 111*(9), 38–44.

46. Kesler, B. (2011) "The Vulnerability of Nuclear Facilities to Cyber Attack." *Strategic Insights*. Vol 10 Issue 1.

47. Kesler, B. (2011) "The Vulnerability of Nuclear Facilities to Cyber Attack." *Strategic Insights*. Vol 10 Issue 1.

48. Kesler, B. (2011) "The Vulnerability of Nuclear Facilities to Cyber Attack," p. 17. *Strategic Insights*. Vol 10 Issue 1.

49. Kesler, B. (2011) "The Vulnerability of Nuclear Facilities to Cyber Attack." *Strategic Insights*. Vol 10 Issue 1.

50. Kesler, B. (2011) "The Vulnerability of Nuclear Facilities to Cyber Attack." *Strategic Insights*. Vol 10 Issue 1.

51. Kesler, B. (2011) "The Vulnerability of Nuclear Facilities to Cyber Attack." *Strategic Insights*. Vol 10 Issue 1.

52. Kesler, B. (2011) "The Vulnerability of Nuclear Facilities to Cyber Attack," p. 21. *Strategic Insights.* Vol 10 Issue 1.

53. Kesler, B. (2011) "The Vulnerability of Nuclear Facilities to Cyber Attack." *Strategic Insights.* Vol 10 Issue 1.

54. Kim, D. (2013) "Cyber Security Issues Imposed on Nuclear Power Plants." *Annals of Nuclear Energy* Vol. 65.

55. Kesler, B. (2011) "The Vulnerability of Nuclear Facilities to Cyber Attack." *Strategic Insights.* Vol 10 Issue 1.

56. Kesler, B. (2011) "The Vulnerability of Nuclear Facilities to Cyber Attack." *Strategic Insights.* Vol 10 Issue 1.

57. Holt, M. & Andrews A. (2014, January 3). "Nuclear Power Plant Security and Vulnerabilities." Congressional Research Service Report (CRS) RL34331. Retrieved online at www.crs.gov.

58. Kim, D. (2013) "Cyber Security Issues Imposed on Nuclear Power Plants." *Annals of Nuclear Energy* Vol. 65.

59. Holt, M. & Andrews A. (2014, January 3). "Nuclear Power Plant Security and Vulnerabilities." Congressional Research Service Report (CRS) RL34331. Retrieved online at www.crs.gov.

60. Holt, M. & Andrews A. (2014, January 3). "Nuclear Power Plant Security and Vulnerabilities." Congressional Research Service Report (CRS) RL34331. Retrieved online at www.crs.gov.

61. Holt, M. & Andrews A. (2014, January 3). "Nuclear Power Plant Security and Vulnerabilities." Congressional Research Service Report (CRS) RL34331. Retrieved online at www.crs.gov.

62. Holt, M. & Andrews A. (2014, January 3). "Nuclear Power Plant Security and Vulnerabilities." Congressional Research Service Report (CRS) RL34331. Retrieved online at www.crs.gov.

63. Holt, M. & Andrews A. (2014, January 3). "Nuclear Power Plant Security and Vulnerabilities." Congressional Research Service Report (CRS) RL34331. Retrieved online at www.crs.gov.

64. Kesler, B. (2011) "The Vulnerability of Nuclear Facilities to Cyber Attack." *Strategic Insights.* Vol 10 Issue 1.

65. Kim, D. (2013) "Cyber Security Issues Imposed on Nuclear Power Plants." *Annals of Nuclear Energy* Vol. 65.

66. Parfomak, P.W. (2013) "Keeping America's Pipelines Safe and Secure: Key Issues for Congress. CRS Report R41536.

67. Jerome, S. (2013, December) "Cyber Attacks Up by 60 Percent at Water Utilities" *Water Online.*

68. Department Homeland Security (DHS) Financial Sector Overview. Retrieved online at: www.dhs.gov.

69. H.R. 3696 The National Cybersecurity and Critical Infrastructure Protection Act 2014, Bill Summary. Retrieved online at www.govtrack.us.

Chapter 11

Immigration Policy and the American-Mexican Border: Humanitarian Crisis or US Invasion?

Introduction

In the fall of 2013, there was a steady increase in the number of Unaccompanied Alien Children (UAC) crossing the US-Mexican border and entering the US. The numbers continued to steadily increase until the early months of 2014, particularly from March onward. By June of 2014, it was clearly evident to not only those working the border, but the entire world, that there was a crisis on the American frontier.[1] Once again, the US was embroiled in a controversy over illegal immigrants entering the country. What made this one so unexpectedly different and more controversial, however, was the high number of unaccompanied children entering the US.

Very quickly the controversy divided into two camps.[2] On the one hand, this was a humanitarian crisis, caused by repressive governments in Latin America and gang warfare which necessitated good parents to send their children north to America in the hopes of a better life. The children coming across the border needed to be cared for, treated, and reunited with family and friends that were already living in US, and it was the responsibility of the federal government to accomplish this goal.

On the other hand, the other side argued that when President Obama could not get the DREAM Act passed by Congress, he violated the Constitution by issuing a memorandum allowing children already in the US illegally to remain and not be deported. When Latin American parents heard that children would not be deported from the US, they sent their kids to America for a better life.

As the UAC flooded into the US, it was an illegal immigration crisis that America was facing, bordering on an invasion. The border needed to be made more secure, and the children needed to be reunited with their parents.

Caught at what could be called ground zero was the US Customs and Border Protection, the Border Patrol, and Immigration and Customs Enforcement, all part of the Department of Homeland Security. The crisis of the summer of 2014, whether a humanitarian crisis or illegal immigration crisis, was now an issue placed squarely in the hands of homeland security. Out of this crisis also came controversy after controversy that have to do, at its core, with American immigration policy. This chapter will wrestle with the controversy of immigration in America by focusing on the crisis of the summer of 2014.

History of Immigration/Border Protection

America, it is true, has long been a nation of immigrants, as early English settlers fled England's tyrannical rule to make a new life in a new world. When America declared itself independent in 1776, it became its own sovereign nation and it established its own laws. When the Articles of Confederation failed, the US Constitutional Convention was held in 1787, from which was created the US Constitution, the supreme law of the land. The Constitution gave the power of US citizenship and the protection of the borders to the national government. It is a specified power that appears in multiple locations within the Constitution.

In regard to immigration, Congress is given the authority to "provide for the common defense," to "establish an uniform Rule of Naturalization," and "to provide for calling forth the Militia to execute the Laws of the Union, suppress Insurrections, and repel Invasions." The president's role is simply that "he shall take Care that the Laws be faithfully executed," those laws passed by Congress and signed into law by his pen. In regard to the issue of invasions, under Article IV, Section 4, it states, "The United States shall guarantee to every State in this Union a Republican Form of Government, and shall protect each of them against Invasion; and on Application of the Legislature, or of the Executive (When the Legislature cannot be convened) against domestic Violence."

Initially, the US had little to worry about in terms of immigration for there was relatively little from the establishment of the country in 1776 until about 1830.[3] The estimates from the census records for these time periods is that about 60,000 immigrants entered the US each decade. The first major wave would occur in the 1840s, when Europe became more unstable, with a failed revolution in Germany and the Potato Famine in Ireland. In fact, until about

1849, the majority of immigrants to the US remained European. That all changed in 1849 with the discovery of gold and people from all over the world began to arrive in the US.

The second major wave started to arrive in the US in the 1850s, but the Civil War slowed down the progress until the 1870s. From then until 1930, millions of German, British, and Irish began flooding into America, and many other European countries also witnessed mass migration out of their countries. The only thing that slowed this down was yet another war, this time, World War I (1914–1918). In order to deal with the mass immigration that resulted in the aftermath of this war, Congress began to change the policies related to immigration into America.

In 1917, to control the type of person coming into America, a literacy requirement was passed, and then in 1921, an emergency quota act was passed. The intent of the former was to avoid bringing in the uneducated, while the latter was to slow down the numbers that were flooding into the country. Both of these were temporary stop-gap measures, before the Immigration Act of 1924 was passed. This act established permanent sets of quotas for how many people would be allowed to enter the US by assigning numbers based on national origins. Additional laws in the coming decades made changes to the numbers or made allowances in certain events, such as displaced people after World War II or for American GIs who brought home "war brides."

All of this came to an end when the Hart-Cellar Act of 1965 was passed.[4] The act did away with the quotas based on national origins as it was deemed too "race-based." It was, however, replaced with a new system. This system was based on family relationships and job skills. If a member of the immigrant's family was already living in America, the relatives would be given preferential treatment. If certain immigrants had a job skill America needed, as determined by a political process, then those individuals would also be admitted. It was anticipated that this would bring in more Europeans (families) and the best and brightest (job skills). What happened, however, was that after a brief spurt of Europeans coming into the country, immigrants now began coming to America from Asia and Africa, and most of them had low to no job skills.[5]

As more and more immigrants began coming into the country, the laws were also being circumvented by illegal immigrants crossing the borders without authorization and remaining in America.[6] Catching the illegal immigrants and deporting them became a game of cat-and-mouse. By the 1980s, there was a strong desire on the part of the Republicans to control the flow of illegal immigrants. The Democrats, however, wanted to see more reforms that allowed those here illegally to be able to gain American citizenship. This is the process known as "amnesty." When a person enters the country illegally, but is still allowed to gain American citizenship, then they are being given amnesty for their crime of violating federal laws regarding entry into the country without legal authorization. The Democratic-held Congress worked with the Reagan Administration to pass the Immigration Reform and Control Act of 1986, which promised to both control the number of illegal immigrants coming into the country, and to reform the laws allowing for amnesty of those already in the US. The reality, however, was that it allowed for the reforms, but it did not provide for the control. The reforms and amnesty elements were quickly implemented, but the funding to enhance border security was slowed and almost non-existent. It was actually not until the 1990s, under the Clinton Administration, that any real effort on the part of Congress to fund border security began to take hold and the number of border patrol agents increased.[7] In the end, while the new law was intent on fixing the controversies surrounding immigration policy, the reality is, all it managed to do was to exacerbate them.[8]

DREAM Act & Border Incursion 2014

On January 29, 2013, President Obama in a speech regarding border security made the statement that, "We strengthened security at the borders so that we could finally stem the tide of illegal immigrants. We put more boots on the ground on the southern border than at any time in our history. And today, illegal crossings are down nearly 80 percent from their peak in 2000."[9] To a degree, this was true. In 2012, there were 21,394 Border Patrol agents employed, which was up from the 17,499 agents employed when Obama took office in 2009. This was more than double the number than was employed just four years earlier, in 2004, when just over 10,000 agents were employed. The majority of these agents were then assigned to the southern border, while only some were assigned to the northern border. While these figures all sound like the southern borders were made more secure, they were not.

The reason the southern border was not made more secure was highlighted by the Associated Press when they conducted an investigation. They found that in San Diego, with 2,500 agents, on one day, they arrested ninety-seven illegal immigrants. On the same day in the Rio Grande Valley, 3,200 agents made 1,422 arrests.[10] As it turns out, in the San Diego region, a majority of the Border Patrol agents are not working on the border between the US and Mexico, but rather they are working anywhere from 50 to 250 miles inland, away from the border. Whereas, in the Rio Grande Valley, the majority of agents are assigned on the border itself, although nearly 30 percent are also working further inland, up to fifty miles. Many of the agents work "checkpoints" as far as sixty miles inland, on major highways, stopping not only illegal immigrants, but American citizens as well.[11] In fact, even these checkpoints have become controversial for agents are not only stopping ordinary American citizens committing no crimes, but they have also been said to be racially profiling people, which means an American citizen who is of Hispanic origin will receive more scrutiny.[12]

Then, when the 2014 border crisis occurred, it was estimated by Border Patrol Agent Hector Garza that 70 percent of the agents were being pulled off of the border in order to handle administrative paperwork, thus reducing the actual number of agents on the border.[13] So, despite the fact that the US Border Patrol has seen the number of agents double since the end of the Bush administration and through the Obama administration, it is estimated that 35 percent of the agents assigned to the border are not actually performing their duties on the border, but further inland. This has also been considered as one explanation for why the number of illegal immigrant apprehensions declined from 2007 to 2011, for if agents are not located where illegal immigrants cross the border, than they are less likely to catch them.[14] The alternative, of course, is that the increase in agents has sent a message to the would-be illegal immigrants not to even try crossing the border in the first place.

Controversies

One of the controversies associated with the UAC erupted when it was learned in June of 2014 that the US government was paying to have these immigrant children flown to other cities further inside the US. Rather than dealing with their detention and hearings along the border and in the states where they were captured, the federal government ordered that other cities and towns take in the illegal immigrant children. They began setting up camps, opening up closed facilities, and building news ones in order to house these immigrant children in places as far from the border as Massachusetts, Alaska, and Hawaii.[15] The estimates have been at least 37,000 of the illegal immigrant minors have been so transported. When looking at the numbers provided by the Office of Refugee Resettlement (an office of the Department of Health & Human Services), the numbers of illegal immigrants children being moved away from the borders is rather shocking.[16] Over 3,800 children were sent to Florida; 2,804 were sent to Maryland; 4,244 were sent to New York; and 2,856 were sent to Virginia. When looking at it from the county level, Los Angeles County received 1,993 of these children, while Nassau County and Suffolk counties in New York received 1,096 and 1,181 children respectively. And while others received smaller numbers, for instance Kings County, New York, received fifty-nine, while Westchester County received 226, the fact that the distance being flown is often what makes this so controversial. From Brownsville, Texas, the closest point on the Mexican-US border to New York City is a five hour and twenty minute airplane flight. Every country in Central America, from Mexico to Panama, is located within a five hour and twenty minute flight. And since nearly every unaccompanied minor is coming from Central America, they could be flown back to their country of origin for the same cost as flying them throughout the US.[17]

The fact that the federal government has decided to fly them further into the US has also become controversial with local governments. Many cities and towns began fighting back in the summer of 2014 as the federal government did not disclose to state or local authorities that they were bringing these children to their communities.[18] Uproars over this have occurred all over the country, including in places such as Newtown, Kansas,[19] Bourne, Connecticut,[20] and Lawrenceville, Virginia.[21] The latter resulted from the undisclosed coordination between the Department of Health & Human Services (HHS) and a closed college to reopen the college campus in order to house at least 500 illegal immigrant teenagers. When the contract was leaked to the public, over 1,000 citizens showed up at the next town meeting to protest. As a result of the public backlash, the HHS withdrew the contract. And just as in Lawrenceville, Virginia, all over the US there have been cases where because the public backlash was too great, the federal government changed course and found other locations to house the illegal immigrants.[22]

Where the controversy also became divisive was when it was learned that not only was the federal government flying the UAC to other cities, but they were chartering commercial flights in order to move them. In order for an ordinary US citizen to fly on an airplane in the US today, the Transportation Security Administration (TSA) mandates that every person have some form of picture identification. Without a picture identification, whether it is driver's license or passport, no American citizen is allowed to fly. However, when it came to the UAC, the TSA allowed these children to board commercial flights based on a piece of paper they received at the border from the US Border Patrol, a piece of paper that is known as a "Notice to Appear" form, one that is easily copied, forged, and one that carries no picture. When the story broke in July 2014, a spokesman for TSA, Ross Feinstein, tweeted that "You can't fly by just showing a 'Notice to Appear.'"[23] Throughout July and most of August, TSA continued to tell news reporters that illegal unaccompanied minors could not fly with just a Notice to Appear.[24] When representatives of the National Border Patrol Council (NBPC) (a union for members of the Border Patrol) were asked, however, they affirmed that illegal immigrants were being allowed onto flights without proper identification, whereas American citizens would not be so allowed.[25] TSA stated that the NBPC and border patrol agents were wrong in these assertions.

In late July, Congressman Kenny Marchant (R-TX) made a request of the Department of Homeland Security to try and get to the truth. He wanted to know if illegal immigrants were being allowed to fly on commercial flights with only the Notice to Appear, Form I-862. On August 7, 2014, TSA's John S. Pistole replied in a letter that confirmed that if the passenger could only present the I-862, they would try to use other "corroborating information" in order to identify the individual and then that passenger "is permitted into the screening checkpoint to undergo screening."[26] In other words, the simple answer was, yes, illegal immigrants were being allowed to board the planes without proper identification. If a US citizen did not have a picture identification, they would never be permitted by TSA to enter the screen checkpoint, they would be turned away. Congressman Louie Gohmert (R-TX) reacted to the letter by asking, "Why do we have to undergo groping, thorough review of our photo IDs, and long infernal lines while the TSA is figuratively closing its eyes and waving people [through] with no regard for US law right onto airplanes?"[27] The spokesman for the National Border Patrol Council, Hector Garza, also noted, "Shame on Ross Feinstein and the TSA for lying to the American public and for saying that border patrol agents … were liars."[28]

There are other controversies surrounding the use of the term "Unaccompanied Alien Children," as well as their number counts. The first controversy stems from the fact that the UAC, despite DHS originally using the term "children" and many others using the term "kids," are really mostly anything but. While there have been reports of children as young as six years old coming across the borders, most of the people crossing the border are, in reality, teenagers or older. Many of the "children" have been found to be in their twenties, but are posing as being under eighteen in order to qualify for the benefits and to be able to attend high schools.[29]

The second controversy is in the name itself. The name Unaccompanied Alien Children (UAC) comes from the original Senate bill that passed the Senate in 2005 and was titled the Unaccompanied Alien Child Protection Act. The bill did not pass the full Congress, but it was incorporated into the Wilberforce Trafficking Victims Protection Reauthorization Act of 2008, under section 235, which details and defines the use of the term Unaccompanied Alien Children.[30] In other words, it has become a legal term that is codified in federal law, laws that the Department of Homeland Security enforce. Where the controversy lies is in the fact that the Department of Homeland Security has ordered the Immigration and Customs Enforcement (ICE) to stop calling the UAC, "aliens."[31] There has been a push to avoid using the term "aliens" because it is considered insensitive.[32]

One more controversy regarding UAC is the actual number count. The US Customs and Border Protection records data accounting for the number of UAC. When the border patrol picks up a UAC, they are given a Notice to Appear, a piece of paper that has their information and requires them to appear in court for a hearing. Officially, they are used by the Department of Homeland Security to officially charge a UAC with illegally entering the country and are used for purposes of holding a court hearing to determine if they should be removed from the US. Copies of the Notice to Appear are then sent on to the Department of Justice's Executive Office for Immigration Review for tracking of those required to appear in court. A FOIA request for the number of UAC apprehensions from fiscal year 2013 through June of fiscal year 2014 found that the US Customs and Border Protection had made a total of 85,000 apprehensions of UAC. Each of those UACs should have received a Notice to Appear. However, according to the DOJ Executive Office for Immigration Review, they reported only having 41,952 total receipts during the same time frame. In other words, approximately half of all the Notices to Appear appear to have been lost and over 40,000 children have been allowed into the US with no ability to track them.[33] This is not all too surprising, for the Department of Homeland Security has admitted to losing track of 6,000 foreign nationals who have come to America legally on student visas.[34]

In addition to having lost track of over half of the UACs through the Notices to Appear, the estimates range from around 30 and 40 percent, to as high as 90 percent, that the UAC, despite receiving a Notice to Appear, will simply not show up for their court hearings. Using the lower estimate, that means that of the 41,952, over 12,000 will not appear in court, on top of the 40,000 that will not be required to show because there is no Notice to Appear.[35] And, even if they do appear, it is evident they are not being deported, despite statements to the contrary by the Obama Administration. According to the statistics from HHS, from January to July of 2014, compared to the 37,477 illegal immigrants kids released into the US, during the same time period only 280 were actually deported.[36]

Another aspect of the summer of 2014 border incursion controversy centered on the issue of health. One of the reasons that the US has always controlled the number of immigrants coming into the country is to ensure that it has the capabilities and resources for screening these individuals for communicable diseases that may threaten the health of all Americans. This has long been a priority of border control in America. One historical example is Ellis Island. The island located near the Statute of Liberty, Ellis Island, became a gateway for millions of immigrants coming into the US from 1892 to 1954. As Ellis Island began screening immigrants, one of the realizations was that many immigrants bring with them communicable diseases, diseases that threaten the health of all Americans. That threat is very real, as there have been various epidemics in American history, such as the 1918 flu pandemic, when returning World War I soldiers brought back with them the so-called Spanish Flu in 1919, and in which an estimated 500,000 Americans died. To prevent this, Ellis Island began quarantining any immigrant coming into the country until they were healthy. By 1902, on the south side of the island, the Ellis Island Immigrant Hospital was opened, which again, served as a measure for protecting the American people.

One of the policy areas of concern for the executive branch, according to the White House website, is homeland security, which states that "The president's highest priority is to keep the American people safe."[37] Further down, the website notes that it intends to strengthen the security of America in regard to "outbreaks of a pandemic disease" by "ensuring that decision-makers have the tools they need to manage disease outbreaks by linking health care providers, hospitals, and public health agencies. By building on America's unparalleled talent and through international partnerships, we can create new drugs, vaccines, and diagnostic tests, and manufacture them more quickly and efficiently."[38]

In order to achieve these goals, the executive branch authorizes the Centers for Disease Control (CDC) to oversee the process of the examinations of immigrants coming into the US. According to the CDC's own website, "The Center for Disease Control and Prevention (CDC) is responsible for providing the technical instructions to Civil Surgeons and Panel Physicians who conduct medical examinations for immigration."[39] Still further, it notes that "The purpose of the medical examination is to identify applicants with inadmissible health-related conditions for the Department of State (DOS) and US Citizenship and Immigration Services (USCIS). The health-related grounds for inadmissibility include persons who have a communicable disease of public health significance, who fail to present documentation of having received vaccination against vaccine-preventable diseases, who have or have had a physical or mental disorder with associated harmful behavior, or who are a drug abuser or an addict."[40] So, for those people immigrating to the US legally, they must undergo the medical examination and they must pay for the examination themselves. Anyone who is determined to have an "inadmissible health-related condition" is not allowed into the country. The question that has been raised then is why the current incursion of illegal immigrants bringing communicable diseases into the US do not have to pay for the medical examination but receive it for free from American taxpayers and, despite having these diseases, are still allowed into the country in violation of the CDC's own legal requirements.

The first issue of the issues inherent within this controversy is whether or not the illegal immigrant youth crossing into the US in the summer of 2014 are really bringing with them diseases. Some have dismissed the statements as being "wildly overstated" and that they are coming from Republicans and conservatives trying to use the communicable diseases as a scare tactic.[41] The rhetoric that illegal immigrants bring diseases into the US has been labeled as nothing more than "restrictionists" using "hateful rhetoric to blame immigrants for all of our nation's ills."[42] Even many doctors began to criticize the "rumors" that illegal immigrants were carrying diseases into the country as nothing more than "hysteria."[43] It would seem from all of these reports, that the Unaccompanied Alien Children had no communicable diseases, they were all healthy, and most had received vaccinations against these diseases.

All of these reports, however, do not seem to comport with evidence coming from those working with the UAC and the families coming across the border. In fact, even federal government reports contradict this belief that the UACs are carrying no disease across the border. The Office of Inspector General for the Department of Homeland Security conducting onsite inspections along the US-Mexican border filed a report to the secretary of Homeland Security dated July 30, 2014. In that memorandum, the inspector general made the following observations: "Many UAC and family units require treatment for communicable diseases, including respiratory illnesses, tuberculosis, chicken pox, and scabies."[44] This straightforward statement by the inspector general means one of two things: either the other people reporting no diseases are wrong or the Inspector General of the Department of Homeland Security who sent people to the border to investigate the situation is lying.

The memorandum continued that "UAC and family unit illnesses and unfamiliarity with bathroom facilities resulted in unsanitary conditions and exposure to human waste in some holding facilities."[45] These types of living conditions help to further the spread of communicable diseases, which is evident it did when the memorandum further states that "DHS employees reported exposure to communicable diseases and becoming sick on duty. For example, during a recent site visit to the Del Rio USBP Station and Del Rio Port of Entry, CBP personnel reported contracting scabies, lice, and chicken pox. Two CBP Officers reported that their children were diagnosed with chicken pox within days of the CBP Officer's contact with a UAC who had chicken pox.

In addition, USBP personnel at the Clint Station and Santa Teresa Station reported that they were potentially exposed to tuberculosis."[46] According to the CDC website, tuberculosis is one of the "communicable diseases of public health significance" and poses a threat to the American people.[47] But again, if the reports of UAC carrying communicable diseases are nothing more than rumors, why did the inspector general report these findings from site visits by the Office of Inspector General?

The issue of communicable diseases coming across the southern border of the US became an even more controversial issue in the summer of 2014 with the outbreak of the Ebola virus in West Africa. Ebola is one of the most serious viruses known, for once a person is infected they develop flu-like symptoms. It is fatal for approximately 50–90 percent of those who contract the virus, many of whom begin to hemorrhage and bleed to death internally, although others do not experience these specific symptoms. Ebola is not an airborne pathogen, but rather, one that is picked up from contact with the bodily fluids of an infected patient, typically under unsanitary living conditions. Since March of 2014, over 3,000 people have contracted Ebola and as of September 2014, over half have died. All the initial fatal cases were in the West African nations of Guinea, Liberia, Sierra Leone, and Nigeria.[48]

When confronted with the questions about people bringing Ebola into the US across the southern US border, Dr. Tom Frieden, the Director of the Centers for Disease Control dismissed the notion outright. He stated very simply, "This is not happening."[49] He then elaborated that "As far as we know the two patients flown in from Liberia are the first two patients in this hemisphere to ever have Ebola."[50] Frieden was referring to the doctor and nurse who were in Africa, helping with the epidemic, when they contracted the disease. They were flown to Atlanta under the auspices of the Centers for Disease Control and both recovered from the virus. Frieden seemed to be suggesting it was not a threat. Yet, as it turns out the threat was very real, even when Frieden so quickly dismissed the possibility. Less than two weeks later, CDC admitted that over the previous month it had faced sixty-eight Ebola scares in the US.[51] These were cases where doctors thought they were witnessing the signs and symptoms of Ebola and alerted CDC.[52] By September 1, 2014, Dr. Frieden then testified before Congress that "it is the world's first Ebola epidemic and it is spiraling out of control."[53]

One other reason that the quick dismissal has become controversial is because at approximately the same time as Frieden dismissed the possibility of Ebola coming into the US, a Border Patrol agent leaked some documents to the media that were labeled Unclassified: For Official Use Only. The documents present the number of illegal immigrants coming into the US that were caught by the

Border Patrol by country.[54] Noting that the Ebola outbreak began in late 2013, in the first six months of 2014, when the Ebola outbreak was growing, of the four countries experiencing the outbreak, thirty-eight illegal immigrants from Guinea were caught by Border Patrol coming across the border with Mexico. There were thirty-nine caught from Liberia, nineteen from Sierra Leone, and 874 from Nigeria.[55] These are the illegal immigrants that were caught, so the numbers of people from countries experiencing the Ebola outbreak coming into the US are assuredly higher.

In addition to the illegal immigrants coming from the four countries experiencing the Ebola outbreak, the report also finds that people are coming from countries all over the world into America, illegally, through the southern border. These include illegal immigrants from as far away as China.[56] Where this is becoming a very serious threat is in regard to the rising terrorist group ISIS (the Islamic State in Iraq and Syria) which is an arm of al-Qaeda that was thrown out of that terrorist group as being too radical. Secretary of Defense Chuck Hagel has stated that ISIS poses a greater threat than al-Qaeda and "is beyond anything that we've ever seen."[57] It has been revealed that ISIS is familiar with the porous southern border and there are plans to potentially exploit the current situation. At the end of August of 2014, it was leaked by federal agents from the Department of Homeland Security that a threat was imminent from ISIS coming through the southern border and the same information was released to the Texas Department of Public Safety.[58] Whether or not an attack is imminent, clearly the border crisis created in the summer of 2014 has created an opportunity that terrorist groups such as ISIS could exploit.

While terrorists coming across the border is assuredly a threat, so too is the amount of criminals coming across the border. There is a serious debate over this particular issue for many have argued that it is myth that illegal immigrants coming across the border are not criminals.[59] At the core, there is an argument that a person entering the US, without going through a proper inspection, is not committing a criminal act. However, Section 1325 of the US Code, states that "(a) Improper time or place; avoidance of examination or inspection; misrepresentation and concealment of facts any alien who (1) enters or attempts to enter the United States at any time or place other than as designated by immigration officers, or (2) eludes examination or inspection by immigration officers, or (3) attempts to enter or obtains entry to the United States by a willfully false or misleading representation or the willful concealment of a material fact, shall, for the first commission of any such offense, be fined under Title 18 or imprisoned not more than six months."[60] In other words, anyone who is not a US citizen, an alien, who enters this country by avoiding examination or concealing the fact they are an alien, has, in fact, committed a crime. That is why they have long been called "il-legal aliens," although even the use of the term has become controversial.[61]

Once moving beyond the violation of federal law, what many argue is that illegal immigrants are not criminals, just people looking for a better life. While they are assuredly not all criminal-types, there is evidence that many are crim-inals and many of them have committed crimes in the US. One Border Patrol agent who has worked for years on the southern border and is vice president of the National Border Patrol Council has described it in this manner, "These are not people just coming here to work as the so-called line is fed to us. These people are coming here to do horrible things."[62] Another Border Patrol agent, Chris Cabrera, was far more specific when he tried to explain the situation that "if they have family in the United States, they'll release them to the fam-ily, even if they're admitted gang members. We've had a couple that had ad-mitted to murders in their home country. They were seventeen years old, sixteen years old, and the United States government thought it fit to release them to their parents here in the United States."[63] The Border Patrol faces this threat each day and they have lost many of their own to illegal alien criminals. Most re-cently, Border Patrol agent Javier Vega, Jr. was off-duty and went on a fishing trip in Santa Monica with his family. Two illegal aliens, Gustavo Tijernina, who had been deported four times already, and Ismael Hernandez, who had already been deported twice, attempted to rob Javier, Jr. at gunpoint.[64] Vega moved to protect his family and a firefight ensued, and while he managed to keep his family alive, he died in the process.[65] The two illegal aliens are facing murder charges, the mother of Agent Javier Jr. had to bury her son, and the family has had to fight the Border Patrol to have his death ruled in the line-of-duty.[66] It would appear that there are at least some illegal aliens who are criminals.

While these are isolated events, the scope of the problem grows much larger. In February and March of 2013, there were reports that the US Immigration and Customs Enforcement (ICE) had released over 2,000 illegal immigrants into the US population who had criminal convictions. When the issue rose to prominence by the summer of 2013, the inspector general of the Department of Homeland Security launched an investigation. The findings from that in-vestigation confirmed that it was true, that 2,226 illegal immigration detainees with criminal convictions had been released into the US general population between February 9 and March 1, 2013, because they did not have enough bed space to house the criminals. These criminals were released from ICE facilities all over the country and they were released only on the weekends. ICE, ac-cording to the report, took it upon themselves to just release the individuals without notifying DHS or the executive office.[67]

This particular news media event and the Inspector General Investigation then led others to begin looking into the validity of these reports. The Center for Immigration Studies was one of these organizations.[68] What they found was that ICE, in 2013, had caught a number of criminals that they then released back into the US without filing any immigration charges against them in what is known as "catch and release." The total number of illegal aliens caught for some type of offense and then release back into the population was over 36,000 in 2013. The majority of these were for traffic offenses (17,228), but many were for driving under the influence (15,635). Rather than pursue deportation, they simply took them into custody, recorded their information, and then let them go. While traffic offenses and DUIs may not be reason enough to deport, over 5,000 were caught and released for larceny, 2,600 for assaults, and over 2,000 for burglary. All caught and released. Still further, there were over 1,000 cases of aggravated assault, nearly 800 cases of robbery, and over 400 cases of sexual assault. Robbery and rape apparently are not crimes worthy of people being deported. Apparently, neither is murder. There were dozens of cases of murder, and yet all of these individuals were caught and released back into the public. While those figures were reported by the Center for Immigration Studies, they came from the records of the Department of Homeland Security.

Further government evidence also demonstrates the problems of criminality among illegal immigrants in the US. A majority of both legal and illegal immigrants entering the US on the southern border remain in the vicinity of the Mexican-American border. According to the US Department of Justice's US Attorney's Office, of the 61,529 criminal cases filed against defendants, the border region had more convictions than any other districts in the US. The government's own report shows that in fiscal year 2013, 6,341 cases were filed in western Texas, 6,130 in southern Texas, 4,848 in Southern California, 3,889 in New Mexico, and 3,358 in Arizona.[69] That accounts for approximately 40 percent of all cases filed by US Attorneys in the US. Of the ninety-four federal court districts, the five located on the Mexican-American border had the largest number of criminal cases and the largest number of actual convictions. The most common crime out of all of these was immigration violations (23,744), followed by drug-related crimes (13,383). Based on this, crime appears to remain high on the US-Mexican American border, yet when looking at crime statistics, many have argued that illegal aliens committing crimes is a myth because reported crime rates are actually down on the border. This appears to be somewhat of a paradox.

The reality, however, is that while US crime is down, the types of criminal cases and convictions being sought by the US Attorneys do not show up in the

Federal Bureau of Investigation's Uniform Crime Reports, the official crime statistics in the US. In the main crime data (Part I Crimes), there is no category for immigration violations. In addition, the UCR does not record violations such as trespassing, one of the common charges. Still further, while one would think that drug-related offenses would be part of the official crime rates, unless the individual has committed a robbery, larceny, or murder in association with the drug offense, the drug trafficking charges do not appear as part of the UCR data. Thus, crime may even be rising along the border, but it does not show in the official statistics because of what gets counted as a crime, and what does not.

Returning to the original controversy of the summer of 2014 wave of illegal aliens, the UAC, one has to question why this sudden surge in "children" coming across the border occurred in the first place. Even that has become controversial. Some have argued that there never was a surge, that it was a continual stream of people coming across the borders, and that it was the media, in particularly what is labeled as the "right-wing" media, that artificially created the crisis where none ever existed.[70] According to official numbers kept by the US Border Patrol, however, there was in fact a dramatic increase in the number of illegal aliens crossing the US-Mexican border in the summer of 2014, in some cases by as much as 152 percent.[71] Another argument has been that it is because of the increase in gangs and drug violence in Latin America that has driven the children to flee their countries and come to the US[72] Yet, many have pointed out that crime and violence in Latin America has always been high and there has been no recent surge in the violence to warrant a mass exodus from Latin America.[73] The most controversial of the issues, however, centers on the president of the US and his actions with what is known as the DREAM Act.

The DREAM Act, which stands for Development, Relief, and Education for Alien Minors, was first introduced in 2001, but failed to pass Congress. When Barack Obama became president, Congress reintroduced the bill. The idea was that many children are brought to the US illegally when they are young and they often grow up not knowing they are in the US illegally. Usually they discover this fact when they try to go to college and they realize they are not US citizens. Raised in our culture, language, and environment, it makes little sense to deport them to a country and culture they are no longer intimate with. So, the DREAM Act was intent on allowing these children (up to age 35) to remain in the US. The opposition to this bill made the argument that it was a blanket bill that provided amnesty to too many people, many of whom we would not want to retain. The argument was for a bill that would not allow blanket amnesty but discretion to allow those on a case-by-case basis, with the one requirement that border security be enhanced first so as not to allow more people to come into the country to take advantage of this law.

The Democrats introduced it a number of times, but the bill was defeated mostly by Republicans. The Republicans counteroffered to pass border security first, but the Democrats defeated those bills. Because Congress could not pass a bill, there was no law for the president to sign, hence until the legislative branch acted, he was powerless to do anything. He even tried to explain that on Univision television in an interview when he that "the president doesn't have the authority to simply ignore Congress and say, 'We're not going to enforce the laws that you've passed.'"[74] Still further, he stated, "I can't, again, just wave away the laws that Congress has put in place."[75] He said this in January of 2012. Then Congress, once again, failed to pass the DREAM Act.

On June 15, 2012, President Obama then issued a memorandum known as the Deferred Action for Childhood Arrivals (DACA), which ordered Department of Homeland Security Secretary Janet Napolitano to direct the US Customs and Border Protection (CBP) to not remove individuals from the US who were under the age of thirty-one on June 15, 2012, and had arrived in the US before their 16th birthday.[76] President Obama had just issued, by decree, the DREAM Act which Congress would not pass into law. President Obama had just ordered the Department of Homeland Security to ignore the current laws, on the books, passed by Congress, which he, six months earlier, had said as president he could not simply ignore. The president had taken unilateral action and violated the US Constitution.[77]

In 2011, there were an estimated 6,000 UAC who entered the US. In 2012, that number rose to approximately 17,000, with a noticeable increase coming in the last quarter. In 2013, the number rose to approximately 30,000, and in 2014, the most noticeable of increases, the number had increased to 60,000 by the end of the summer and was expected to reach 90,000 by year's end, especially when the weather along the southern border cooled off in the last quarter of the year.[78] The summer of 2014, presented what was being called a crisis and finding bed space for the surge in UAC was becoming problematic. Because President Obama's DACA memorandum allowed for children to stay in the US and not be deported, it is believed that many families in Latin America made the choice to send their children either with other children, by themselves, or through the use of hired immigrant smugglers called "coyotes" to America, on the word spreading that the US would no longer deport the children.

Immigration Policy at the American-Mexican Border: Humanitarian Crisis or US Invasion?

This then leads to one of the most controversial issues surrounding the border crisis of 2014. Many people have argued that the president's issuance of DACA caused the border crisis, including such business analysts as Lou Dobbs, the Heritage Foundation, and many Congressmen, especially Pete Sessions (R-TX).[79] Yet, despite the timing, many continue to argue that the issuance of DACA and the doubling of children crossing the border are unrelated, simply bad timing, a coincidence.[80] There is, however, some evidence to suggest that the White House even understands that administration's policy caused the border crisis.

The evidence comes from Vice President Biden's speech in Guatemala on June 20, 2014, where he met with Central American leaders. A part of his speech explained that "these minors that have recently come are not eligible [for DACA]—they are not eligible to what's referred to as deferred action. A deferred action process. Not if they arrive in the past seven months. Let's get this straight. Any minor who arrived in the past seven years is not eligible for deferred action."[81] Yet, if the Administration was convinced that the DACA policy had nothing to do with the border crisis, then why was it included in the speech? Perhaps the speech could be dismissed as Vice President Biden has been known to say some odd things in his speeches, but three days later, Secretary of Homeland Security Johnson issued "An Open Letter to the Parents of Children Crossing Our Southwest Border." It was translated into Spanish and stated, "the long journey is not only dangerous; there are no 'permisos,' 'permits,' or free passes at the end. The US Government's Deferred Action for Childhood Arrivals program, also called 'DACA' does not apply to a child who crosses the US border illegally today, tomorrow, or yesterday. To be eligible for DACA, a child must have been in the US prior to June 15, 2007, seven years ago."[82] Again, if the administration truly believe that DACA was not the cause of the border crisis regarding UAC, then why write an open letter to the "Parents of Children Crossing Our Southwest Border" mentioning DACA?

Several additional controversies that arose from the border crisis, especially in regard to the huge influx of children entering the US, has to do with resources. First and foremost, if the Border Patrol has become so busy with taking care of the children, who is minding the border? This was found to be a true question posed by the Office of Inspector General for the Department of Homeland Security. The American Civil Liberties Union filed a complaint against the US Customs and Border Protection alleging that the UAC were being abused.

The Office of Inspector General conducted a study and found no evidence that these allegations were true. What it did find, however, was that the CBP's resources were spread so thin that more of their time and resources was being dedicated to the children and that it was detracting from their mission of securing the border.[83]

The other issue that has arisen is where the children end up in the US is taxing the local towns and cities, which are already strapped for cash because of the recession and the anemic economic recovery. These UAC not only are ending up in local public schools, but they are also in need of shelter, health care services, basic supplies, food, etc. There are some cities where over 1,000 kids have been transported by the US Border Patrol and Immigration and Customs Enforcement, and the sudden increase in students in September of 2014, the start of the new school year, is creating a serious funding crisis. One example is Fairfax County, where normally they take in approximately 1,000 new children each year. In September 2014, they found themselves faced with 2,200 new children; 1,023 were UAC. Even one of the richest counties in the nation is facing an economic strain because of the influx.[84]

In the end, one voice that must be heard within this controversy is the American people. Public opinion regarding the opening of the southern border to the UAC and the overall issue of immigration has received strong attention from the American electorate. In the summer of 2014, as this latest crisis unfolded, immigration once again returned to the number one problem facing the US according to the Gallup Poll.[85] In June of 2014, the issue of immigration lagged behind other issues at 5 percent, but by July of 2014, with the reporting of the crisis continuing unabated, the concern rose to 17 percent stating it was the most important problem.[86] This poll, however, is open-ended, it simply asks people what is the most important problem and people are not given any particular topics from which to choose. When Gallup asked the question more directly of the American people, they found "nearly 90% of Americans felt that illegal immigration is a serious problem confronting the nation."[87]

Other public opinion polls have reported that the American people were not happy with President Obama and the administration's handling of immigration, for a CBS poll found that 57 percent of Americans disapproved of his handling the crisis, while an Associated Press poll put that percentage at 68 percent of Americans disapproving.[88] Still another poll, this one from Reuter's, found that "70% of Americans, including 86% of Republicans, believe illegal immigrants 'threaten traditional US beliefs and customs.' "[89] Moreover, 63 percent of respondents to the Reuter's poll also noted that they believe "immigrants place a burden on the economy."[90] Another poll furthered this observation when 90 percent reported feeling that it threatened jobs for legal citizens in

America, and over half of Americans simply wanted the government to put a pause on allowing new immigrants into the country.[91] Public opinion, it would seem, based on the high percentages reported above, is not in favor of the current administration's policy, and whenever government policy and public opinion disagree, there is assuredly a controversy present.

Conclusion

The issue of immigration, both legal and illegal, into America has always been a controversial issue in the US. Illegal immigration and the securing of America's border is an issue that is ever present. The border crisis of 2014 was a bit unique when it comes to the issue because the vast majority of people coming across the border were teenagers and children, labeled by law Unaccompanied Alien Children. The reaction to the issue has decidedly fallen into two camps, which has generated a very divisive controversy in regard to homeland security. One side sees these children fleeing repressive regimes and gang violence, having come to America as refugees, seeking a better life, and that what happened on the southern border in 2014 was a humanitarian crisis. In order to respond, it is best that we take these children into America and provide for them and find some way to allow them to stay. The other side sees this as a violation of the US Constitution in that President Obama did not have the authority to issue the DACA memorandum (which he said himself in 2012), but after doing so, sent the message to Latin America that if the children make it into the US they will not be deported, which created the great migration. Now that the border is overwhelmed with these children, there is the potential for both terrorists and criminals to take advantage of the weak border protection and infiltrate into America. Which narrative is the correct one is the current controversy in homeland security; the core question in the controversy, however, is what America should do with illegal immigrants coming across the border.

Endnotes

1. Zurcher, A. (2014). Child immigrants creating US border crisis. *BBC News*. Retrieved from http://www.bbc.com/news/blogs-echochambers-27874901.

2. Chomsky, A. (2014). America's continuing border crisis: The real story behind the "invasion" of the children. *Moyers & Company*. Retrieved from http://billmoyers.com/2014/08/26/americas-continuing-border-crisis-the-real-story-behind-the-invasion-of-the-children/.

3. For a good history of immigration see: Daniels, R. (2002). *Coming to America: A history of immigration and ethnicity in American life.* 2nd ed. New York, NY: Harper Perennial.

4. Wasem, R.E. (2013). *U.S. immigration policy: Chart book of key trends.* Washington, D.C.: Congressional Research Service.

5. Daniels, R. (2002). *Coming to America: A history of immigration and ethnicity in American life.* 2nd ed. New York, NY: Harper Perennial; Wasem, R.E. (2013). *U.S. immigration policy: Chart book of key trends.* Washington, D.C.: Congressional Research Service.

6. Wasem, R.E. (2013). *U.S. immigration policy: Chart book of key trends.* Washington, D.C.: Congressional Research Service.

7. See for instance U.S. Border Patrol statistics, budgets, etc., across time at Customs Border Protection. (2014). United States Border Patrol. Retrieved from http://www.cbp.gov/sites/default/files/documents/U.S.%20Border%20Patrol%20Fiscal%20Year%20Staffing%20Statistics%201992-2013.pdf.

8. See for instance: Cooper, B. & O'Neil, K. (2005). Lessons from the immigration reform and control act of 1986. *Migration Policy Institute.* Retrieved from file://winfshd2/users$/icc_wmo/Downloads/PolicyBrief_No3_Aug05.pdf; Heritage Foundation. (2013). The Senate's comprehensive immigration bill: Top 10 concerns. *The Heritage Foundation.* Retrieved from http://www.heritage.org/research/reports/2013/06/the-senates-comprehensive-immigration-bill-top-10-concerns.

9. Obama, B. (2013). Continuing to strengthen border security. *The White House.* Retrieved from http://www.whitehouse.gov/issues/immigration/border-security.

10. Associated Press. (2014). Border Patrol has lots of agents—in wrong places. *USA Today.* Retrieved from http://www.usatoday.com/story/news/nation/2014/06/29/border--patrol-has-lots-of-agents—in-wrong-places/11705315/.

11. U.S. Border Patrol. (2014). Being detained. Retrieved from http://www.usborderpatrol.com/Border_Patrol300.htm.

12. Lieberman, A. (2014). Arizona's checkpoint rebellion. *Slate.* Retrieved from http://www.slate.com/articles/news_and_politics/politics/2014/07/arizona_immigration_checkpoint_criticism_border_patrol_harasses_people_and.html.

13. Key, P. (2014). BP Agent: 70% of agents being pulled off patrols for paperwork. *Breitbart.* Retrieved from http://www.breitbart.com/Breitbart-TV/2014/07/12/Border-Patrol-Agent-70-Precent-of-Agents-Being-Pulled-Off-Patrols-For-Paperwork.

14. U.S. Government Accountability Office. (2012). *Border patrol: Key elements of new strategic plan not yet in place to inform border security status and resource needs.* Washington D.C., US GAO; Wasem, R.E. (2013). *U.S. immigration policy: Chart book of key trends.* Washington, D.C.: Congressional Research Service.

15. Boss, O. & Dwinell, J. (2014). Illegal immigrants flown to bay state. *Boston Herald.* Retrieved from http://bostonherald.com/news_opinion/local_coverage/2014/07/illegal_immigrants_flown_to_bay_state; Howell, K. (2014). Feds flying illegal immigrant minors to Hawaii, Alaska; 30K transported across U.S.

16. Office of Refugee Resettlement. (2014). Unaccompanied children released to sponsors by state. Retrieved from http://www.acf.hhs.gov/programs/orr/programs/ucs/state-by-state-uc-placed-sponsors.

17. Office of Refugee Resettlement. (2014). About unaccompanied children's services. Retrieved from http://www.acf.hhs.gov/programs/orr/programs/ucs/about.

18. Starnes, T. (2014). Medical staff warned: Keep your mouths shut about illegal im-

migrants or face arrest. *Fox News.* Retrieved from http://www.foxnews.com/opinion/ 2014/07/02/medical-staff-warned-keep-quiet-about-illegal-immigrants-or-face-arrest/.
    19. Broyles, J. (2014). Child Immigrants. *Kansas First News, NBC.* Retrieved from http://kansasfirstnews.com/2014/08/02/kansas-town-says-no-to-housing-unaccompanied-illegal-minors/.
    20. Rausch, M.J. (2014). Bourne selectmen say no to immigrant children. *CapeNews.* Retrieved from http://www.capenews.net/bourne/bourne_selectmen_residents_say_no_to_immigrant_children.
    21. Moran, R. (2014). Townfolk say 'no' to HHS dumping illegal minors at local college. *PJ Media.* Retrieved from http://pjmedia.com/tatler/2014/06/21/townfolk-say-no-to-hhs-dumping-illegal-minors-at-local-college/.
    22. Associated Press. (2014). Virginia community confronts feds over plan to house immigrant kids at shuttered college. *Fox News.* Retrieved from http://www.foxnews.com/ us/2014/06/20/virginia-community-confronts-feds-over-plan-to-house-immigrant-kids-at/; Ramos, V.M. (2014). Feds pay Long Island nonprofit to house immigrant kids. *Newsday.* Retrieved from http://www.newsday.com/long-island/nassau/feds-pay-long-island-nonprofit-to-house-immigrant-kids-1.8899017; Shaw, J. (2014). Syracuse NY mayor to Obama: Send those immigrant kids up here! *Hot Air.* Retrieved from http://hotair.com/ archives/2014/07/19/syracuse-ny-mayor-to-obama-send-those-immigrant-kids-up-here/.
    23. For exchange between Breitbart's Brandon Darby and TSA Ross Feinstein see Twitchy. (2014). Surprise, surprise! TSA trashes Brandon Darby's Border Patrol sources. *Twitchy Media.* Retrieved from http://twitchy.com/2014/07/11/surprise-surprise-tsa-trashes-brandon-darbys-border-patrol-sources/.
    24. Custer, A. (2014). TSA denies claims of undocumented immigrants boarding flights with no ID. *Valley Central.* Retrieved from http://www.valleycentral.com/news/ story.aspx?id=1070140#.U_y1Hfl7J8F; Hoft, J. (2014). TSA misled: Letter confirms illegals allowed to fly without id, just 'notice to appear.' *Gateway Pundit.* Retrieved from http://www.thegatewaypundit.com/2014/08/tsa-misled-letter-confirms-illegals-allowed-to-fly-without-id-just-notice-to-appear/.
    25. Preysing, C.V. (2014). BP union claims released immigrants are without photo identification. *NBC News, KGNS.* Retrieved from http://www.kgns.tv/home/headlines/BP-union-claims-immigrants-are-without-photo-identification-267067001.html.
    26. Tate, K. (2014). TSA admits lying about illegal aliens flying without proper id. *Breitbart Texas.* Retrieved from http://www.breitbart.com/Breitbart-Texas/2014/08/22/TSA-Admits-Illegal-Aliens-Boarding-Planes-Using-Notice-to-Appear-Forms.
    27. Tate, K. (2014). Gohmert slams TSA for allowing illegals to fly without valid id then lying about it. *Breitbart Texas.* Retrieved from http://www.breitbart.com/Breitbart-Texas/2014/08/23/Gohmert-Slams-TSA-for-Allowing-Illegals-to-Fly-Without-Valid-ID-Then-Lying-About-It.
    28. Tate, K. (2014). Gohmert slams TSA for allowing illegals to fly without valid id then lying about it. *Breitbart Texas.* Retrieved from http://www.breitbart.com/Breitbart--Texas/2014/08/23/Gohmert-Slams-TSA-for-Allowing-Illegals-to-Fly-Without-Valid-ID-Then-Lying-About-It.
    29. Associated Press. (2014). Undocumented minors are enrolling in public schools big-time. *Politix.* Retrieved from http://politix.topix.com/story/13082-undocumented-minors-are-enrolling-in-public-schools-big-time; Lovelace, R. (2014). Adult illegal immigrants posing as children to enroll in high school. *National Review.* Retrieved from

http://www.nationalreview.com/article/382483/adult-illegal-immigrants-posing-children-enroll-high-school-ryan-lovelace.

30. Zamora, L. (2014). Unaccompanied alien children: A primer. *Bipartisan Policy Center*. Retrieved from http://bipartisanpolicy.org/blog/immigration/2014/07/21/unaccompanied-alien-children-primer.

31. Klimek, C.C. (2014). ICE can no longer call illegal immigrant children 'aliens.' *Bizpac Review*. Retrieved from http://www.bizpacreview.com/2014/07/04/ice-can-no-longer-call-illegal-immigrant-children-aliens-129593.

32. Guskin, E. (2013). 'Illegal,' 'undocumented,' 'unauthorized': News media shifts language on immigration. *Pew Research Center*. Retrieved from http://www.pewresearch.org/fact-tank/2013/06/17/illegal-undocumented-unauthorized-news-media-shift-language-on-immigration/.

33. Lovelace, R. (2014). Government has no receipts for thousands of unaccompanied alien children. *National Review*. Retrieved from http://www.nationalreview.com/article/385016/government-has-no-receipts-thousands-unaccompanied-alien-children-ryan-lovelace.

34. Ernst, D. (2014). 6,000 foreign nationals who overstayed student visas have dropped off DHS radar. *The Washington Times*. Retrieved from http://www.washingtontimes.com/news/2014/sep/2/6000-foreign-nationals-who-overstayed-student-visa/.

35. Politifact. (2014). Sen. Jeff Lake says 90 percent of immigrants given court dates fail to show up. *Tampa Bay Times*. Retrieved from http://www.politifact.com/truth-o-meter/statements/2014/jul/10/jeff-flake/sen-jeff-flake-says-90-percent-immigrants-given-co/.

36. Bedard, P. (2014). In just 6 months, 37,477, illegal immigrant kids released, only 280 deported. *Washington Examiner*. Retrieved from http://washingtonexaminer.com/in-just-6-months-37477-illegal-immigrant-kids-released-only-280-deported/article/feed/2160642.

37. White House. (2014). Homeland security. *The White House, President Barack Obama*. Retrieved from http://www.whitehouse.gov/issues/homeland-security.

38. White House. (2014). Homeland security. *The White House, President Barack Obama*. Retrieved from http://www.whitehouse.gov/issues/homeland-security.

39. Centers for Disease Control. (2014). Medical Examinations. Retrieved from http://www.cdc.gov/immigrantrefugeehealth/exams/medical-examination-faqs.html#medical

40. Centers for Disease Control. (2014). Medical Examinations. Retrieved from http://www.cdc.gov/immigrantrefugeehealth/exams/medical-examination-faqs.html#medical

41. Pearson, R. (2014). Disease threat from immigrant children wildly overstated. *Texas Observer*. Retrieved from http://www.texasobserver.org/disease-threat-immigrant-children-wildly-overstated/.

42. Cantor, G. (2014). Restrictionists spread unfounded rumors about migrant children and disease. *American Immigration Council*. Retrieved from http://immigrationimpact.com/2014/07/25/restrictionists-spread-unfounded-rumors-about-migrant-children-and-disease/.

43. Fox, M. (2014). Vectors or victims? Docs slam rumors that migrants carry disease. *NBC News*. Retrieved from http://www.nbcnews.com/storyline/immigration-border-crisis/vectors-or-victims-docs-slam-rumors-migrants-carry-disease-n152216.

44. Office of Inspector General, Department of Homeland Security. (2014). Memorandum for the Honorable Jeh C. Johnson, Secretary. Retrieved from http://www.oig.dhs.gov/assets/Mgmt/2014/Over_Un_Ali_Chil.pdf.

45. Office of Inspector General, Department of Homeland Security. (2014). Memo-

randum for the Honorable Jeh C. Johnson, Secretary. Retrieved from http://www.oig.dhs.gov/assets/Mgmt/2014/Over_Un_Ali_Chil.pdf.

46. Office of Inspector General, Department of Homeland Security. (2014). Memorandum for the Honorable Jeh C. Johnson, Secretary. Retrieved from http://www.oig.dhs.gov/assets/Mgmt/2014/Over_Un_Ali_Chil.pdf.

47. Centers for Disease Control. (2014). Medical Examinations. Retrieved from http://www.cdc.gov/immigrantrefugeehealth/exams/medical-examination-faqs.html#medical.

48. New York Times. (2014). What you need to know about the Ebola outbreak. *New York Times*. Retrieved from http://www.nytimes.com/interactive/2014/07/31/world/africa/ebola-virus-outbreak-qa.html?_r=0.

49. May, C. (2014). CDC director brushes off concerns that ebola could come across southern U.S. border. *Breitbart*. Retrieved from http://www.breitbart.com/Big-Government/2014/08/07/CDC-Director-Brushes-Off-Concerns-that-Ebola-Could-Come-Across-Southern-U-S-Border.

50. May, C. (2014). CDC director brushes off concerns that ebola could come across southern U.S. border. *Breitbart*. Retrieved from http://www.breitbart.com/Big-Government/2014/08/07/CDC-Director-Brushes-Off-Concerns-that-Ebola-Could-Come-Across-Southern-U-S-Border.

51. Lupkin, S. (2014). US hospitals have had 68 Ebola scares, CDC says. *ABC News*. Retrieved from http://abcnews.go.com/Health/us-hospitals-68-ebola-scares-cdc/story?id=25039023

52. Lupkin, S. (2014). US hospitals have had 68 Ebola scares, CDC says. *ABC News*. Retrieved from http://abcnews.go.com/Health/us-hospitals-68-ebola-scares-cdc/story?id=25039023.

53. CBS News. (2014). CDC director: Ebola outbreak 'is spiraling out of control.' *CBS News*. Retrieved from http://atlanta.cbslocal.com/2014/09/02/cdc-director-ebola-outbreak-is-spiraling-out-of-control/.

54. Darby, B. (2014). Leaked CBP report shows entire world exploiting open US border. *Breitbart*. Retrieved from http://www.breitbart.com/Breitbart-Texas/2014/08/03/Leaked-CBP-Report-Shows-Entire-World-Exploiting-Open-US-Border.

55. Darby, B. (2014). Leaked CBP report shows entire world exploiting open US border. *Breitbart*. Retrieved from http://www.breitbart.com/Breitbart-Texas/2014/08/03/Leaked-CBP-Report-Shows-Entire-World-Exploiting-Open-US-Border.

56. Oberg, T. (2014). Texas border crossers: Kids, but Chinese, other nations too. *ABC News*. Retrieved from http://abc13.com/politics/border-children-migration-slowing-but-kids-still-coming/248117/.

57. Wong, K. (2014). Defense secretary: ISIS threat 'beyond anything we've seen.' *The Hill*. Retrieved from http://thehill.com/policy/defense/215724-hagel-isis-beyond-anything-weve-seen.

58. Winter, J. (2014). Online posts show ISIS eyeing Mexican borders, says law enforcement bulletin. *Fox News*. Retrieved from http://www.foxnews.com/us/2014/08/29/online-posts-show-isis-eyeing-mexican-border-says-law-enforcment-bulletin/; Judicial Watch. (2014). Imminent terrorist attack warning update: Ft. Bliss increases security. *Judicial Watch*. Retrieved from http://www.judicialwatch.org/bulletins/imminent-terrorist-attack-warning-feds-us-border/.

59. Maloney, K. (2013). 8 of the most vicious myths about illegal immigrants. *Pol-

icy.Mic. Retrieved from http://mic.com/articles/43599/8-of-the-most-vicious-myths-about-illegal-immigrants; Poverty Law Center. (2014). 10 myths about immigration. *Teaching Tolerance.* Retrieved from http://www.tolerance.org/immigration-myths; Rumbaut, R.G. & Ewing, W.A. (2007). *The myth of immigrant criminality and the paradox of assimilation.* Washington, D.C.: American Immigration Law Foundation.

60. 8 USC 1325: U.S. Code—Section 1325: Improper entry by alien. *Findlaw.* Retrieved from http://codes.lp.findlaw.com/uscode/8/12/II/VIII/1325.

61. Garcia, C. (2012). Why 'illegal immigrant' is a slur. *CNN Opinion.* Retrieved from http://www.cnn.com/2012/07/05/opinion/garcia-illegal-immigrants/.

62. Hanchett, I. (2014). Border patrol agent: 'These people are coming here to do horrible things.' *Breitbart.* Retrieved from http://www.breitbart.com/Breitbart-TV/2014/08/08/Border-Patrol-Agent-These-People-are-Coming-Here-to-do-Horrible-Things

63. CBS News. (2014). Border patrol agent: Federal government releasing murderers into the U.S. *CBC News.* Retrieved from http://washington.cbslocal.com/2014/08/07/border-patrol-agent-federal-government-releasing-murderers-into-us/.

64. Winter, J. (2014). Suspects in murder of Border Patrol agent arrested and deported numerous times. *Fox News.* Retrieved from http://www.foxnews.com/us/2014/08/05/suspects-in-murder-border-patrol-agent-arrested-and-deported-numerous-times/.

65. Payne, W. (2014). 'I will not rest until these worthless pieces of s**t are dead': Anguished vow of mother who watched two illegal immigrants—who had been deported SIX times before—gun down her off-duty Border Patrol son. *Mailonline.* Retrieved from http://www.dailymail.co.uk/news/article-2719011/I-not-rest-worthless-pieces-s-t-dead-Anguished-vow-mother-watched-duty-Border-Patrol-son-gunned-two-illegal-immigrants-deported-SIX-times-before.html.

66. Ortiz, I. (2014). Border Patrol union fights for agent killed by illegal aliens. *Breitbart.* Retrieved from http://www.breitbart.com/Breitbart-Texas/2014/08/09/Border-Patrol-Union-Fights-For-Agent-Killed-by-Illegal-Aliens.

67. Office of Inspector General, Department of Homeland Security. (2014). *ICE's release of immigration detainees.* Washington, D.C.: Office of Inspector General, Department of Homeland Security.

68. Vaughn, J.M. (2014). ICE document details 36,000 criminal alien releases in 2013. *Center for Immigration Studies.* Retrieved from http://cis.org/sites/cis.org/files/vaughan-criminals-5-14_2.pdf; See also Vaughn, J.M. (2014). Catch and release: Interior immigration enforcement in 2013. *Center for Immigration Studies.* Retrieved from http://cis.org/sites/cis.org/files/vaughan-ice-3-14_0.pdf.

69. U.S. Attorneys, U.S. Department of Justice. (2014). *United States Attorneys' annual statistical report.* Washington D.C.: U.S Department of Justice; See also Judicial Watch. (2014). DOJ report: Nearly half of fed crimes near Mexican border. *Judicial Watch.* Retrieved from http://www.judicialwatch.org/blog/2014/08/doj-report-nearly-half-fed-crimes-near-mexican-border/?utm_source=facebook&utm_medium=post&utm_campaign=080514; Tate, K. (2014). DOJ: Regions near Mexico border most crime ridden in US. *Breitbart.* Retrieved from http://www.breitbart.com/Breitbart-Texas/2014/08/06/DOJ-Regions-Near-Mexico-Border-Most-Crime-Ridden-in-US.

70. See for instance Chomsky, A. (2014). The real story behind the 'invasion' of the children. *North American Congress on Latin America.* Retrieved from https://nacla.org/blog/2014/8/25/real-story-behind-%E2%80%9Cinvasion%E2%80%9D-children.

71. U.S. Customs and Border Protection. (2014). Southwest border unaccompanied alien children. Retrieved from http://www.cbp.gov/newsroom/stats/southwest-border-unaccompanied-children.

72. See for instance Tobia, P.J. (2014). No country for lost kids. *PBS Newshour.* Retrieved from http://www.pbs.org/newshour/updates/country-lost-kids/; Ortega, B. (2014). 5 answers: Why the surge in migrant children at border? *AZ Central.* Retrieved from http://www.az-central.com/story/news/politics/immigration/2014/06/09/immigrant-children-arizona-border-answers/10246771/.

73. Bacon, D. (2014). Debunking 8 myths about why central American children are migrating. *In These Times.* Retrieved from http://inthesetimes.com/article/16919/8_reasons_u.s._trade_and_immigration_policies_have_caused_migration_from_ce.

74. San Francisco Gate. (2014). Barack Obama said he doesn't have authority to ignore Congress. *SF Gate.* Retrieved from http://blog.sfgate.com/djsaunders/2014/07/08/barack-obama-said-he-doesnt-have-authority-to-ignore-congress/.

75. Latina Lista. (2014). Transcript: Univision interview with President Obama after State of the Union address. *Latina Lista.* Retrieved from http://latinalista.com/media-2/transcripts/transcript-univision-interview-with-president-obama-after-state-of-the-union-address.

76. Obama, B. (2014). Remarks by the President on immigration. Washington, D.C.: The White House.

77. Slattery, E. & Kloster, A. (2014). An executive unbound: The Obama administration's unilateral actions. *The Heritage Foundation.* Retrieved from http://www.heritage.org/research/reports/2014/02/an-executive-unbound-the-obama-administrations-unilateral-actions#_ftn1; Turley, J. (2014). Jonathan Turley, Shapiro Professor of Public Law George Washington University, "Enforcing the President's Constitutional Duty to Faithfully Execute the Laws." Washington, D.C.: U.S House of Representatives. Retrieved from http://judiciary.house.gov/_cache/files/6e6b1b93-8c14-4ddd-a89b-d36ada121352/turley-testimony.pdf.

78. Cowan, R. (2014). Waves of immigrant minors present crisis for Obama, Congress. *Reuters.* Retrieved from http://www.reuters.com/article/2014/05/28/us-usa-immigration-children-idUSKBN0E814T20140528; Lee, T. (2014). White House preparing for increase in illegals as the weather cools. *Breitbart.* Retrieved from http://www.breitbart.com/InstaBlog/2014/07/23/The-White-House-Itself-Thinks-DACA-Played-a-Role-in-the-Border-Crisis.

79. Carafano, J.J. (2014). Obama' destructive immigration policy. *The Heritage Foundation.* Retrieved from http://www.heritage.org/research/commentary/2014/8/obamas--destructive-immigration-policy; Sessions, J. (2014). Sessions: President Obama is personally responsible for 'rising crisis' at border. Retrieved from http://www.sessions.senate.gov/public/index.cfm/2014/6/sessions-president-obama-is-personally-responsible-for-rising-crisis-at-border; Tampa Bay Times. (2014). Dobbs: Obama policy on young immigrants 'created' the crisis on the border. *Punditfact.* Retrieved from http://www.politifact.com/punditfact/statements/2014/jul/23/lou-dobbs/dobbs-obama-policy-young-immigrants-created-crisis/.

80. Nowrasteh, A. (2014). DACA did not cause the surge in unaccompanied children. *Cato Institute.* Retrieved from http://www.cato.org/blog/daca-did-not-cause-surge-unaccompanied-children.

81. Sexton, J. (2014). The White House itself thinks DACA played a role in the border

crisis. *Breitbart.* Retrieved from http://www.breitbart.com/InstaBlog/2014/07/23/The-White-House-Itself-Thinks-DACA-Played-a-Role-in-the-Border-Crisis.

82. Johnson, J. (2014). An open letter to the parents of children crossing our southwest border. *Department of Homeland Security.* Retrieved from http://www.dhs.gov/news/2014/06/23/open-letter-parents-children-crossing-our-southwest-border.

83. Dinan, S. (2014). Homeland lacks recourses to both secure border, care for kids, probe finds. *The Washington Times.* Retrieved from http://www.washingtontimes.com/news/2014/sep/2/dhs-didnt-abuse-illegal-immigrant-children-audit/; Office of Inspector General. (2014). Memorandum for Honorable Jeh C. Johnson, August 28, 2014. *U.S. Department of Homeland Security.* Retrieved from http://www.oig.dhs.gov/assets/pr/2014/Sig_Mem_Over_Unac_Alien_Child090214.pdf.

84. Miller, S. & Dinan, S. (2014). Illegal border children taxing resources inside U.S. schools. *The Washington Times.* Retrieved from http://www.washingtontimes.com/news/2014/sep/3/influx-of-illegal-immigrant-children-presents-chal/?utm_source=RSS_Feed&utm_medium=RSS.

85. Saad, L. (2014). One in six say immigration most important U.S. problem. *Gallup.* Retrieved from http://www.gallup.com/poll/173306/one-six-say-immigration-important-problem.aspx.

86. Saad, L. (2014). One in six say immigration most important U.S. problem. *Gallup.* Retrieved from http://www.gallup.com/poll/173306/one-six-say-immigration-important-problem.aspx.

87. Saad, L. (2014). One in six say immigration most important U.S. problem. *Gallup.* Retrieved from http://www.gallup.com/poll/173306/one-six-say-immigration-important-problem.aspx.

88. Lee, T. (2014). WH spins: Dismal approval ratings on illegal immigration 'strengthens' Obama's hand on exec amnesty. *Breitbart.* Retrieved from http://www.breitbart.com/Big-Government/2014/08/08/WH-Spins-Dismal-Approval-Rating-on-Illegal-Immigration-Strengthens-Obama-s-Hand-on-Exec-Amnesty.

89. Bell, A. (2014). Americans worry that illegal migrants threaten way of life, economy. *Reuters.* Retrieved from http://www.reuters.com/article/2014/08/07/us-usa-immigration-worries-idUSKBN0G70BE20140807; Lee, T. (2014). WH spins: Dismal approval ratings on illegal immigration 'strengthens' Obama's hand on exec amnesty. *Breitbart.* Retrieved from http://www.breitbart.com/Big-Government/2014/08/08/WH-Spins-Dismal-Approval-Rating-on-Illegal-Immigration-Strengthens-Obama-s-Hand-on-Exec-Amnesty.

90. Bell, A. (2014). Americans worry that illegal migrants threaten way of life, economy. *Reuters.* Retrieved from http://www.reuters.com/article/2014/08/07/us-usa-immigration-worries-idUSKBN0G70BE20140807; Lee, T. (2014). WH spins: Dismal approval ratings on illegal immigration 'strengthens' Obama's hand on exec amnesty. *Breitbart.* Retrieved from http://www.breitbart.com/Big-Government/2014/08/08/WH-Spins-Dismal-Approval-Rating-on-Illegal-Immigration-Strengthens-Obama-s-Hand-on-Exec-Amnesty.

91. Lee, T. (2014). WH spins: Dismal approval ratings on illegal immigration 'strengthens' Obama's hand on exec amnesty. *Breitbart.* Retrieved from http://www.breitbart.com/Big-Government/2014/08/08/WH-Spins-Dismal-Approval-Rating-on-Illegal-Immigration-Strengthens-Obama-s-Hand-on-Exec-Amnesty.

Chapter 12

How Do We Make US Transportation Networks Safer?

Introduction

In April 2013, one week after the Tsarnaev brothers wreaked havoc at the Boston Marathon, two suspected terrorists were arrested in Canada in a foiled bomb plot on Canada's transit system. Chiheb Esseghaier and Raed Jasser, who both lived in Montreal and Toronto, were planning to derail a Via Rail passenger train scheduled from New York to Toronto.[1] The attack was thwarted by a cross-border joint task force between Canadian police, the intelligence branch, the FBI and the US Department of Homeland Security.[2] Authorities claim the would-be attack was supported by an al-Qaeda element in Iran, though there was no evidence that it was state-sponsored. The exact route of the targeted train is up for speculation, though many believe it was the New York to Toronto route that was selected for the attack. Both suspects were charged in Canada with conspiracy to commit murder for the benefit of a terrorist group, participating in a terrorist group, and conspiring to interfere with transportation facilities for the benefit of a terrorist group.[3]

The thwarted plot to derail a Canadian passenger train shed light on the vulnerabilities that still exist in America's commuter system and prompted counterterrorism analysts to renew calls to tighten security on America's mass transit lines.[4] It also revealed how this transportation sector has been overshadowed by security efforts in the aviation and airport industries.

Historically, transportation in the US has relied on the private sector for safety and security. The 9/11 attacks demonstrated the vulnerabilities of the nation's transportation network and spurred a massive change in existing safety and security approaches.[5] While much attention has been paid to air travel safety, what about other transportation networks? How are they being made safer and what technologies are being used to enhance security measures?

The US Transportation Network

"Transportation" is an all-purpose term used to describe a wide variety of systems, structures, vehicles, and actions. Although the majority of passenger travel in the US occurs by automobile, air travel and railways are used for longer distances. Cargo is most often transported by railroad, truck, pipeline, or boat. Air shipping is typically reserved for perishables and premium express shipments. To say the US transportation system is vast is an understatement.

Prior to the attacks of September 11, 2001, transportation security was the responsibility of the Department of Transportation (DOT). Established in 1966 by President Lyndon B. Johnson, the DOT is the primary agency in the federal government with the responsibility for shaping and administering policies and programs to protect and enhance the safety, adequacy, and efficiency of the transportation system and services.[6] Shortly after 9/11, President Bush signed The Aviation and Transportation Security Act (Public Law 107-71) creating the Transportation Security Administration (TSA) within the Department of Transportation (DOT). TSA operated in that location until the opening of the Department of Homeland Security (DHS) in 2003, when it was absorbed into the now-dissolved Directorate for Border and Transportation Security.[7] Since that time, TSA has been returned to its independent status as a standalone agency within DHS and is tasked with strengthening the security of the nation's transportation systems.

Because of the nature of the 9/11 attacks, the aviation industry has received most of the attention in terms of security. Other transportation networks, though also important, have been seemingly lower on the priority list. Mass transit and passenger rail and our maritime transportation systems are also key infrastructures that need to be secured. In fact, one of the final recommendations made by the 9/11 Commission Report characterized the federal focus on aviation spending as "fight[ing] the last war," noting that "opportunities to do harm are as great, or greater, in maritime or surface transportation."[8] In this next section we will examine these less noted sectors and explore how they are protected and what technologies are being used to enhance security measures.

Mass Transit and Passenger Rail

Mass transit and passenger rail are one of seven key modes identified by the US Department of Homeland Security (DHS). This sector includes service by buses, rail transit (commuter rail, heavy rail—also known as subways or metros—and light rail, including trolleys and streetcars), long-distance rail—namely Amtrak and Alaska Railroad—and other, less common types of service (cable cars, inclined planes, funiculars, and automated guided systems).[9] The Transportation Security Administration (TSA) is responsible for security in all modes of transportation, including mass transit and passenger rail systems.

Rail and mass transit systems have long been an attractive target for terrorists and criminal actors. Since 9/11, there have been more than 2,000 terrorist attacks worldwide against mass transit and rail targets resulting in over 3,900 deaths and more than 14,000 injuries.[10] The March 11, 2004, bombing of Madrid's commuter trains by al-Qaeda linked jihadists, which over ten years ago killed 191 people, has continued to be a source of inspiration.[11] On July 7, 2005, four al-Qaeda inspired suicide bombers carried out bombings on London's public transportation system, killing fifty-two people. Mumbai, India, was a similar scene in 2006 when 8 bombs planted aboard a commuter train killed over 200 people and injured more than 700. Other notable international attacks were in Moscow (2010) and Belarus (2011), which collectively killed over 50 and injured close to 300.

Plots in the US include a 2003 al-Qaeda plot to disperse gas in New York's subways, a 2004 plot to bomb New York's Herald Square subway stations, a 2006 plot to blow up the subway tunnel under the Hudson River, a 2008 plot to carry out a terrorist attacks against the Long Island Railroad, a 2009 plot to carry out suicide bombings on New York's subways and a 2010 plot to bomb the Washington, D.C., Metro system.[12] Al-Qaeda has long studied the possibility of attacks on railroad systems—seeing them as cheap, relatively easy to carry out, and with potentially devastating results.[13] A document seized during the raid in Pakistan that left Osama bin Laden dead was evidence of an al-Qaeda discussion to target rail lines in the US. According to the documents, plans were in place to derail trains in the US by placing obstructions on tracks over bridges and valleys. The plan was to be executed to coincide with the 10th anniversary of the September 11 attacks.[14]

Furthermore, of forty-four homegrown jihadist terrorist plots in the US as of March 2014, five were directed against subways or commuter trains. One of these was discovered when the FBI arrested a California National Guard reservist on March 17, 2014, as he headed for the Canadian border on his way to Syria. Nicholas Michael Teausant, a student at San Joaquin Delta Community College, was planning to join the Islamic State of Iraq and the Levant (ISIL). Teausant told a confidential informant working for the FBI that he had previously planned to bomb the Los Angeles subway and had inquired about purchasing powerful fireworks, presumably to use in an improvised explosive device.[15]

Mass transit systems tend to be less secure than the aviation sector for a number of reasons. First, rail travel revolves around routine, scheduled stops along fixed routes and its normal operation relies on passengers having ready access to both stations and trains.[16]

Second, there are over 32,000 stations and more than 20,000 miles of track. Combine this with the impracticality and cost of screening every passenger, and it leaves US subways and rails exposed to the type of terrorist attacks other nations have experienced in past years.[17] Third, mass transit systems, like Amtrak, operate in an open environment with easy access, convenient locations, and intermodal connections. These advantages make rail and mass transit systems completely different from the structure and organizations of the airline transportation industry.[18] Finally, the high ridership, expensive infrastructure, economic importance, and location in large metropolitan areas or tourist destinations also make passenger rail systems attractive targets for terrorists.[19]

It has been suggested that the only way to secure subway and rail cars is to screen every passenger. Most security experts agree that screening all subway and rail passengers is impractical and too costly. Thus far, TSA is not considering requiring it. One argument estimates that it would cost between eight to ten dollars to screen a single passenger, which when added to a subway fare would put public transportation out of business.[20] Others maintain that it is not feasible for passengers with a twenty-minute ride or less to stand in a twenty-minute line for a security check. Instead, random screening has been favored by the TSA as an alternative.

Because TSA has focused its attention on aviation security, mass transit, and railway security has been left primarily to transit authorities, local governments, and rail operators. At times, this has put a real strain on state and local budgets. For example, after the London attacks in 2005, the nation's rail and mass transit systems went under alert. For thirty-six days, Atlanta's MARTA system spent an additional $10,000 a day on security costs in addition to its normal operating budget. Over the years, public transportation systems have faced challenges with budget shortfalls. Many are not in good financial condition. Some have been forced to cut back on services, raise fares, and lay-off employees.[21] Furthermore, only a small amount of the TSA budget is allocated for surface transportation security. While the funding has increased under the Obama administration, the amount still only constitutes about 2 percent of the overall budget, compared to about 85 percent for aviation.[22] Critics argue that this is troubling since fewer than two million airline passengers fly daily compared to about thirty-four million rail and transit passengers trips taken each day.

Managing surface transportation risk is not a lost cause. Despite the vulnerabilities, there has not been a significant attack in the US on mass transit or passenger rail. Risk management, consequence mitigation, and deterrence and vulnerability assessments along with emergency response planning and training have all contributed to a safer network. Rail companies have taken measured precautions to help prevent attacks. These include random searches of passengers and baggage, increased presence of security officers and bomb-sniffing dogs, increased video surveillance, removal or hardening of trash cans so they cannot hide bombs, and encouraging passengers to report suspicious activity through the "If You See Something, Say Something™" campaign. The slogan was created for the Metropolitan Transit System (MTA) as part of their security-awareness campaign in 2002. It gained rapid attention from the public and other transportation systems and was soon plastered across subways, buses, and billboards. In 2010, MTA licensed the slogan to the Department of Homeland Security (DHS). DHS has since used the slogan as a campaign to raise public awareness of indicators of terrorism and terrorism-related crime, and to emphasize the importance of reporting suspicious activity to the proper state and local law enforcement authorities.[23]

In 2013, the Transportation Security Administration (TSA) commended sixteen rail and mass transit agencies from across the nation for earning TSA's highest rating of "Gold Standard" on their most recent Baseline Assessments for Security Enhancement (BASE) for their dedication to a strong security program.[24] The BASE program was developed to increase domain awareness, enhance prevention and protection capabilities, and further response preparedness of transit systems nationwide.

While screening every rail passenger is clearly impractical, technology is offering innovative ways to provide security. One area gaining attention is the rapidly developing field of intelligent video analysis (IVA). Developed in the 1980s as an attempt by systems designers to overcome "bored-guard syndrome," this technology allows suspicious individuals, abandoned objects, and unauthorized vehicles to be detected with unprecedented accuracy.[25] The IVA software monitors video streams in near real time and automatically creates security alerts or analyzes historical data to identify specific incidents and patterns.[26] This technology takes surveillance to the next level and is effective when combined with other methods such as high visibility police patrols, random searches, and trained search dogs.

While not new, the TSA's Visible Intermodal Prevention and Response (VIPR) Teams continue to be an effective line of defense against potential terrorist attacks. Following the 2004 Madrid train bombings which killed 191 people and wounded 1,800 more, TSA developed the VIPR program to help law enforcement when needed. Since then, the teams have been deployed at the request of local, state, and federal law enforcement to support their efforts and enhance the security presence during specific alert periods or major high-profile events. The exact makeup of VIPR teams is determined jointly with local authorities and can include Federal Air Marshals, Transportation Security Officers, Behavior Detection Officers, TSA certified explosive detection canine teams, Transportation Security Inspectors, Transportation Security Specialists—Explosives, as well as local law enforcement.[27] Deploying VIPR teams in today's environment of evolving threats provides an effective and visible deterrent to anyone planning an attack.

Maritime Transportation

Awareness about the vulnerability of US ports and ships to a terrorist attack was heightened after September 11, 2001. In the months following the attacks, congressional committees held several hearings on the issue. In August 2002, the US Government Accountability Office (GAO) conducted field investigations of several US seaports and found that ports are inherently vulnerable to terrorist attacks because of their size, easy accessibility by water and land, and the tremendous amount of cargo that is typically transferred through them.[28]

This sector of the transportation system consists of about 95,000 miles of coastline, 361 ports, 25,000 miles of waterways, 3.4 million square miles of Exclusive Economic Zone, and intermodal landside connections, which allow the various modes of transportation to move people and goods to, from, and on the water.[29] The major features of the US maritime system can be categorized as: US ports, commercial ships using US ports, and cargo containers.

US Ports

The US maritime system includes more than 30 sea and river ports with more than 3,700 cargo and passenger terminals and more than 1,000 harbor channels spread along thousands of miles of coastline. Port security is handled jointly by the US Coast Guard (USCG) and the US Border and Customs Protection (CBP). The top 50 ports in the US account for about 90 percent of all cargo tonnage and twenty-five US ports account for 98 percent of all container shipments.[30] Energy products tend to be concentrated at particular ports. For example, the Louisiana Offshore Oil Port (LOOP) is the single largest point of entry for waterborne crude oil coming into the US. LOOP receives and stores oil from tankers carrying domestic crude oil produced in the Gulf of Mexico. LOOP is the only port in the US capable of offloading deep draft tankers known as Ultra Large Crude Carriers (ULCC) and Very Large Crude Carriers (VLCC).[31]

DHS considers the securing of goods imported and exported via maritime transport to be a critical task. The SAFE Port Act of October 2006 tasked DHS with the responsibility of assuring maritime transport security and protecting the nation's ports.[32] Since that time, a variety of risk mitigation efforts, vulnerability assessments, and preventative measures have been established.

Commercial Ships Using US Ports

In 2011, approximately 7,836 commercial ships made more than 68,000 calls at US ports. Vessel calls were up 7.9 percent from five years earlier, but 13.6 percent from the year before. Of the 2011 calls, 35 percent were by tankers, 32.5 percent were by containerships, 16.1 percent were by dry bulk vessels, 9.1 percent were by Roll-On/Roll-Off (Ro-Ro) vessels, and 5.9 percent were by general cargo ships. In 2011, 98.0 percent of the tanker calls were by double-hull tankers, up from 83.7 percent five years earlier.[33]

Cargo Containers

Container ships are a growing segment of maritime commerce and the focus of much debate over security. Container ships carry stacks of marine containers loaded with a wide variety of goods. A large container ship can carry more than 3,000 containers, of which several hundred might be offloaded at any given port.[34] Given these numbers, how does cargo flow securely to the US? The US Customs and Border Protection Agency (CBP) website describes the transit process in the following manner:

In the US

- More than eleven million cargo containers arrive on ships and are offloaded at US seaports each year.
- CBP uses risk-based analysis and intelligence to pre-screen, assess, and examine 100 percent of suspicious containers.
- Remaining cargo is cleared for entry to the US using advanced inspection technology.
- The Customs-Trade Partnership Against Terrorism ensures another layer of secure treatment for cargo entering the US.

Overseas

- Shipping companies are required, twenty-four hours in advance, to provide manifest data for all cargo containers destined for the US.

- 100 percent of this data is then transmitted to the US National Targeting Center Cargo for screening to identify high-risk cargo.
- Under the Container Security Initiative (CSI), CBP partners with foreign customs authorities to examine all US-bound high-risk cargo while it is still at foreign ports.[35]

Potential Port Security Threats

A Congressional Research Service Report, "Port and Maritime Security: Background and Issues for Congress" established a list of potential port security threat scenarios.[36] According to the CRS, security experts are concerned about a variety of terrorist threat scenarios at US ports. Among other things, they are concerned that terrorists could:

- Use commercial cargo containers to smuggle terrorists, nuclear, chemical, or biological weapons, components thereof, or other dangerous materials into the US;
- Seize control of a large commercial cargo ship and use it as a collision weapon for destroying a bridge or refinery located on the waterfront;
- Sink a large commercial cargo ship in a major shipping channel, thereby blocking all traffic to and from the port;
- Attack a large ship carrying a volatile fuel (such as liquefied natural gas) and detonate the fuel so as to cause a massive in-port explosion;
- Attack an oil tanker in a port or at an offshore discharge facility so as to disrupt the world oil trade and cause large-scale environmental damage;
- Seize control of a ferry (which can carry hundreds of passengers) or a cruise ship (which can carry more than 3,000 passengers, of whom about 90 percent are usually US citizens) and threaten the deaths of the passengers of a demand is not met;
- Attack US Navy ships in an attempt to kill US military personnel, damage or destroy a valuable US military asset, and (in the case of nuclear-powered ships) cause a radiological release; or
- Use land around a port to stage attacks on bridges, refineries located on the waterfront, or other port facilities.[37]

These terrorist threat scenarios can be categorized along five common dimensions: perpetrators, objectives, locations, targets, and tactics. These dimensions are useful for discussing both historical instances of maritime terrorism and potential scenarios for future maritime attacks. Taken together, they pro-

Table 12.1. Example Maritime Attack Characteristics

Dimensions	Example Characteristics	
Perpetrators	Al-Qaeda and affiliates Foreign nationalists Others	Islamist unaffiliated Disgruntled employees
Objectives	Mass casualties Trade disruption	Port disruption Environmental damage
Locations	360+ US ports 9 key shipping	165 foreign trade partners bottlenecks
Targets	Military vessels Fuel tankers Port area populations Port Industrial plants	Cargo vessels Ferries/cruise ships Ship channels Offshore platforms
Tactics	Explosives in suicide boats Ramming with vessels Underwater swimmers Exploding fuel tankers WMDs in cargo ships	Explosives in light aircraft Harbor mines Unmanned submarine bombs Explosives in cargo ships

Source: CRS Report for Congress "Maritime Security: Potential Terrorist Attacks and Protection Priorities."

vide a set of illustrative characteristics which could serve as the basis for the development of potential attack scenarios. Table 12.1 illustrates the possibility of generating numerous unique, yet credible attack scenarios based on different combinations of perpetrators, objectives, locations, targets, and tactics.[38]

Table 12.1 demonstrates the virtually unlimited number of potential attack scenarios which must be considered when planning for security in the maritime transportation sector. To address this challenge, federal agencies have committed to a number of approaches led by the US Coast Guard (USCG).

Maritime Security Initiatives

The US Coast Guard (USCG) is the lead federal agency for maritime homeland security efforts, and is integral to DHS's port and shipping security efforts.[39] The USCG, along with the Navy and other federal agencies, conduct ongoing port security training exercises domestically and overseas.[40] Initially these were conducted under a pilot program called, the Port Security Training and Exercise Program (PortSTEP), a joint endeavor developed by the TSA and USCG to help meet the mandates of the 2002 Maritime Transportation Security Act.[41] PortSTEP began in 2005 as a pilot program to develop the Intermodal Security Training Exercise Program (I-STEP) for TSA's Transportation Sector Network Management (TSNM). PortSTEP studied a number of different ports based on size and complexity, as well as mixed mode of transportations to determine the best environment for conducting security exercises. Out of that program I-STEP was born. I-STEP is designed to address the unique transportation security issues found in the intermodal environment of the nation's transportation security network. It provides tools and services for security exercises and has the ability to support a mix of Basic Tabletop, Advanced Tabletop and Functional Exercises.[42] I-STEP supports not only the maritime sector, but all sectors including aviation, mass transit, freight rail, and highway motor carrier, and pipeline industries.[43]

In 2007, one of the more controversial pieces of maritime security legislation was passed by Congress in the Implementing Recommendations of the 9/11 Commission Act. Included in the bill's provisions was a mandate that DHS scan 100 percent of the approximately 32,000 cargo containers entering US ports each day.[44] The bill mandated that the program be phased in over a five year period with a deadline of July 2012.

Given the extensive economic importance of the maritime supply chain, the vulnerability of maritime cargo to terrorist and other malicious attacks has long been a concern.[45] Initially, Congress and the administration took a risk-based approach to strengthen maritime security after 9/11. This approach centered on analyzing cargo attributes, such as contents and origin of the cargo container, to single out high-risk cargo for further inspection.[46] However, in 2006 this changed with the passage of the Security and Accountability for Every Port Act, which called for the testing of the feasibility of scanning 100 percent of US-bound cargo, a requirement that was fulfilled through the creation of the Secure Freight Initiative pilot program.[47] The results of the program showed that scanning containers could be accomplished—but on a limited basis. Despite these findings, Congress moved to mandate that 100 percent of all US-bound maritime cargo be scanned by July 1, 2012 (prior to the pilot program ever reaching completion).[48]

Those who supported the 100 percent mandate compared it to the supposed success of the air cargo mandate, which also mandated 100 percent screening of air cargo. One of the major differences between these two mandates is that the air cargo only called for 100 percent *screening* whereas the maritime cargo mandate calls for 100 percent *scanning*.[49] This means that each of the approximately 11.6 million maritime cargo security containers entering US ports each year must be physically scanned. Compounding the issue is that many containers often measure some forty feet in length. So while the basic technology exists to effectively scan containers, the advanced technology to include larger containers does not. Another factor is cost. A single x-ray scanner used for cargo screening costs about $4.5 million, plus an estimated operating costs of $200,000, add to that roughly $600,000 per year for the personnel required to run the equipment and you have a monumental price tag.[50]

The other side of the argument is that the 100 percent screening is useless since the majority of cargo traveling through the maritime supply chain constitutes legitimate goods. A large part of the post-9/11 anxiety regarding this issue has centered on the "nuke in a suitcase" scenario, which has an extremely low probability of being carried out.[51] Those against the mandate argue that is simply unrealistic to treat every piece of cargo as a genuine threat.

In May 2012, then Secretary of Homeland Security Secretary Janet Napolitano issued a twenty-four-month waiver of the mandate for all non-US seaports. She cited as her reason a $16 billion price tag for establishing detection systems at close to 700 international shipping facilities sending goods to the US.[52] The extension was renewed for another two years in June 2014, by Secretary Jeh Johnson. After a review of the port security system, Johnson concluded that DHS's ability to fully comply with the unfunded mandate of 100 percent scanning is highly improbable, hugely expensive, and not the best use of taxpayer resources to meet port security and homeland security needs.[53] Rather than meeting the mandate, Homeland Security now employs data collection and assessment to single out "high-risk" freight boxes for scrutiny prior to placement on carrier vessels.[54] Secretary Johnson has also instructed DHS to increase screening abroad, improve targeting, engage stakeholders, and address other political vulnerabilities.[55]

How Do We Make US Transportation Networks Safer?

For well over thirteen years, the US has made great strides in strengthening the nation's transportation network. Most of the attention has been paid, and for good reason, to air security. The 9/11 attacks brought down four jetliners, destroyed the Twin Towers, demolished a portion of the Pentagon, and scarred a Pennsylvania field. 2,996 lives were lost and protecting air travel became a top priority. Within a year after the attacks, the Transportation Security Administration (TSA) assumed responsibility for security at the nation's airports and deployed a federal workforce to screen all commercial airline passengers and baggage.[56]

Airport and aviation security has not been without its challenges and while the implementation of new technologies has not been perfect, these efforts have managed to keep the skies safe. There has not been an attack on US soil since September 11, 2001, and luckily no one has successfully turned a plane into a bomb. But while much attention has been paid to air travel safety, what about the other transportation networks? How do we keep them safe?

The thwarted plot to derail a Canadian passenger train not only exposed vulnerabilities that still exist in America's commuter system, but revealed how the surface transportation sector has been overshadowed by security efforts in the aviation sector. The amount of DHS funding going to aviation security surpasses that of any other transportation mode. Over 85 percent of the TSA budget is allocated to aviation, with a mere 20 percent going to surface transportation. And yet it is estimated there are only two million air passengers per day compared to about thirty-four million rail and transit passengers that use public transportation on a daily basis.

A 2010 report from the Obama administration stressed the need for more work to be done to maintain safety on the nation's mass transit lines. The recommendations included modernizing the information technology infrastructure used to vet the identity of the travelers and transportation workers and completing blast analyses for all underwater passenger rail tunnels.[57] Some critics argue this is just presidential politics and point to cuts in federal funding over the years as major security concerns. Public ridership continues to go up, yet federal funding has decreased.

Although there has not been an attack on the US surface transportation network, events like the 2004 bombing of a Madrid commuter train and the 2005 coordinated bombings of the London public transit system have heightened awareness that US mass transit and passenger rail systems are at risk. The very nature of public transit systems makes them harder to defend because of their open architecture, multiple access points, and heavy volume of passengers. But recent events, like the Canadian plot to blow up a passenger train and the arrest of the ISIS sympathizer who planned to bomb the Los Angeles subway highlight the need to make changes.

Changes also need to be made to security measures in the maritime sector. No attacks have been conducted at our nation's ports. However federal mandates of 100 percent screening of all containers are proving to be impossible. Two extensions made on this mandate, first by Secretary Napalitano in 2012 and recently by Secretary Johnson in 2014, clearly demonstrate that the mandate is unmeetable.

It is not feasible to identify every passenger boarding a subway or passenger train, nor is it realistic to scan every cargo container entering US ports. However, more attention needs to be paid to the surface transportation sector. Some experts have argued that policies in both sectors (mass transit and maritime) should return to a risk-based approach. High visibility police patrols, random searches, and trained search dogs are some measures that mass transit and rail systems can implement. Analyzing manifest and other data to single out only high-risk cargo for further inspection is a risk-based alternative to scanning every piece of cargo. Making the surface transportation sector safer will require more federal dollars and a commitment to innovative technologies to enhance risk-based measures.

Conclusion

How do we make the US transportation systems safer? This is a question that is not easily answered and will most likely continue to bring debate. While the aviation sector has received most of the federal funding and attention, critics warn that the surface transportation sector, particularly mass transit and rail, are even more vulnerable to a terrorist attack. Federal mandates like the 100 percent container screening are not realistic and newer technologies are needed to effectively stop any determined adversary who wants to get a weapon of mass destruction into the US. Unfortunately technologies are costly and funding cuts to transportation and other sectors are a major concern. The ability to make the transportation sector more secure will require cooperation from both the public and private sectors and a realistic, cost-effective strategy.

Endnotes

1. Knowles, B., Smith G.B. & Simaszko G. (2013, April 22) "U.S. and Canada foil Al Qaeda Terrorist Plot to derail New York to Toronto passenger train, two suspects arrested," *The New York Daily News* Retrieved online at http://www.nydailynews.com/news/world/u-s-canada-terror-attack-foiled-article-1.1324305.

2. Doucet, I. (2013, April 22). "Two arrested in Canada over alleged passenger train terrorist plot" *The Guardian.*

3. Zuckerman, J. Bucci, S.P. & Carafano, J.J. (2013, July 22) "60 Terrorist Plots Since 9/11: Continued Lessons in Domestic Terrorism." *The Heritage Foundation Special Report.*

4. Chakraborty B. (2013, April 22). "Counterterrorism analyst want US mass transit security tightened in wake of plots," *FOX News/politics* retrieved at www.foxnews.com/politics.

5. Bullock, J.A., Haddow G.D., & Coppola, D.P. *Introduction to Homeland Security* 4th edition.

6. U.S. Department of Transportation. Office of the Historian.

7. Bullock, J.A., Haddow G.D., & Coppola, D.P. *Introduction to Homeland Security* 4th edition.

8. U.S. National Commission on Terrorist Attacks Upon the U.S. *The 911 Commission Report.*, p. 391.

9. Department of Homeland Security *Transportation Systems Sector—Sector Overview.* Retrieved at: www.dhs.gov.

10. Mineta Transportation Institute.(NTSCOE) Annual Report 2011–2012.

11. Jenkins, B.M. & Butterworth B. (2014) "Mineta Transportation Institute Says Subways Are Still in Terrorists' Sight." Report prepared by the *Mineta Transportation Institute.*

12. Jenkins, B.M. & Butterworth B. (2014) "Mineta Transportation Institute Says Subways Are Still in Terrorists' Sight." Report prepared by the *Mineta Transportation Institute.*

13. Carter, C.J. (2013, April 22). "Congressman: Thwarted terror plot targeted train from Canada to U.S." Retrieved at: CNN.com.

14. Carter, C.J. (2013, April 22). "Congressman: Thwarted terror plot targeted train from Canada to U.S." Retrieved at: CNN.com.

15. Jenkins, B.M. & Butterworth B. (2014) "Mineta Transportation Institute Says Subways Are Still in Terrorists' Sight." Report prepared by the *Mineta Transportation Institute.*

16. "Terrorism: The Ever Evolving Threat" (June 2010) *Railway Technology Market & Customer Insight* Retrieved online at www.railway-technology.com.

17. Stoller, Gary (2010, December 27) "Can trains, subways be protected from terrorists?" Retrieved at: *USATODAY.com.*

18. Stoller, Gary (2010, December 27) "Can trains, subways be protected from terrorists?" Retrieved at: *USATODAY.com.*

19. Stoller, Gary (2010, December 27) "Can trains, subways be protected from terrorists?" Retrieved at: *USATODAY.com.*

20. Stoller, Gary (2010, December 27) "Can trains, subways be protected from terrorists?" Retrieved at: *USATODAY.com.*

21. American Public Transportation Association (2009) "Challenge of State and Local Funding Constraints on Transit Systems: Effects on Service, Fares, Employment and Ridership."

22. Stoller, Gary (2010, December 27) "Can trains, subways be protected from terrorists?" Retrieved at: *USATODAY.com.*

23. Department of Homeland Security, "If You See Something, Say Something™" Retrieved at: www.dhs.gov.

24. Department of Homeland Security, TSA Press Release: "TSA Commends 16 Mass Transit and Rail Agencies for Highest Security Levels." www.tsa.gov.

25. "Terrorism: The Ever Evolving Threat" (June 2010) *Railway Technology Market & Customer Insight* Retrieved online at www.railway-technology.com.

26. IBM Intelligent Video Analytics: features. http://www-03.ibm.com/software/products/en/intelligent-video-analytics.

27. Department of Homeland Security *Transportation Security Administration*—Visible Intermodal Prevention and Response (VIPR) www.dhs.gov.

28. Fritilli, J.F. (2004) "Port and Maritime Security: Background and Issues for Congress." CRS Report RL31733.

29. Department of Homeland Security *Transportation Systems Sector—Sector Overview.* http://www.dhs.gov"www.dhs.gov.

30. Fritilli, J.F. (2004) "Port and Maritime Security: Background and Issues for Congress," CRS Report RL31733, p. 10–11.

31. Crude Offloading Suspended at LOOP" *MarineLog.* Retrieved at: www.marinelog.com.

32. Bullock, J.A., Haddow G.D., & Coppola, D.P. *Introduction to Homeland Security,* p. 263. 4th edition.

33. U.S. Department of Transportation Maritime Administration (2013) "2011 U.S. Water Transportation Statistical Snapshot." www.marad.dot.gov.

34. Fritilli, J.F. (2004) "Port and Maritime Security: Background and Issues for Congress." CRS Report RL31733.

35. Department of Homeland Security (2007) How Cargo Flows Securely to the United States CBP www.cbp.gov.

36. Fritilli, J.F. (2004) "Port and Maritime Security: Background and Issues for Congress." CRS Report RL31733.

37. Fritilli, J.F. (2004) "Port and Maritime Security: Background and Issues for Congress," CRS Report RL31733, p. 10–11.

38. Fritilli J.F. & Parfomak P.W. (2007) "Maritime Security: Potential Terrorist Attacks and Protection Priorities. CRS Report RL33787.

39. Bullock, J.A., Haddow G.D., & Coppola, D.P. *Introduction to Homeland Security* 4th edition.

40. Fritilli J.F. & Parfomak P.W. (2007) "Maritime Security: Potential Terrorist Attacks and Protection Priorities. CRS Report RL33787.

41. Transportation Security Administration, Intermodal Security Training and Exercise Program—(I-STEP). Retrieved at: www.tsa.gov.

42. Transportation Security Administration, Intermodal Security Training and Exercise Program—(I-STEP). Retrieved at: www.tsa.gov.

43. Transportation Security Administration, Intermodal Security Training and Exercise Program—(I-STEP). Retrieved at: www.tsa.gov.

44. Carafano, J.J. & Zuckerman, J. (2012, February 2) "Maritime Cargo Scanning Folly: Bad for the Economy, Wrong for Security." *WebMemo, The Heritage Foundation.*

45. Carafano, J.J. & Zuckerman, J. (2012, February 2) "Maritime Cargo Scanning Folly: Bad for the Economy, Wrong for Security." *WebMemo, The Heritage Foundation,* p. 1.

46. Carafano, J.J. & Zuckerman, J. (2012, February 2) "Maritime Cargo Scanning Folly: Bad for the Economy, Wrong for Security." *WebMemo, The Heritage Foundation,* p. 1.

47. Carafano, J.J. & Zuckerman, J. (2012, February 2) "Maritime Cargo Scanning Folly: Bad for the Economy, Wrong for Security." *WebMemo, The Heritage Foundation,* p. 1

48. Carafano, J.J. & Zuckerman, J. (2012, February 2) "Maritime Cargo Scanning Folly: Bad for the Economy, Wrong for Security." *WebMemo, The Heritage Foundation,* p. 1.

49. Carafano, J.J. & Zuckerman, J. (2012, February 2) "Maritime Cargo Scanning Folly: Bad for the Economy, Wrong for Security." *WebMemo, The Heritage Foundation,* p. 1.

50. Carafano, J.J. & Zuckerman, J. (2012, February 2) "Maritime Cargo Scanning Folly: Bad for the Economy, Wrong for Security." *WebMemo, The Heritage Foundation,* p. 2.

51. Carafano, J.J. & Zuckerman, J. (2012, February 2) "Maritime Cargo Scanning Folly: Bad for the Economy, Wrong for Security." *WebMemo, The Heritage Foundation,* p. 2.

52. Homeland Security Posed to Breach Port Cargo Screening Mandate" (2012, July 16) *Global Security Newswire.* Retrieved at: www.nti.org.

53. Berman, J. (2014, June 3). "Mandate for 100 percent ocean container screening blasted by shippers." *Logistics Management.* Retrieved at: www.logisticsmgmt.com.

54. "Homeland Security Posed to Breach Port Cargo Screening Mandate" (2012, July 16) *Global Security Newswire*. Retrieved at: www.nti.org.

55. "Homeland Security Posed to Breach Port Cargo Screening Mandate" (2012, July 16) *Global Security Newswire*. Retrieved at: www.nti.org.

56. TSA Transportation Systems Overview. www.tsa.gov.

57. Chakraborty B. (2013, April 22). "Counterterrorism analyst want US mass transit security tightened in wake of plots," *FOX News/politics*. Retrieved at www.foxnews.com/politics.

Index